THE MAGNIFICAT®
YEAR OF FAITH
COMPANION

Edited by Fr. Peter John Cameron, o.p.

OCTOBER 11, 2012 TO NOVEMBER 24, 2013

Table of Contents

Essays

The Year of Faith

This text is an excerpt of the Apostolic Letter Porta Fidei *of Pope Benedict XVI.*

EVER SINCE THE START of my ministry as Successor of Peter, I have spoken of the need to rediscover the journey of faith so as to shed ever clearer light on the joy and renewed enthusiasm of the encounter with Christ....

The Year of Faith...is a summons to an authentic and renewed conversion to the Lord....

Faith grows when it is lived as an experience of love received and when it is communicated as an experience of grace and joy. It makes us fruitful, because it expands our hearts in hope and enables us to bear life-giving witness....

Only through believing...does faith grow and become stronger; there is no other possibility for possessing certitude with regard to one's life apart from self-abandonment, in a continuous crescendo, into the hands of a love that seems to grow constantly because it has its origin in God....

Reflection on the faith will have to be intensified, so as to help all believers in Christ to acquire a more conscious and vigorous adherence to the Gospel, especially at a time of profound change such as humanity is currently experiencing....

We want this Year to arouse in every believer the aspiration to *profess* the faith in fullness and with renewed conviction, with confidence and hope.… At the same time, we make it our prayer that believers' *witness* of life may grow in credibility. To rediscover the content of the faith that is professed, celebrated, lived and prayed, and to reflect on the act of faith, is a task that every believer must make his own, especially in the course of this Year.

Faith is choosing to stand with the Lord so as to live with him. This "standing with him" points towards an understanding of the reasons for believing. Faith, precisely because it is a free act, also demands social responsibility for what one believes.…

Knowledge of the content of faith is essential for giving one's own *assent*, that is to say for adhering fully with intellect and will to what the Church proposes.…

We must not forget that…very many people, while not claiming to have the gift of faith, are nevertheless sincerely searching for the ultimate meaning and definitive truth of their lives and of the world. This search is an authentic "preamble" to the faith, because it guides people onto the path that leads to the mystery of God. Human reason, in fact, bears within itself a demand for "what is perennially valid and lasting." This demand constitutes a permanent summons, indelibly written into the human heart, to set out to find the One whom we would not be seeking had he not already set out to meet us. To this encounter, faith invites us and it opens us in fullness.

The joy of love, the answer to the drama of suffering and pain, the power of forgiveness in the face of an offence received and the victory of life over the emptiness of death: all this finds fulfillment in the mystery of [Christ's]…becoming man, in his sharing our human weakness so as to transform it by the power of his Resurrection….

Through faith, we can recognize the face of the risen Lord in those who ask for our love…. It is…his love that impels us to assist him whenever he becomes our neighbor along the journey of life….

[Faith] is the lifelong companion that makes it possible to perceive, ever anew, the marvels that God works for us…. Faith commits every one of us to become a living sign of the presence of the Risen Lord in the world. What the world is in particular need of today is the credible witness of people enlightened in mind and heart by the Word of the Lord, and capable of opening the hearts and minds of many to the desire for God and for true life, life without end….

May this Year of Faith make our relationship with Christ the Lord increasingly firm, since only in him is there the certitude for looking to the future and the guarantee of an authentic and lasting love…. Let us entrust this time of grace to the Mother of God, proclaimed "blessed because she believed" (Lk 1:45).

Editorial

Father Peter John Cameron, O.P.

J ournalist J. F. Pisani tells the story of what he calls "a torturous dinner party." His account appears in the February 27, 2012 edition of *The Catholic Transcript*. Pisani found himself seated at table next to "a strident anti-Catholic fallen Catholic." From the salad to the dessert course, his fellow dinner guest "went from one complaint about the Catholic Church to another, as if she were obsessed."

As the disgruntled person persisted in airing her seemingly endless list of grievances and gripes ("the topics were all familiar ones"), the journalist sat there quietly, taking it all in. But apparently his silence got to her, because at a certain point, writes Pisani, "she looked at me with intense questioning in her eyes as if to ask, 'Aren't you going to argue with me?'" He perceived that one goal of her tirade was to provoke him into defending the Church. And then, at last, came the direct question, "Why do you still go to that Church?"

Here is what Mr. Pisani replied: "The novelist Walker Percy converted to Catholicism, and when reporters asked him why he did it, he would always respond, 'What else is there?'"

And before the woman could launch in to a fresh rant, Pisani said simply, "I believe in the True Presence, I believe that the Eucharist is the Body of Christ and I don't want to live without it." He concluded their conversation by saying this: "Pray to be shown the truth, because if Christ is truly present in the Eucharist—and I believe he is—receiving him is about the most important thing you can do in life. Anything I say won't convince you, but if you pray with an open heart, you'll get the answer you need."

The Year of Faith

Pope Benedict XVI has designated from October 2012 to November 2013 as the "Year of Faith." The Year of Faith is "a summons to an authentic and renewed conversion to the Lord." The Holy Father tells us that "a task that every believer must make his own, especially in the course of this Year," is "to rediscover the content of the faith that is professed, celebrated, lived, and prayed, and to reflect on the act of faith."

The Pope asks that this Year of Faith may "make our relation with Christ the Lord increasingly firm." At the same time, he expresses his desire for this Year "to arouse in every believer the aspiration to profess the faith in full-ness and with renewed conviction." For faith "makes us fruitful, because it expands our hearts in hope and enables us to bear life-giving witness." More than anything, that is what is required at this critical moment in time. "What the world is in particular need of today is the credible witness of people…capable of opening the hearts and minds of many to the desire for God and for true life, life without end."

We want to be able to do what the journalist did for that lost soul over an arugula salad.

How to use this book

Pope Benedict counsels that "reflection on the faith will have to be intensified, so as to help all believers in Christ to acquire a more conscious and vigorous adherence to the Gospel." To aid in such intensive reflection, Magnificat has published the *Year of Faith Companion*. The *Companion* assists you in living out your Year of Faith by providing a certain special "something" for each day of the Year: reflections on Sacred Scripture, profiles of the holy men and women of the Bible, short explanations on the *Catechism of the Catholic Church*, essays on different aspects of faith, spiritual meditations geared to faith, devotions, prayers, and original poems.

You will find in this little booklet a treasury of riches to enhance your personal prayer, to share with your whole family, and to make an integral part of study or prayer groups you belong to. The convenient table of contents gives you quick access to those entries you may want to return to again and again during the course of the Year.

Let us, then, pray for the grace this Year "to rediscover the journey of faith so as to shed ever clearer light on the joy…of the encounter with Christ." What else is there?

Adam

"O APPLE who alone were formed mature, O ancient father Adam!" cries Dante in *Paradise*, as he beholds a brilliant light wherein dwells the first human soul.

Why such honor for our father in sin? Adam is the first of the lost sheep, but also the first to be born again as a little child. Consider that Adam knew something we know only by the example of Mary and Jesus. He was mature, yet innocent. In love he named the animals; and when God brought him the first woman, he burst out happily, "This one, at last, is bone of my bones/ and flesh of my flesh," and named her *ishshah*, "woman," because she came from *ishah*, "her man" (Gn 2:23). They were naked as babes, and knew no harm.

When God pronounces the punishment for his sin, Adam doesn't sulk. He "called his wife Eve, because she became the mother of all the living" (Gn 3:20). It's as if Adam, remembering the childlike time, could see the long line of children to come, and regard it as a great blessing. This is Adam's faith: the simple trust of a man who had been a child such as we can but hope to be.

– Anthony Esolen

*F*AITH INCORPORATES the unknown into our everyday life in a living, dynamic, and actual manner. The unknown remains unknown. It is still a mystery, for it cannot cease to be one. The function of faith is not to reduce mystery to rational clarity, but to integrate the unknown and the known together in a living whole, in which we are more and more able to transcend the limitations of our external self.

Hence the function of faith is not only to bring us into contact with the "authority of God" revealing; not only to teach us truths "about God," but even to reveal to us the unknown in our own selves, in so far as our unknown and undiscovered self actually lives in God, moving and acting only under the direct light of his merciful grace.

This is, to my mind, the crucially important aspect of faith which is too often ignored today. Faith is not just conformity, it is *life*. It embraces all the realms of life, penetrating into the most mysterious and inaccessible depths not only of our unknown spiritual being but even of God's own hidden essence and love. Faith, then, is the only way of opening up the true depths of reality, even of our own reality.

– Father Thomas Merton, O.C.S.O.

I BRING this prayer to you, Lord,
For you alone can give
What one cannot demand from oneself.
Give me, Lord, what you have left over,
Give me what no one ever asks you for.
I don't ask you for rest,
Or quiet,
Whether of soul or body;
I don't ask you for wealth,
Nor for success, nor even health perhaps.
That sort of thing you get asked for so much
That you can't have any of it left.
Give me, Lord, what you have left over,
Give me what no one wants from you.
I want insecurity, strife,
And I want you to give me these
Once and for all.
So that I can be sure of having them always,
Since I shall not always have the courage
To ask you for them.
Give me, Lord, what you have left over,
Give me what others want nothing to do with.
But give me courage too,
And strength and faith;
For you alone can give
What one cannot demand from oneself.

– Lieutenant André Zirnheld

"When Jesus heard this, he was amazed and said to those following him, 'Amen, I say to you, in no one in Israel have I found such faith.'" (Mt 8:10)

At some level, faith is perfectly normal. Even Gentiles have no excuse for not believing: "What can be known about God is evident to them, because God made it evident to them" (Rom 1:19). This is why in Charles Péguy's work, *The Portal of the Mystery of Hope*, faith leaves God disaffected: "Faith doesn't surprise me," God says. "It's not surprising." Apart from this scene with the centurion, in fact, the only time Jesus is "amazed" in the Gospels is at Nazareth when he faces boggling *unbelief*: "He was amazed at their lack of faith" (Mk 6:6).

What then is so special about the centurion? Mechtilde of Hackeborn once heard these words: "I tell you the truth that I am very pleased when men trustingly expect great things from me." The centurion expects great things—and as a pagan *he expects more than he deserves*. This is what fills Jesus with joy. The Gentile trusts in God's *boundless* goodness. He thus becomes the Son's first taste of his unbounded universal mission. Jesus saves all by faith, apart from works of the Law. This includes us. We too make Christ wonder in gladness by expecting of him *much more than we deserve*: "Lord I am not worthy, but only say the word…"

– Father J. Anthony Giambrone, O.P.

The Christian faith is not a "religion of the book."
Christianity is the religion of the "Word" of God,
a word which is…incarnate and living"
(Saint Bernard, S. missus est hom. 4, 11:PL 183, 86). (CCC 108)

THE FIRST COMMANDMENT of the Law of Moses makes us aware of a basic principle of our Catholic Faith: that there is no other god besides the Lord our God. Why then do we set up anything in place of him? It is a danger then to see anything in this life, including the Bible, the inspired words of our Lord God, as an end in itself, or to understand the practice of our religion as a matter of memorizing verses of Sacred Scripture. Christianity is not a religion of words gathered together, but rather the religion of the Word of God who became man for our salvation, and in fact gathers us to himself. Christianity is the religion that begins here on earth our eternal life in heaven.

The Word of God makes this possible by speaking to us, by revealing himself to us so that by the power of the Holy Spirit we might come to know the Father, just as the Word, the eternal Son of the Father, knows him. The Father spoke to us before Christ with words of prophecy and promise, but in Christ we find the definitive Word of all fulfillment.

– Father James M. Sullivan, O.P.

A Litany of Faith

(Based on the writings of Pope Benedict XVI)

℟ *Lord, increase my faith.*

◖ In faith something meets us that is greater than anything we can think up for ourselves. ℟

◖ Faith is a new Yes that becomes possible when we are touched by God. ℟

◖ Faith is the finding of a You who bears me up and gives me the promise of an indestructible love. ℟

◖ Faith means union with him whose power holds us fast and carries us over the elements of death. ℟

◖ Faith is a breaking out of the isolation of my "I," and a resurrection of my true self. ℟

◖ Faith is reaching that point in which we recognize we need to be given something. ℟

◖ Faith means opening our hand in trust and accepting a gift. ℟

◖ Faith involves every domain of our existence: our mind, our will, our feelings, our love. ℟

◖ Faith entails the shift from dependence on the visible and practicable to trust in the invisible. ℟

◖ Faith is the opening up of the inner powers of understanding that await the light of Truth. ℟

◖ Faith is a call to community. ℟

◖ Faith has to do with forgiving—we can find ourselves only in the receiving and giving of forgiveness. ℟

◖ Faith must mature by suffering anew, at every stage of life, the oppression and the power of unbelief. ℟

◖ Faith expands our hearts in hope and enables us to bear life-giving witness. ℟

◖ Faith makes us light—to be a believer means to escape our own gravity. ℟

– Father Peter John Cameron, O.P.

The Nature of Faith

FAITH IS A GIFT FROM GOD. This gift has three dimensions. First of all, it lights up our minds so that we know the truth about God. Second, it brings about a relationship with God we could never otherwise have. Third, it propels us forward into eternal life which begins even now.

Faith allows us to know the truth about God which we could never have known unless he had wanted to reveal it to us. Here God is not related to as the answer to a philosophical riddle but instead is related to as a friend. Friendships involve self-disclosure. So when God gives the gift of faith he tells us something personal about himself. He tells about his own inner and thrice personal life of knowledge and love as Father, Son, and Spirit. He tells us that he made everything not out of need but out of a desire to share his own life. He tells us about our sins and about his Son who saves us from our sins. He tells us about his plans and dreams for us, realized in Jesus as the Bridegroom of the Church and Lord of the New Creation.

He communicates treasures beyond the range of human or angelic minds.

But precisely because faith allows us to know God personally in a relationship of trust, faith is a dangerous gift. Everything depends on whether or not the gift of faith is accepted. "I believe it" becomes "I believe you." Saying "Yes" to the offer says "Yes" to the offered friendship. On the other hand, saying "No" to the offer says "No" to the offered friendship. Friendship has to be free and so God will not force our minds or our wills. If we say "Yes" in faith, it is not because our minds have been compelled but because our hearts have been so invited by God, whom we both trust because we know and also know because we trust. This "Yes" of faith is our basic relationship with God.

Faith is like a seed. It is alive and growing and pregnant with the promise of harvest even when buried in mid-winter soil. Faith is like a lamp shining in the middle of darkness. With its aid, we can truly see, even though it is midnight. Right now we see as in a glass darkly. But dawn is coming and our faith is the very beginning of eternal life.

– Father John Dominic Corbett, O.P.

Eve

ADAM BLAMED EVE, and Eve blamed the serpent. G. K. Chesterton said that when he accepted Christian tradition, including the doctrine of the Fall, "I could hear bolt after bolt over all the machinery falling into its place with a kind of click of relief."

Chesterton also observed that the problem with the world is not that it is unreasonable; rather that it is "nearly reasonable, but not quite." If only Eve had turned and said, "Adam, my love, forgive me!" If only she had bowed her head before God and said, "Yes, my Lord, we were both wrong." The split in our psyche is not our "fault," and yet we must take responsibility for it. What if we tell the truth and they don't love us anymore! What if we act with integrity and they kick us out? In failing to act with integrity, we have been kicked out—have kicked ourselves out—already.

It took Mary, eons later, to look God in the eye and proclaim an unqualified "Yes!" I will not blame the serpent. I will say "Yes" to all the joy, all the pain, all the unknown. I will eat fully of the tree of life.

– Heather King

J AM A TRADITIONALIST in that I do not like to see Mass offered with a large coffee cup as a chalice. I suppose I am a romantic too, since I loved the Arthur legend as a child and reverenced the Holy Grail and the search for it. I feel with Newman that my faith is founded on a creed, as Reverend Louis Bouyer wrote of Newman in that magnificent biography of his.

"I believe in God, the Father Almighty, Creator of heaven and earth. And of all things visible and invisible, and in his Only Son Jesus Christ, our Lord."

I believe too that when the priest offers Mass at the altar, and says the solemn words, "This is my body, this is my blood," that the bread and the wine truly become the Body and Blood of Christ, Son of God, one of the Three Divine Persons. I believe in a personal God. I believe in Jesus Christ, true God and true man. And intimate, oh how most closely intimate we may desire to be. I believe we must render most reverent homage to him who created us and stilled the sea and told the winds to be calm, and multiplied the loaves and fishes. He is transcendent and he is immanent. He is closer than the air we breathe and just as vital to us. I speak impetuously, from my heart, and if I err theologically in my expression, I beg forgiveness.

– Dorothy Day

Abel

Don't we first see Abel's blood that "cries out to [God] from the soil" (Gn 4:10)? But to esteem this proto-man of faith, let us look instead at the blood he shed from his flock. It's only a few short years from the laid-back air of Eden, where Abel's parents resting in the grass would hear the soft steps of their easygoing Lord on his daily stroll in the evening's cool. How times have changed. Now in the barren waste, with no taste of paradise in the appetite of memory, Abel senses the Lord as a serious God owed awesome respect, grave engagement, sacrifice that costs him dearly. It's not death that he offers here, but life at its best: the first-born from his estate. But life at its finest comes at the price of blood, and blood comes at the price of death.

The lamb is this man; the offering is this person. All the more striking that this law of adoration arises not from divine mandate, but human desire. Abel receives no command from God, yet he knows what to do. At a deeper level in the heart, God is heard. The sacrifice of the dearest this shepherd owns is the submission of himself to the Lord, who is due far more than he requests. It is fitting that our grandfather in faith is enabled to offer the total sacrifice of self—the greatest expression of faith and sign of the perfect sacrifice to come.

– Father Lawrence J. Donohoo

*F*AITH IS NOT PURE PRIVATE DECISION, which as such does not really concern anyone else. It will and can show its credentials. It wishes to make itself understandable to others. It lays claim to being a *logos* and, therefore, to the never-failing capacity to become apo-logy. But at a deeper level, this apologetic interpretation of theology is a missionary one, and the missionary conception, in its turn, brings to light the inner nature of faith. Faith has the right to be missionary only if it truly transcends all traditions and constitutes an appeal to reason and an orientation toward the truth itself. However, if man is made to know reality and has to conduct his life, not merely as tradition dictates, but in conformity to the truth, faith also has the positive duty to be missionary. With its missionary claim, the Christian faith sets itself apart from the other religions which have appeared in history; this claim is implicit in its philosophical critique of the religions and can be justified only on that basis.…

Faith can wish to understand because it is moved by love for the one upon whom it has bestowed its consent. Love seeks understanding. It wishes to know ever better the one whom it loves.… Christian faith can say of itself, I have found love. Yet love for Christ and of one's neighbor for Christ's sake can enjoy stability and consistently only if its deepest motivation is love for the truth. This adds a new aspect to the missionary element: real love of neighbor also desires to give him the deepest thing man needs, namely, knowledge and truth.

– Pope Benedict XVI

Caravaggio's
Calling of Saint Matthew

O sing him a song that is new, play loudly,
with all your skill. (Ps 33:3)

M<small>E</small>?
I see his hand
pointing
No
reaching
for me?
Others on the lookout
see only accusation
for they know that they are guilty
and the pointer is to blame.
Others sense invasion
as they huddle and squint in shadows
protecting their collection,
tallying their gain.
But me?
I have left everything
counted in the dark,
protected by shade.
I have left everything
to know the face behind
the higher hand,
to know the heart of God
that reaches like a man.

– Rita A. Simmonds

Enoch

ENOCH IS A MYSTERIOUS FIGURE. The Book of Genesis says, "Enoch walked with God, and he was no longer here, for God took him" (Gn 5:24). The Epistle to the Hebrews says of him, "By faith Enoch was taken up so that he should not see death; and he was not found, because God had taken him. Now before he was taken he was attested as having pleased God" (Heb 11:5 RSV). Thus Hebrews introduces a new note, faith, for Enoch. Or is it so new? Genesis says that Enoch "walked with God," which surely means to live in a way that pleases God, to let God lead us.

The first eleven chapters of Genesis, in which Enoch is named, might be called "damnation history"; they recount how human beings fell ever more deeply into sin. Salvation history begins at chapter 12 of Genesis, with the resounding words, "The LORD said to Abram: 'Go forth from the land of your kinsfolk and from your father's house'" (Gn 12:1): leave behind your security, your safety, your familiar surroundings, and put your trust in me.

In a shadowy way, Enoch anticipates Abraham; despite the darkness of sin, Enoch has faith. The author of the Epistle to the Hebrews, who tells us of Enoch's faith, also tells us that "faith is the assurance of things hoped for, the conviction of things not seen" (Heb 11:1 RSV).

– Father Joseph T. Lienhard, S.J.

Be attentive to the analogy of faith *(Cf. Rom 12:6).*
*By "analogy of faith" we mean the coherence of the truths
of faith among themselves and within the whole plan of
Revelation. (CCC 114)*

THE "ANALOGY OF FAITH" might be explained by something we find in the daily newspaper. One of the most recent games to appear is a number crossword of sorts called KenKen. Like Sudoku, it is made up of a square grid with some numbers filled in and some numbers not. The goal of the puzzle is to put all the right numbers where they belong. The twist about KenKen is that the numbers are determined by mathematical equations within certain areas. In other words, all of the numbers in a certain section and indeed throughout the entire grid have to "add up."

Our Catholic Faith is similar in the sense that all of its doctrines are interconnected and, taken together, they all "add up." This means, for example, that the doctrine of the Immaculate Conception teaches us something about the Eucharist. The reality of marital love reflects some truth about the Blessed Trinity. We can no more take apart pieces from our faith as we could take apart a number puzzle, and still have it make sense. God gives us the theological virtue of faith precisely to see how it all fits together, and then to live according to what has been revealed.

– Father James M. Sullivan, O.P.

Noah

NOAH IS LIKE THE KID who we all knew, and perhaps who we ourselves were, in school. He was the one who just could not get with the program, who was always on the sidelines. He was the strange one who seems to be in a daydream, not keeping up with all of the fads, moods, and activities of the other kids. His gaze is somewhere else.

In his day, the activities of men were mindless of God, but Noah is not (Gn 6:8). To him, who is not one of the "in" crowd, God commands the building of the ark so that after the destruction, the world might be populated once again. Perhaps Noah's neighbors, even as they laugh at him, have a sinking feeling inside that, in his oddness, Noah has his eye on something important that the rest have overlooked. In this case it is true. All of them perish, except for Noah and his family and the animals they save on the ark (Gn 7:21).

There is usually a price to be paid for opening our hearts and minds to the one whose ways are not our ways (Is 55:8). But it is no sacrifice, when our joy, like Noah's, is in finding favor with our God.

– Father Vincent Nagle, F.S.C.B.

HE FRUIT OF PRAYER IS FAITH.
   If we pray,/ then we will believe.
...   If we believe,/ then we will love—
because the fruit of Faith is love,
and the fruit of love is service.
Similarly, if we want to deepen our Faith,
we must deepen our oneness with Christ.

Without seeing him/ we pray to him,
we turn to him,/ we cling to him,
we love him/ without seeing him.

Faith
is the most beautiful gift God can give
   to a human being—
to believe that he *Is*,/ and that Christ *Is*...
God from God/ Love from Love,
true God from true God,/ begotten, not made;
one in substance with the Father,
by whom all things were made....

And yet he became so small,
he became a human being like us,
to make it possible for us to believe.
To increase our Faith
he made himself the Bread of Life—
even a child can break that Bread,
even a child can eat that Bread.
This is humility in the action of Faith,
and Faith in the action of humility....

– Blessed Teresa of Calcutta

FATHER,
I abandon myself into your hands;
do with me what you will.
Whatever you may do, I thank you:
I am ready for all, I accept all.
Let only your will be done in me,
and in all your creatures—
I wish no more than this, O Lord.
Into your hands I commend my soul:
I offer it to you with all the love of my heart,
for I love you, Lord, and so need to give myself,
to surrender myself into your hands without reserve,
and with boundless confidence,
for you are my Father.

– Blessed Charles de Foucauld

Abraham

ABRAHAM'S LIFE is the template for faith in action. When his name is changed from Abram, or probably Abu-ramu, he has not only moved from Haran to the new territory of Canaan, he has also moved from vague belief in higher powers to trust in one Creator who guides human affairs.

His willingness to sacrifice his only son Isaac is a test of faith that foreshadows the sacrifice of God's own Son: "Because you acted as you did in not withholding from me your beloved son, I will bless you abundantly" (Gn 22:16-17). God demands the same life-changing faith of us. To those who claim to be faithful because they are descended from the first patriarch, our Lord will say, "If you were Abraham's children, you would be doing the works of Abraham" (Jn 8:39).

In the American Civil War, people were inspired by Lincoln's steady confidence in his cause, and so he became to them "Father Abraham." The deepest faith, though, is trust in the True God and True Man who says, "Before Abraham came to be, I AM" (Jn 8:58). The mysterious Melchizedek, who offers bread and wine to "our Father in faith," is whispering that some day Christ will offer his own Body and Blood to those whose faith makes them true heirs of Abraham.

– Father George William Rutler

"Amen, I say to you, if you have faith the size of
a mustard seed, you will say to this mountain,
'Move from here to there,' and it will move.
Nothing will be impossible for you." (Mt 17:20)

THE MOUNTAIN IS A METAPHOR. Jesus here has just re-buked his disciples and their entire "unfaithful" genera-tion, for they failed to cast out a demon through lack of faith. The great immovable mountain is thus an image for the recalcitrant presence of evil. It is like a huge haughty demon staging a sit-in, refusing to budge even an inch. The miniscule mustard seed then portrays the irresistible force of faith, which can pry loose and evict such a mon-ster without even lifting a finger.

Jesus' teaching exposes the bewildering dispropor-tion of faith's power. Faith for the Christian is like David's small stone; it will lay low the most menacing Philistine. If the tiniest speck works such marvels, just imagine what a healthy dose might do! "Nothing will be impossible for you," Jesus audaciously promises. If the mountain is a meta-phor, it must yet challenge our weak imagination. Miracles are not out of the question. Archimedes said, "Give me a place to stand, and I will move the world." Faith gives more leverage than Archimedes ever dreamt, for by faith the soul reaches to God. The saints knew the trick of faith's miracle lever.

– Father J. Anthony Giambrone, O.P.

*With his whole being man gives his assent to God
the revealer. Sacred Scripture calls this human response
to God, the author of revelation, "the obedience of faith"*
(Cf. Rom 1:5; 16:26). (CCC 143)

IN COMING TO UNDERSTAND what the theological virtue of faith actually is, we first have to bracket the many meanings of "faith" we might encounter in our daily lives. To some people "faith" seems to be a sort of confidence: "You can do it, I have faith in you." For others, it denotes a broad statement of belief such as, "I practice the Christian faith," forgetting any denominational reference.

What the theological virtue of faith is, however, is quite different from these two examples. Faith, simply put, is our being obedient to what God has revealed to us to be true. Faith unites us to God through what he has chosen to reveal to us, what is necessary for our salvation. We give assent of intellect and will, from our head and our heart, to God, who can neither deceive nor be deceived. The obedience of faith is our hearing God speak to us personally and our freely surrendering to him and to his revelation. We believe in what is spoken to us not because of ourselves but simply because of who it is that is speaking, namely, God himself.

– Father James M. Sullivan, O.P.

Sarah

SARAH IS ABRAHAM'S WIFE and Isaac's mother. She conceives in her old age. She is afraid people will laugh at her. She has the job of mothering Isaac after his traumatic experience on the mountain.

We have to wonder: What would it do to a child to go up on a mountain with his father, ostensibly to offer sacrifice, and for the father to end up holding a knife to the child's neck? What kind of a child leaves with Abraham that morning, and what kind of a child does Abraham bring back to Sarah?

Just so, life traumatizes all of us. Like Sarah, in our old age, we are better poised to nurse the psychic wounds of others. And like Sarah, our job is to withstand the laughter of others, in spite of our suffering, and to learn to laugh at ourselves.

After Abraham comes down from the mountain, the angel of the Lord says, "[B]ecause you acted as you did in not withholding from me your beloved son, I will bless you abundantly and make your descendants as countless as the stars of the sky and the sands of the seashore" (Gn 22:16-17).

Good news for Abraham, perhaps. As for the *mother* of all these children—in her old age, no less!—we can only hope that Sarah had a sense of humor.

– Heather King

Beatitudes to the Sunflowers

THESE SEALED SUNFLOWERS
stand to the sermon of the sun,
attentive they lean,
silent as seed.
How blessed
are the poor,
the meek,
the pure.
This earth will be theirs;
their eyes will see.
How blessed
and tall,
their heads still green.
They wait
for the sun
on faces unseen.

– Rita A. Simmonds

*P*ERHAPS IN THE LAST ANALYSIS it is impossible to escape a paradox whose logic is completely disclosed only to the experience of a life based on faith. Anyone who entrusts himself to faith becomes aware that both exist: the radical character of the grace that frees helpless man and, no less, the abiding seriousness of the responsibility that summons man day after day. Both together mean that the Christian enjoys, on the one hand, the liberating, detached tranquility of him who lives on that excess of divine justice known as Jesus Christ. There is a tranquility that knows: in the last analysis, I cannot destroy what *he* has built up. For in himself man lives with the dreadful knowledge that his power to destroy is infinitely greater than his power to build up. But this same man knows that in Christ the power to build up has proved infinitely stronger. This is the source of a profound freedom, a knowledge of God's unrepentant love; he sees through all our errors and remains well disposed to us. It becomes possible to do one's own work fearlessly; it has shed its sinister aspect because it has lost its power to destroy: the issue of the world does not depend on us but is in God's hands.

– Pope Benedict XVI

Melchizedek

In a book rife with genealogies, Melchizedek, King of Salem, appears out of nowhere. The bread and wine he offers is neither the lambs of Abel nor the grain of Cain, but part peace-offering, part sacrifice which earth has offered and human hearts have made. In nine ways Melchizedek points to the future Christ: greater than Abraham, without beginning or end of days, a priest for ever, a priest who sacrifices to the true God, of a sacred lineage directly from God, a priest who is also a king, a king of Salem or peace, as king of Jerusalem a king of the Jews, a king of the pagans he serves.

Yet this cryptic figure is an archetype with a difference, for he stands at the crossroads of paganism and belief. His "God Most High" (Gn 14:18) names both the Canaanite deity and the true God whom Abram worships. Melchizedek points to the heathen in our own hearts who is foreign to Christ, who also shines on our lands of sunrise and sunset that have not seen the great light. These are not found near Meribah—that place of rebellion within that *has* heard the Word, but holds out defiantly in disobedience. No, they are arid wastes full of promise still waiting for the waters of grace. Melchizedek beckons us to track the mysterious pagan in our own souls, bring it to the altar of faith, and apportion it to Christ.

– Father Lawrence J. Donohoo

*R*EAL FAITH, faith which inspires all one's actions, faith in the supernatural which strips the world of its mask and reveals God in all things; which abolishes the notion of "impossible," and empties the words "anxiety," "danger," and "fear" of their meaning; which gives life calm, peace, deep joy, like a child holding its mother's hand; which detaches the soul so completely from earthly things by showing up their total lack of importance and their childishness; which bestows such confidence in prayer, the confidence of a child asking its father for something useful; the faith which shows that "apart from doing what is agreeable to God, everything is vanity"…oh, how rare that is!… My God, give me real faith! My God, I believe, help the little faith I have!

– Blessed Charles de Foucauld

Hagar

Hagar is the Egyptian slave of Sarah, wife of Abraham. Sarah is barren and orders Hagar to give herself to Abraham. Hagar submits, and then conceives, after which, understandably, she "looked on her mistress with disdain" (Gn 16:4).

"The angel of the Lord said to her further, "Behold, you are with child, and shall bear a son; and you shall call his name Ishmael, because the Lord has given heed to your affliction" (Gn 16:11 rsv).

The Lord gives heed to our affliction. We are sometimes up against a rock and a hard place. A move in any direction will mean suffering; any choice we make will be partly right and partly wrong. If Hagar resists her mistress, she may be put to death. If she submits, she faces humiliation, repulsion, the possibility of pregnancy, emotional entanglement, and more risks ahead.

But the spiritual path always means risk, always contains both a yes and a no. God gives us a "child"—of one sort or another—and the child will be a "wild ass of a man/ his hand against everyone" (Gn 16:12). We are given unsolvable conundrums. We are given crosses that seem impossible to bear. But we are never alone.

The Lord gives heed to our affliction.

– Heather King

> *"Whatever you ask for in prayer with faith,*
> *you will receive."* (Mt 21:22)

FAITH AND PERSEVERANCE ARE CLOSE COUSINS. This means that asking with belief is not by nature a one-shot prospect, a magic wand for playing fairy godmother. That idea is the invention of faith-healers and Gospel quacks. In truth, asking and asking without hesitation, when the prospects only get dimmer and dimmer, is the deepest sort of faith. Seen from this perspective, Jesus' teaching here is no different from his teaching in the parable of the pestering woman. To pray faithfully is like knocking untiringly at God's door. A true believer knows he is always home. Those who waver, however, will sigh and walk away if he hasn't answered after whatever dose of banging. Of course, the reason God at times waits to answer is that walking away is sometimes best for us. In other words, unworthy prayers, prayers that ask for what we ought not to receive when put to the test by God naturally wither and die. Since prayer itself is the work of the Spirit, God simply withholds the grace of our asking like the importunate widow for what might in fact harm us. The infallible gift of praying with perseverant faith, in contrast, is simply the grace to know who God truly is and thus what he is always sure to give—even if we must stand awhile and knock.

– Father J. Anthony Giambrone, O.P.

*F*OR YOU MUST UNDERSTAND: he desires nearness; he would like to live in you and commingle his breath with your breathing. He would like to be with you until the end of the world. He knocks at all the souls. He makes himself small and inconspicuous so as to be able to partake of all their little transactions and concerns. He approaches quietly so as not to disturb or be recognized; he comes to be present incognito in the full hubbub of the earth's annual fair. He seeks trust, intimacy; he is a beggar for your love. Here is where you must really stand firm so that the boundaries won't be blurred. He is God and he must remain such. He ought not demean himself. It is a God-fearing thing to remind him of what he owes to himself. When he suddenly jumps out of his ambush and grips at your heart with one of his famous handholds, and your heart goes wild with throbbing, then you must quickly cast yourselves down and say with all humility: "Lord, go away from me. I am a sinful man!" That's an obvious distance, you see. And when he looks at you sorrowfully and silently attempts to make his solitude visible to you, remain strong. Do him homage and say: "I am not worthy that you should come under my roof" (but leave the rest out!).

– Father Hans Urs von Balthasar

The Virgin Mary most perfectly embodies
the obedience of faith. (CCC 148)

ONE OF THE BLESSED MOTHER'S TITLES used in a recent collection of Masses is "Pillar of Faith." At first, this may strike us an unusual title for our Lady. A pillar doesn't sound very feminine; it sounds rather cold and lifeless. Yet this title says a great deal about the role of Mary in our lives. A pillar is built for only one purpose in a building: for support. Because of this, the pillar has to be strong. It is built with the purest materials because any weakness in the pillar itself will cause the structure to weaken and even collapse. That is why Mary is created sinless, of the purest materials, from the first moment of her Immaculate Conception. She is created in this fashion for the benefit of the entire "building" of the Church.

We call upon Mary as a source for our own strength in faith because we too make up the building of the Church along with her. We ask the Blessed Mother to make us "pillars of faith" alongside herself, to be obedient to the Lord in all that he has revealed. The closer we are to her, that strongest pillar, the more certain we are of the strength of the entire building.

– Father James M. Sullivan, O.P.

Isaac

LIKE HIS FATHER ABRAHAM and Jacob his own son, Isaac is one of the three patriarchs in the tradition of faith. He is among a great cloud of witnesses because he passes on what he has learned from his father, fidelity to God's design, which was perfected in Jesus (cf. Heb 12:1-2).

His birth turns his aged parents' incredulity to rejoicing. His name, meaning "he laughs/ will laugh," extends their delight. They realize then what their three mysterious visitors had told them and the fulfillment of the promise about Abraham fathering a nation as vast as the stars. Referring to Isaac, who unlike his elder brother is not born of a slave, Saint Paul sees him as a model of the joyous freedom of God's children (Gal 4:22ff.).

When Abraham's faith is tested, so is that of Isaac, who meekly submits to his life being sacrificed. In his being spared by God, the Church Fathers see prefigured Jesus' Resurrection, the pivot of faith.

When old and blind, through his wife Rebecca's deception, Isaac blesses Jacob, the younger of his twin sons. His mistake is justified, since the elder brother Esau forfeited his birthright for defying God's ordinance in marrying women not of the chosen race. Isaac's blindness thus signifies faith through which we see dimly God's wise ways that aren't ours.

– Father Michael L. Gaudoin-Parker

*L*IKE ME, you need a faith capable of destroying all the obstacles the world will present, and hell as well, for besides all the communities that have already been founded, there are appeals from all over the world, there are foundations about to begin and others planned for later on.... It's a real storm wind driving our sails. Are you going to furl the sails in order to shelter your boat in the port, for fear that the going will get too rough, or are you going to let yourself sail out onto the open sea, driven by the powerful wind of God's Spirit?

Don't be afraid. Don't just look at the present state of things, which could destroy you completely; start getting ready to rebuild.... The Lord is with you. Ask him for faith that can tear up and move mountains because it stands on his power and on his love...a faith that does not trust in self at all, for it knows itself in truth—that humble faith which never fails to touch the Lord's heart.... Tell him often: "I am nothing, but you are all. I have nothing, but you possess all. I can do nothing, but you can do all things. What I'm asking you today is so much easier than moving mountains, and you promised to grant that much as a reward for faith no bigger than a mustard seed."

– Little Sister Magdeleine of Jesus

THE GOAL OF OUR LIFE is to live with God forever./ God, who loves us, gave us life./ Our own response of love allows God's life/ to flow into us without limit.

All the things in this world are gifts from God,/ presented to us so that we can know God more easily and make a return of love more readily./ As a result,/ we appreciate and use all these gifts of God/ insofar as they help us to develop as loving persons./ But if any of these gifts become the center of our lives,/ they displace God/ and so hinder our growth toward our goal.

In everyday life, then, we must hold ourselves in balance/ before all of these created gifts insofar as we have a choice/ and are not bound by some obligation./ We should not fix our desires on health or sickness,/ wealth or poverty, success or failure, a long life or a short one./ For everything has the potential of calling forth in us/ a deeper response to our life in God.

Our only desire and our one choice should be this:/ I want and I choose what better leads/ to God's deepening his life in me.

– Saint Ignatius of Loyola

Rebekah

ATTENTIVE READERS OF GENESIS have noticed that it is Rebekah, even more than Isaac, who imitates the style of Abraham's faith. Abraham is an exemplary man of action. Isaac is a contemplative. When he meets his future wife in Genesis 24, Isaac is going "to meditate in the field in the evening" (Gn 24:63 RSV). Rebekah, meanwhile, has just completed a journey of faith that mirrors Abraham's, coming out of Mesopotamia to the Promised Land. Like the patriarch, she is called out of her country to an unknown future. She has never met Isaac, whom Abraham does not let go back to his old land: "Never take my son back there" (Gn 24:6, 8). Isaac is the promised son, the future by which the Lord's promise of land and descendants will be fulfilled. He may not go "back there" into the past. Instead a servant goes and finds Rebekah, with the Lord's help: "So they called Rebekah, and asked her, 'Do you wish to go with this man?' She answered, 'I do'" (Gn 24:58).

Rebekah knows that this marriage is not a matter of human calculation but of the divine plan. With that simple trust, which embraces the unknown in faith, she is propelled into the future of the Father. Thus she shows herself to be a true daughter of Abraham, our father in faith, who accepted the adventure of God's plan with a total trust.

– Angela Franks

Faith is first of all a personal adherence of man to God....
It is a free assent to the whole truth
that God has revealed. (CCC 150)

IMAGINE that after the death of your Great-Aunt Martha, you find in her attic a hope chest filled with family heirlooms. In it you come upon something that fills in all the "blanks" of your family's history; it could be a crinkled photograph, an immigration document, or a piece of well-worn jewelry. That "something" shows the turning point in your family's history, and perhaps how your entire family had come into being at all.

Now imagine the Church being that hope chest filled with the mysteries of the faith. You find all sorts of things in there, from moral teachings to sacramental graces, from words of Scripture to those of prayers. What would be the "something" that would make sense of it all? The "whole truth that God has revealed" can only be understood in the light of the cross of Christ. The "whole truth" can only be seen from the cross. Without the cross, Scripture would be a dead letter, prayers would be empty superstitions, and the moral code of the Church would be sheer torture. We give assent to the whole truth God has revealed because he has saved us and made it possible to say, "I believe."

– Father James M. Sullivan, O.P.

Jacob

How often does destiny reach into a mother's womb? Will life's trajectory be fixed by the movements of a fetus? It certainly happened to Jacob, son of Isaac and Rebecca, third patriarch of the Chosen People, whose hand took hold of his twin brother's heel in a fierce struggle to be born. Further usurpations follow, including the seizure of Esau's birthright and blessing in order to fulfill God's prophecy that "the older shall serve the younger" (Gn 25:23). A covenant is thus made with one whose name means "heel-catcher," "leg-puller." From his loins we trace not merely the Twelve Tribes of Israel, but the Church herself, founded upon the faith of the Twelve Apostles.

Then in the struggle with the angel from whom he will not desist until a blessing be given, a new name is vouchsafed, that of Israel, "because you have contended with divine and human beings and have prevailed" (Gn 32:29). Here is the great theme of Jacob's life, that of continual wrestling with God, "who answered me in my hour of distress and who has been with me wherever I have gone" (Gn 35:3). Such faith in God's "steadfast love" (Gn 32:10 RSV) shall shape the outcome of the world's destiny.

– Regis Martin

The Predisposition to Faith

THOUGHTFUL HUMAN beings need to understand the world and their place within it. Numerous different answers to this search for meaning exist—and the last century is littered with the burned-out remains of many such theories.

Today, people continue to search for meaning. Some find it in tribalism—the withdrawal of loyalty to a particular racial, ethnic, or religious group. Others adopt a materialistic, evolutionary interpretation of life—but one that provides no meaning, since life results from randomness or determinism. Many give up on meaning, except for their own personally created meaning—a relativism made to fit their own preferences. All these views are secular: none of them has any use for God or religion. Nevertheless, millions of intelligent, idealistic people have committed themselves with great intensity to such forms of faith—faiths from which God has been exiled.

The need for meaning—and for faith—remains. And if for many years the dominant groups in society have rejected God—especially Christianity—it is time for thoughtful minds to rethink this rejection.

There are many reasons to appreciate again the strengths of Christianity: it views all human beings as members of the same family; it is genuinely universal and rejects no one. Christianity is also very particular: it has many beautiful local forms and welcomes different cultural traditions. As a Catholic, I note the wide range of expressions within Catholicism, from different parts of the world, and inspired by different religious orders and groups. Nevertheless, the universality—the all-embracing character—of Catholic Christianity is what matters the most.

In addition, Catholicism has a great intellectual—rational and spiritual—tradition, which remains vibrant and growing; it reaches out in reason and truth to the minds of people throughout the world. Christianity also offers a foundational emphasis on the interpersonal—namely, the love of God and of neighbor. Self-giving love is at the center of the Christian understanding of life.

Christianity is an adventure: it will challenge you to a relationship with God, and to new, loving relationships with others. Like any true adventure, it poses some serious dangers—including the risk of death. It is not likely that you will die a martyr, but what may die is what you understand to be your self; you may have to bury a prideful understanding of yourself and your narcissistic fantasies. Finally, Christianity promises you wonderful fellowship with other human beings, and the great hope of genuine fulfillment.

– Paul C. Vitz

"Faith in Christ is the highest form of repentance."
– Saint Cyril of Alexandria

Rachel

RACHEL'S LIFE reads like a soap opera.

She is switched by her father for Leah, her older sister, on her wedding night to Jacob, after which, the "second wife," she stands by as Leah bears Jacob four sons. Unable to conceive, in frustration she gives her maidservant Bilhah to Jacob: Bilhah bears Jacob two more sons and conceives another. Finally Rachel conceives and bears her own son, Joseph.

She then flees with Jacob, Leah, Joseph, and the other children into the land of Canaan, meanwhile secreting away her father's idols. Jacob, unknowing, puts a curse on the thief. Rachel conceives another son and, fulfilling the curse, dies in childbirth, naming her newborn Ben Oni ("son of my mourning").

Thus, Rachel is connected with the slaughter of the innocents, when shortly after Christ's birth Herod orders that all the male children under the age of two be killed.

> *"Then was fulfilled what had been said*
> *through Jeremiah the prophet:*
> *'A voice was heard in Ramah,*
> *Sobbing and loud lamentation;*
> *Rachel weeping for her children...'"* (Mt 2:17-18).

Instead of destroying her child, Rachel is herself destroyed in giving birth. She is the voice of the unborn, and she is the voice of the women whom now, as then, we seldom hear—she is the voice of their repentant mothers.

– Heather King

"Peter said to [Jesus] in reply,
'Though all may have their faith in you shaken,
mine will never be.'"
(Mt 26:33)

THERE IS A FINE LINE between professing deep faith and simply being stubborn. When Jesus prophesies that Peter will deny him, the Apostle responds with this mulish protest and fancies himself supremely faithful. It is evident, though, that he does not trust the Lord's word without question.

The difficulty is that Peter's own weakness is now the matter for assent. He must believe that he is in all truth capable of the lowest betrayal. This is an ugly thought… harder than saying, "You are the Christ!" There is indeed a stubborn protest within all of us faced with the offensive truth that no crime, however despicable, is beyond the scope of our own wickedness. It is only the grace of God that saves us from ourselves and accomplishes the good we do.

Saint Thomas Aquinas says it is a sin to be scandalized by our own sinfulness, since it supposes us to be something we are not. Horrified at the word Jesus speaks to him, Peter strains not to hear it. But truth is not made simply by insisting. Peter supposes his own willpower is enough to fend off moral failure. His self-reliance so shuts down denial as a prospect, that he misses it as it overtakes him. It takes a cock-crow to snap Peter from his Pelagian trance.

– Father J. Anthony Giambrone, O.P.

*F*AITH IS AN ORIENTATION of our existence as a whole. It is a fundamental option that affects every domain of our existence. Nor can it be realized unless all the energies of our existence go into maintaining it. Faith is not a merely intellectual, or merely volitional, or merely emotional activity—it is all of these things together. It is an act of the whole self, of the whole person in his concentrated unity. The Bible describes faith in this sense as an act of the "heart" (Rom 10:9).

Faith is a supremely personal act. But precisely because it is supremely personal, it transcends the self, the limits of the individual.... Any act that involves the whole man also involves, not just the self, but the we-dimension, indeed, the wholly other "Thou," God, together with the self. But this also means that such an act transcends the reach of what I can do alone. Since man is a created being, the deepest truth about him is never just action but always passion as well; man is not only a giver but also a receiver.... Faith is a perishing of the mere self and precisely thus a resurrection of the true self. To believe is to become oneself through liberation from the mere self, a liberation that brings us into communion with God mediated by communion with Christ.

– Pope Benedict XVI

Joseph the Patriarch

AMONG THE STORMS of the house of Jacob, there are few as thrilling as the story of Joseph, the eleventh son, whom Jacob loved more than the others and because of which his brothers sold him into slavery. But God, long accustomed to writing straight with crooked lines, uses their treachery to further his own plans, thus fulfilling the meaning of Joseph's name: "May God increase." Which he triumphantly does during the long years of servitude in Egypt. So steadfast is the Lord's love that Joseph rises to unheard of heights, becoming, after Pharaoh, the most powerful man in the land.

When famine strikes, it is Joseph who, having filled the bins during the time of plenty, brings the sons of Israel into Egypt, there to provide for and reconcile with his brothers amid scenes of matchless pathos. "Do not be distressed," he tells them, "and do not reproach yourselves for having sold me here. It was really for the sake of saving lives that God sent me here ahead of you" (Gn 45:5). The evil they sought failed to undo the good God brought. Do not be afraid, he assures them. "I will provide for you and your children" (Gn 50:21). It is a tale only God could tell. And thanks to the courage and fidelity of Joseph, he is the pencil with which God writes it.

– Regis Martin

> *"Believing is an act of the intellect*
> *assenting to the divine truth by command of the will*
> *moved by God through grace"*
> (St. Thomas Aquinas, STh II-II, 2, 9; cf. Dei Filius 3: DS 3010).
> (CCC 155)

GRATIA UT MOTIO is not a phrase that we come upon every day, but it is a particular grace that God has given every one of us so that we can believe in him and grow closer to him. The reason we need this grace is simple: our reason is not enough.

When Saint Thomas Aquinas describes the beginning of faith in an individual, he points out all the many truths that people encounter in the world that might point to God. There is beauty in the world, there is order, there is progression and maturity. However, none of these experiences can bring us to the conclusion of who God is. For that, we need faith, and for faith we need grace.

It is particularly this *gratia ut motio* which the Lord gives us that helps us to make that free assent of intellect and will in order to believe. This "grace for movement" moves our will to command our intellect to say, "I believe." We need to think about things and we need to desire them too. In the act of faith, we do both, and we think about and desire the greatest of all things: God himself.

– Father James M. Sullivan, O.P.

*D*O YOU NOT KNOW that utter dying to self, to live only in God and for God, can only take place by degrees, through a persistent fidelity in making the sacrifice of the intelligence, of the will, of all our passions and caprices, of our feelings and affections; finally and above all, the sacrifice that comes of a complete submission in all trials, in unceasing interior vicissitudes, and in states, sometimes painful indeed, through which God makes us pass in order to change us completely into him?

Do you not know that the state of pure faith excludes all things that can be perceived by the senses? In that state we go forward stripped of everything, and find no support from any created thing; but the pure light of faith remains for ever in the highest point of the soul; and by this simple light we see not only what we must do and what we must avoid, but we learn further that, by God's grace, we live in a horror of, and flight from, evil, in love and performance of good.... For it is our lot in this life to live always in fear; perfect assurance is possible to no one. God wishes us to glorify him by a self-abandonment full of faith and love: it is the tribute of which he is most jealous.

– Father Jean-Pierre de Caussade, s.j.

Tamar

TAMAR'S INDEFATIGABLE FAITH in the future earns her a place in Matthew's genealogy of Jesus (Mt 1:3)—despite the unsettling way she enters the messianic lineage. How does this come about? Through the outworking of providence and the persistence of faith.

Judah marries his eldest son Er to Tamar, a Canaanite woman. Yet "Er...greatly offended the LORD" (Gn 38:7), and he dies. Onan, the next brother, has the duty to marry Tamar and give her offspring; he too is struck down. Though Tamar is owed the opportunity to have a child by the third son, Shelah, Judah withholds him from her out of fear. Tamar, however, will not be denied. She devises a clever ruse through which she conceives a child from Judah's line—by the unwitting Judah himself! When Tamar reveals her identity, Judah proclaims, "She is more righteous than I" (Gn 38:26 RSV).

Tamar's plucky example points to another Canaanite woman who will look in unwavering hope to Jesus, Judah's offspring, pleading for her child with great pluck and persistence. "Please, Lord, for even the dogs eat the scraps that fall from the table of their masters." Jesus replies, "O woman, great is your faith! Let it be done for you as you wish" (Mt 15:27-28).

– Angela Franks

"Jesus said… 'Everything is possible to one who has faith.'
Then the boy's father cried out,
'I do believe, help my unbelief!'"
(Mk 9:23-24)

THE BOY'S FATHER BELIEVES OR DOES HE NOT? He wants faith to prevail in his wavering and weary heart. Yet Jesus' own disciples have just failed to help his suffering boy; and who knows how many other failed remedies he has tried since his son was a little child? Chances are, the expectation of disappointment has settled on this father like a cloud. Jesus seems to meet him as he is nearing the end of his rope. Indeed, the man's desperation is evident and moving—some ancient manuscripts even (fittingly) add the heartrending detail that the poor father cried out his beautiful, helpless prayer "with tears."

Chastened as he may be by disappointment and uncertain what he really thinks possible anymore, the father's love is still stronger than despair. He thus pleads with the one who promises that all things are possible, for more than faith this father earnestly wants his beloved son to be saved. If we understand the pathos of a parent whose child has suffered terribly all his life, we can also appreciate the way charity fosters deeper faith. One who loves deeply simply needs to believe. Boundless love demands boundless possibilities—and that invites an endless increase in faith.

– Father J. Anthony Giambrone, O.P.

*H*ISTORY IS NOT IN THE HANDS of the powers of darkness, chance, or human decisions alone. When evil energy that we see is unleashed, when Satan vehemently bursts in, when a multitude of scourges and ills surface, the Lord, the supreme arbiter of historical events, arises. He leads history wisely towards the dawn of the new heavens and the new earth....

There is consequently a desire to reaffirm that God is not indifferent to human events but penetrates them, creating his own "ways" or, in other words, his effective plans and "deeds"....

The nations must learn to "read" God's message in history. The adventure of humanity is not confused and meaningless, nor is it doomed, never to be appealed against or to be abused by the overbearing and the perverse....

This attitude of faith leads men and women to recognize the power of God who works in history and thus to open themselves to feeling awe for the name of the Lord. In biblical language, in fact, this "fear" is not fright. It is recognition of the mystery of divine transcendence. Thus, it is at the root of faith and is interwoven with love.... As Saint Hilary of Poitiers, a fourth-century bishop, said: "All our fear is in love."

– Pope Benedict XVI

Moses

IT IS TO MOSES that God first reveals his name: "I am who am" (Ex 3:14), a name that has fascinated believers throughout the ages. Is God saying that his name goes beyond all names, that no name, no finite mind, can grasp him? Yet he tells Moses his name; he entrusts himself to Moses. For the beginning of faith is God's act of trust in us, God entrusting us with the truth that he reveals about himself.

Then Moses comes to Mount Sinai. He ascends the mountain and dwells with God for forty days. Saint Gregory of Nyssa has a beautiful interpretation of this event: he compares the life of Moses to the mystical ascent to union with God. We begin in the darkness of ordinary life. As we ascend the mountain, we leave the darkness behind and climb toward the light. The light grows brighter and brighter; but then, with Moses, we enter the cloud, and darkness envelops us. For at that moment of revelation, we know that we can never know God; it is the mysticism of darkness.

But Moses comes down from the mountain again and for forty years leads the children of Israel through the desert. They will enter the Promised Land, but Moses will never set foot in it. It is the final self-sacrifice of the one who has seen God: to offer himself for others—in other words, to be Jesus Christ.

– Father Joseph T. Lienhard, S.J.

An Examination of Conscience

According to Faith

- Have I been true to my faith through diligent prayer, reception of the sacraments, and works of mercy?
- Do I frequently call on the Holy Name of Jesus and make fervent acts of faith?
- Have I omitted to nourish and protect my faith?
- Do I constantly renew my faith through acts of self-surrender, holy dependence on God, and humility?
- Do I trust in divine providence even amidst hardships?
- Have I committed voluntary doubt by disregarding or refusing to hold as true what God has revealed and the Church proposes for belief?
- Have I deliberately cultivated hesitation in believing what the Catholic faith teaches?
- Have I shied away from the difficulty in overcoming objections connected with the faith?
- Have I let the anxiety aroused by faith's obscurity overwhelm me?
- Have I committed the sin of incredulity by neglecting a revealed truth of the faith or willfully refusing to assent to it?
- Do the actual preferences of my life betray a lack of faith? Have I made compromises that contradict faith?
- Have I been a zealous witness to the faith, withstanding fear or shame?
- Am I grateful to those who led me to my faith and who help sustain my faith?
- Do I truly live by faith, or do I let my emotions, my ideas, my feelings, or my passions predominate?
- Is God the center and main priority of my life?

– Father Peter John Cameron, O.P.

*T*HE ADVENT OF FAITH effects an original and substantial transformation in the moral life. It centers the moral life on a particular person: Jesus, the Christ. In short, he becomes the source and cause of moral excellence for those who believe in him. Jesus is not merely a sage or a model. By means of the personal ties that faith and love initiate, he establishes such a close spiritual communion between himself and his disciples that Saint Paul will present the Christian life as "life in Christ." He even affirms that, "It is no longer I who live, but Christ who lives in me" (Gal 2:20). This view is unique among the moralities and religions of the world: For Christians, the person of Jesus has become the center of the moral life, as he is also the center of prayer and the liturgy that nourishes it.

It is appropriate to note that it is here that faith acquires its full force. Faith does not signify, as it often does today, merely a certain opinion about life or a mental adherence to a creed. Faith is a vital act; it commits one person to another forever.... Faith becomes the interior rule guiding one's creative and constructive actions. It engenders hope, which gives life its energy. Faith in Christ, therefore, is like an interior law for building up the moral life of the Christian.

– Father Servais Pinckaers, O.P.

Aaron

THE PRIEST has no portion but the Lord. Think of your priests, giving up the domestic comfort of wife and children to serve as faithful sons of the Father—who in turn bestows a portion of his flock upon them. The priestly life makes visible the invisible country that is heaven, a land resplendent with the Father's overflowing abundance.

Aaron, Moses' brother and Israel's first high priest, stands at the head of this spiritual lineage. He is the first chosen by God for that exposure on the high rock of faith which is priestly service of God and man. Thus exposed, the priest can fail. The people may clamor for insurance in the face of the demands of holiness, which descend from the heights of invisible love. Why not fashion a golden calf to cover our bases? There are corners in our heart that are Egypt still. The yoke of sin has the advantage of familiarity. Who knows about this far country to which the Father calls us?

Yet the sacred vestments surround Aaron. Faith will be incarnate, pressing into visibility, in the very fabric of our lives. Our failures are swallowed up in this raiment wrought by God. What comes of trusting the Father? Mercy, and definitive ennoblement: "He increased the glory of Aaron/ and bestowed upon him his inheritance…The LORD himself is his portion,/ his inheritance in the midst of Israel" (Sir 45:20, 22).

– J. David Franks

Faith is certain.
It is more certain than all human knowledge.
(*CCC 157*)

IN THE DISCUSSION of the theological virtue of faith, there is always a great temptation to believe the truths of faith because we have reasoned to them all by ourselves. This temptation exalts our own faculty for reasoning far beyond a level it was made to go. We cannot reason to all the truths of our Catholic Faith because God did not create us that way. He created us to need faith. He created us to believe in him.

One of the effects of original sin, as the Catechism describes it, is "self-assertion, contrary to the dictates of reason" (CCC 377). The true use of reason, which is guided and informed by grace, leads us to the conclusion that our faith is certain because it relies on God for its revelation. The false use of reason, which is led astray and deformed by sin, brings us to the conclusion that our faith is faulty, because we ourselves reasoned to its conclusions. It is only in the light of grace that we can see God's revelation as true and certain. This is the working of the theological virtue of faith, which takes away our blindness toward God and, in truth, ourselves.

– Father James M. Sullivan, O.P.

*I*N THE FORMER TIME God proved the inability of our nature to obtain life, and now he has revealed a Savior capable of saving the incapable. For both these reasons he wanted us to believe in his goodness and to look upon him as guardian, father, teacher, adviser, and physician, as our mind, light, honor, glory, strength, and life, and to have no solicitude about what we wear and eat.

This faith, if only you desire it, you can have, and, first of all, the knowledge of the Father.... Anyone can be an imitator of God, if he takes on his own shoulders the burden of his neighbor, if he chooses to use his advantage to help another who is underprivileged, if he takes what he has received from God and gives to those who are in need—for such a one becomes God to those who are helped. When you have faith, you will see that God rules in heaven, even though you are on earth; you will begin to speak of the mysteries of God; you will love and admire those who suffer because they refuse to deny God; you will condemn the deceit and error of the world as soon as you realize that true life is in heaven.

– John the Solitary

Miriam

MIRIAM'S FAITH IS EXUBERANT! In her we see the joy of the people of God who have not been forgotten by him as they labor in the mines of the Egyptians. No, indeed, he has a plan for his people, and Miriam is a privileged witness to his saving work.

As a child hiding amidst the reeds, she witnesses her baby brother Moses floating in a basket on the river Nile, plucked from the waters by the daughter of Pharaoh. As a grown woman, fleeing Egypt with her people, led by that same baby brother, she passes through the waters of the Red Sea, held back by the hand of the Lord. Their Egyptian pursuers are swallowed in those same waters. Miriam, as though filled to the brim with joy, grabs the tambourine and leads the Israelite women in song and dance: "Sing to the LORD, for he is gloriously triumphant;/ horse and chariot he has cast into the sea" (Ex 15:21). Hers is the full-throated praise of the God who is constant and sure. Indeed, he has not forgotten us! His plans are greater than our plans—exceeding all our hopes and expectations!

– Lisa Lickona

It IS NOT for his gifts/ that I continue in my prayers,/ but because he is true Life.

It is not so much by hope/ as by bonds of love that I am drawn./ It is not for gifts,/ but for the Giver that I ever yearn.

It is not glory I aspire to,/ but it is the Glorified One whom I wish to embrace./ It is not by the desire for life,/ but by the remembrance of him who gives life/ that I am ever consumed!

It is not for joyous passions that I yearn,/ but it is because of a desire for him who is preparing them/ that my heart bursts out in tears./ It is not rest that I seek,/ but it is the face of him who offers rest that I seek in prayer.

It is not for the nuptial banquet,/ but it is for the Bridegroom that I long./ Despite the weight of my transgressions/ I believe with indubitable hope,/ trusting in the hand of the Almighty One,/ that not only shall I obtain pardon,/ but that I shall see him in person,/ thanks to his mercy and pity,/ and that I shall inherit heaven/ although I completely deserve to be banished.

Receive with sweetness, O powerful Lord God,/ the prayer of him who was bitterness for you./ Grant that through remembrance of your hope/ I may remain unscathed, protected by you. Amen.

– Saint Gregory of Narek

*W*HEN YOU COME DOWN to hard brass tacks, Advent is meant to be the time of faith. Unfortunately, one of the things missing in the world is faith. Ask a Protestant, a Catholic, a Jew: "Do you *really* have faith?" Many wouldn't know what to say, if they were honest. Ask yourself now, do you have faith? Real faith? Really??

Your faith should be unshakable, like a tree standing near the water, as it says in Psalm One. Your faith should be like a light within your heart to light your path, and the path of your friends, and others around you.

True faith is profound, immutable, unchangeable. *That* is the faith of our fathers, the faith which has been given to us by God via the Second Person of the Trinity, Jesus Christ.

No one can be so ugly, no one so tragic, no one so miserable as not to be beloved by God. That's something extraordinary! Aren't you filled to the brim with this miracle? It is so great!

And the greater your faith, the deeper that miracle. Think about it. Dream about it. Ponder it. And slowly, as you do, without noticing it, you will become a saint.

– Servant of God Catherine de Hueck Doherty

Nahshon

Nahshon is, by fate and his own free initiative, a necessary link in the chain of our salvation story. He was a descendant of Jacob's son, Judah, and the ancestor of King David. In Holy Scripture, we see him assuming leadership of the tribe of Judah when the Israelites leave Egypt under Moses' leadership (Nm 1:7). In the rabbinic commentary, he is the first one to step forward into the Red Sea, even before it has parted. Thus, in Yiddish, people say "To be a Nahshon" to mean a "protagonist." He is the symbol of what every Christian is called to: to take responsibility for the Church so that the story of the Body of Christ might continue in history.

So fully does Nahshon fulfill this role, leading the ranks of his people in procession and battle, that when it comes time for the inauguration of the sacrifices of the Tabernacle, Moses chooses Nahshon to be the first one to present his gift of sacrifice to the Lord (Nm 7:12). It is this offering that gives the beginning of all lawful and righteous offerings to God, fulfilled in Jesus Christ in the fullness of time. Though remembered by few, yet Nahshon shares in the glory of the story of salvation. His example can lead us to say yes to being protagonists of our story in Christ.

– Father Vincent Nagle, F.S.C.B.

*It is intrinsic to faith that a believer desires
to know better the One in whom he has put his faith.*
(CCC 158)

How do we distinguish between a genuine question
of faith and a questioning faith? As the theological virtue
of faith envelops our life there will naturally, or in this
case, supernaturally, be questions that arise. This is the
means by which we grow in faith. Sometimes we have to
wrestle with a truth of the faith in order to understand it
better and to live our faith more fully. There are definitely
sins against faith and the Catechism lists them as: *voluntary doubt, incredulity, heresy, apostasy,* and *schism* (CCC
2088-2089). There are also sins against the truth, which
also harm faith such as: lies, dishonesty, ignorance, cheating, and gossiping.

One helpful marker for our growth in faith and our
avoidance of these sins against faith is our wonder, our
awe before God. When God becomes commonplace in our
life, or when we no longer think of him as awesome and
our faith as truly amazing, we need to ask more questions
and seek "more understanding" of the great mystery that
has been revealed to us. What we know now can never be
enough to fulfill us for ever.

– Father James M. Sullivan, O.P.

Joshua

JOSHUA'S FAITH can best be seen in his relationship to Moses. No Old Testament figure is as united with God as is Moses. In fact, on two occasions the Lord tells Moses, "You shall be as God..." (cf. Ex 4:16, 7:1). Yet, often the people complain and doubt Moses' God-given leadership. Joshua, however, faithfully recognizes Moses' authority as that of the Lord himself.

Joshua is among twelve men sent by Moses to scout out the land of Canaan which, Moses says, the Lord has promised to give to the Chosen People. While the others give discouraging reports about the possibility of entering the land, Joshua, along with Caleb, assures the people they have nothing to fear; he is certain that the Lord is with them.

Joshua's faith is not deterred by Moses' death outside the Promised Land. Joshua knows that Moses' greatness comes from God, and therefore the authority that is present through Moses can continue beyond Moses. Putting his faith in God's call, Joshua fearlessly leads the people into the Promised Land. The authority that Joshua exercises henceforth is the same as that of Moses; it is the true authority that springs from faithful dependence upon God.

– Father Richard Veras

"And the apostles said to the Lord,
'Increase our faith.'" (Lk 17:5)

THERE IS A DELIGHTFUL ANECDOTE in Ronald Knox's book, *Enthusiasm*, in which some obscure religious charlatan, challenged by skeptics, gathered a small group of pious disciples to witness her miraculously walk across a lake. Whipping them up with fervor, she demanded to know whether they *truly believed* she could perform this great sign. They warmly assured they did believe. She accordingly replied that in such case no sign was necessary, then walked away (by land), leaving the crowd rather dumbfounded.

The story raises interesting questions. What stuff does faith live on? Do external signs deepen real faith or just enable immature convictions? How can we differentiate supernatural knowledge from simple self-delusion?

Saint Thomas Aquinas says that external inducements (e.g., sermons, arguments, miracles) are necessary but not sufficient for engendering true faith in our hearts. It is an interior movement of grace that ultimately brings our will to assent with divine insight; for if God does not supply the supernatural gift, we will be left at the level of native discernment—which will likely leave us the dupes of a charlatan. For this reason, it is right that, like the Apostles, we turn directly to the Lord to beg from him an increase in our faith.

– Father J. Anthony Giambrone, O.P.

*T*HE PATRISTIC TRADITION associates the sixth beatitude, "Blessed are the pure in heart, for
they will see God" (Mt 5:8), with theological
faith. For theological faith both purges our emotions
of inordinate affections and dismisses from our minds
fanciful and erroneous representations of what is to be
believed. But this takes place only because God, the
First Truth, shapes our intelligence through the *habitus*
of theological faith and, through minds renewed by a
living faith, effects a radical change in the whole person.
The Church celebrates this purity of heart in her saints,
but especially in the Blessed Virgin Mary who, as Saint
Irenaeus writes, "became by her obedience the cause of
salvation for herself and for the whole human race." In
an effort to suggest the depth of involvement that our
blessed Lady enjoys in the plan of salvation, and therefore in the Church's pilgrim journey of faith, Irenaeus
goes on to develop a theological comparison between
Eve, the first woman, and Mary, the first person to conceive the Word of God in her heart. "The knot of Eve's
disobedience was untied through the obedience of the
Virgin Mary; what the virgin Eve had bound up through
her lack of faith, the Virgin Mary untied by her faith."

– Father Romanus Cessario, O.P.

Rahab

As the Isrealites advance upon Jericho, Joshua sends two men into the city as spies. Rahab, a prostitute, takes them in and, when the king's guard comes to the door, reports that the two have fled. In fact, she has hidden them on her roof under a pile of flax stalks.

Because of her faith, Rahab understands that the parting of the Red Sea and the destruction of the Amorites by Joshua's army are signs of the living God. Upon hearing the news, "our hearts melted" (Jos 2:11 RSV), she told the spies—with love, with awe—which is why she undertakes the potentially fatal risk of harboring them. It's safe to assume that in the melting of her heart, she gives up her life of harlotry. When Jericho is destroyed, Rahab and her family, alone among the inhabitants of the city, are spared.

Thus, Rahab is the precursor to the woman with the alabaster ointment who waters Christ's feet with her tears. "So I tell you, her many sins have been forgiven; hence, she has shown great love. But the one to whom little is forgiven, loves little" (Lk 7:47). May our own hearts melt as well. May we water Christ's feet with tears for our own sins.

– Heather King

I BELIEVE IT IS IMPORTANT to acquire a fresh awareness of the fact that faith is the center of all things—*"Fides tua te salvum fecit,"* the Lord said over and over again to those he healed. It was not the physical touch, it was not the external gesture that was operative, but the fact that those sick people believed. And we too can only serve the Lord energetically if our faith thrives and is present in abundance.

Faith is above all faith in God. In Christianity it is not a matter of an enormous bundle of different things; all that the Creed says and the development of faith has achieved exists only to make our perception of the Face of God clearer. He exists and he is alive; we believe in him; we live before him, in his sight, in being with him and from him. And in Jesus Christ, he is, as it were, with us bodily.

To my mind, this centrality of God must appear in a completely new light in all our thoughts and actions.

Furthermore, this is what enlivens activities which, on the contrary, can easily lapse into activism and become empty.

This is the first point I want to stress: faith actually looks to God with determination and thus impels us in turn to look to God and set out towards him.

– Pope Benedict XVI

*T*HE OTHER THING ABOUT FAITH concerns the fact that we ourselves cannot invent faith, composing it with "sustainable" pieces, but we believe together with the Church. We cannot understand all that the Church teaches, nor must all of it be present in every life.

Yet, it is important that we are co-believers in the great "I" of the Church, in her living "We," and thereby find ourselves in the great community of faith, in that great subject in which the "You" of God and the "I" of man truly touch each other; in which the past of the words of Scripture becomes the present, times flow into one another, the past is present and, opening itself to the future, allows into time the brightness of eternity, of the Eternal One.

This complete form of faith, expressed in the Creed, a faith in and with the Church as a living subject in which the Lord works: it is this form of faith that we must seek to put truly at the heart of our endeavor.

– Pope Benedict XVI

*"Though faith is above reason,
there can never be any real discrepancy
between faith and reason"
(Dei Filius 4:DS 3017). (CCC 159)*

PETER WAS STANDING on the water no doubt wondering why he was not sinking. Then he began to doubt, and he did sink. He calls out to Jesus to save him, and Jesus does just that. Back in the boat, Jesus corrects him: "O you of little faith, why did you doubt?" (Mt 14:31 RSV).

Science cannot explain how Peter was standing on the water, only faith can. Science is limited in its scope because it is limited to man's knowledge of reality. Faith goes beyond those limits because it is made up of God's knowledge of reality. Yet faith and science work in parallel, not contradictory, ways. Peter, you might say, was relying on science as he was sinking on the water. Christ, however, called him in faith to walk on the water. That's why Christ chides him for his lack of faith. You cannot see with the eyes of the body the realities of the soul. If Peter's faith had been strong at that moment, he would have seen Jesus who was in front of him as opposed to the water that was beneath him. Jesus saves us as well, particularly from thinking that we have the proven methods for arriving at all knowledge.

– Father James M. Sullivan, O.P.

Deborah

DEBORAH IS A RARE INDIVIDUAL, a female judge of Israel. The judges lead the Chosen People in the period after Joshua and before the kings. She "used to sit under Deborah's palm tree" and settle disputes (Jgs 4:5). But God needs her not only to reconcile but also to rouse, for he wants to free the Israelites from the Canaanites, and he needs a general. Thus she goes to Barak and says, "This is what the LORD, the God of Israel, commands,…go, march on Mount Tabor'" (Jgs 4:6). But Barak is fearful: "If you come with me, I will go; if you do not come with me, I will not go" (Jgs 4:8). She goes, and it is a good thing, because Barak seems to need much encouragement: "Be off…The LORD marches before you" (Jgs 4:14). Unsurprisingly, the song of Deborah and Barak after the victory exhorts action: "Awake, awake, Deborah!… Arise, Barak" (Jgs 5:12).

The Lord needs us to be peacemakers and also rabble-rousers. First it is our own heart that must be aroused, to shake off fear and sloth. The victory of Deborah and Barak occurs "by the waters of Megiddo" (Jgs 5:19): what will be called "Armageddon" in the book of Revelation (16:16), where the armies opposed to Christ assemble to battle him and his Church. The reality of spiritual battle does not die with the judges.

– Angela Franks

The Creed: A Man

THE CREED IS LIKE A MAN. The first article is the head, the second the chest, and the third the hands and feet.

The first article is the mind, because it states that understanding of the relation of God and the world without which the subsequent articles, detailing faith in the Incarnation, the Church, and the sacraments, cannot make sense. One part of the world cannot become another part without ceasing to be what it is. Only if the eternal Son of God is transcendent to the world can he become a part of the world by taking flesh of Mary without ceasing to be what he is in his divinity. Again, only if the sacraments are the instruments of the transcendent God can they be more than empty signs or bare promises and become channels of a more than human, a more than worldly life. The first article continues to work in the second and third.

The second article is the heart of the creed, the heart of Christianity, for it contains the mystery of the redemption. Without our redemption from sin and death by Christ's cross and Resurrection, all the other organs of Christian life lose their point. The Church becomes a society of mere human affection and remembrance, and the sacraments empty. Without the heart, the blood stops going to the brain, too, and without the mystery of the redemption, we realize neither our predicament as sinners nor the incomparable love with which God has loved us at the price of his Son. Creation itself is flattened out if we no longer appreciate it as the stage for the drama of redemption.

The clauses of the third article of the creed, finally, detail the works of the Spirit with which the article begins. The Holy Spirit makes the Church a communion of holy people, united to God through holy things, living in hope of the resurrection and eternal life. This communion is actualized most of all in the works of love, our daily offering of our body to God, a living sacrifice. This is what it means to be the hands and feet of Christ in the world.

Without the head, we can't see where we have been or where we are going. Without the heart, we are still in our sins, dead. Without the hands and feet, without doing the works of love, we don't make any progress to life everlasting.

– Father Guy Mansini, O.S.B.

"Faith alone, trust in the action of God,
in the goodness of God who does not abandon us,
is the guarantee that we are not working in vain."
– Pope Benedict XVI

Gideon

DID HE EVER THINK, centuries after he battled the Midianites, that a book with his name on it would be found in the nightstand of hotel rooms? Probably not. What Gideon did know was that on the journey of life, God could be trusted. But that did not happen overnight.

When called by God to free the Hebrew people and condemn their worship of idols, Gideon is unsure if he is the right man for the job. Three times Gideon asks God to give proof that he could rise to the occasion and be a leader. It is not the signs he receives that convince Gideon. It is the realization that on every step of the journey God is near: "'I shall be with you,' the LORD said" (Jgs 6:16). Unlike the stone idols that seem so attractive to the people, this is the living God who helps Gideon choose the right men, develop a plan, and lead the people to freedom. The grateful people want to make Gideon their king, but he refuses, saying, "The LORD must rule over you" (Jgs 8:23).

Gideon's story is not confined to the drawer of a hotel room. It is found in the lives of all who believe the true God calls us to trust.

– Monsignor Gregory E. S. Malovetz

WHERE DOES [JOY] COME FROM?… The crucial [factor] is…based on faith: I am wanted; I have a task in history; I am accepted, I am loved.… Man can only accept himself if he is accepted by another. He needs the other's presence, saying to him, with more than words: it is good that you exist. Only from the You can the I come into itself. Only if it is accepted, can it accept itself. Those who are unloved cannot even love themselves. This sense of being accepted comes in the first instance from other human beings. But all human acceptance is fragile. Ultimately we need a sense of being accepted unconditionally. Only if God accepts me, and I become convinced of this, do I know definitively: it is good that I exist. It is good to be a human being. If ever man's sense of being accepted and loved by God is lost, then there is no longer any answer to the question whether to be a human being is good at all. Doubt concerning human existence becomes more and more insurmountable. Where doubt over God becomes prevalent, then doubt over humanity follows inevitably. We see today how widely this doubt is spreading. We see it in the joylessness, in the inner sadness, that can be read on so many human faces today. Only faith gives me the conviction: it is good that I exist. It is good to be a human being, even in hard times.

– Pope Benedict XVI

*"I tell you, he will see to it that justice is done for them
speedily. But when the Son of Man comes,
will he find faith on earth?"*
(Lk 18:8)

CAN WE IMAGINE a world where the faith has been
erased? It is like a science fiction dream. Yet, in every generation, a brave new world struggles to come to birth—
and in vast regions in various ages it has even swallowed
up the Church without a trace. Like the eternal enmity of
Amalek and Israel (Ex 17:16), the City of Man wages unceasing war to raze the City of God.

The gates of hell shall not prevail; but do we know what
this really means? After all, a similar promise was made
to Jerusalem. And Jeremiah preached his famous Temple
sermon (Jer 7:1-15), warning (without effect) that God's
presence and promise can never callously be presumed.

The flame of faith is precarious, for the devil stirs up a
terrible wind. We have all seen the baptismal light snuffed
out in the lives of others. Not by malice, nor an atheistic,
totalitarian state—but by simple inattention, by failing to
guard the gift like a taper in the gale. As Satan, light by
light, quenches the faith in our society, he threatens to
consume us all in total darkness—and worse, to plunge
our world into merciless cold. May our lamps burn ready
with lively faith and love to see and greet the Bridegroom
when he comes.

– Father J. Anthony Giambrone, O.P.

Samson

THERE STOOD SAMSON, eyeless in Gaza at the mill with slaves. He had been dedicated to the Lord from his infancy: no razor was to touch his hair. He had fought mightily for Israel against the Philistines. And now, betrayed by his pagan wife Delilah and by his own weakness, he had lost the favor of God. His hair was shorn while he slept, and he lost his strength. The Philistines gouged out his eyes and thrust him in prison to grind corn.

His hair grew back, and perhaps in prison Samson remembered his duty to God. The Philistines meanwhile were celebrating a feast for their corn-god, Dagon, and thought it would be fine to bring mighty Samson out to entertain them.

Imagine the temple filled with thousands of men and women, laughing. Then Samson has an idea, born of faith. He is blind, but he sees. "Lord GOD," he cries, "remember me!" (Jgs 16:28). He begs for the strength to avenge himself on his enemies. His hands braced between two columns, he pushes—and the temple collapses, killing him and every Philistine there with him.

Samson was far from a saintly man. Yet in his last act of complete trust, he gave his life for his people, as Jesus the greatest warrior of all would do.

– Anthony Esolen

But if you wish to know how these things come about,/ ask grace not instruction,/ desire not understanding,/ the groaning of prayer not diligent reading,/ the Spouse not the teacher,/ God not man,/ darkness not clarity,/ not light but the fire/ that totally inflames and carries us into God/ by ecstatic unctions and burning affections./ This fire is God,/ and *his furnace is in Jerusalem*;/ and Christ enkindles it/ in the heat of his burning passion,/ which only he truly perceives who says:/ *My soul chooses hanging and my bones death.*/ Whoever loves this death/ can see God/ because it is true beyond doubt that/ *man will not see me and live.*/ Let us, then, die/ and enter into the darkness; let us impose silence/ upon our cares, our desires and our imaginings./ With Christ crucified/ let us *pass out of this world to the Father*/ so that when the Father is shown to us,/ we may say with Philip:/ *It is enough for us.*/ Let us hear with Paul:/ *My grace is sufficient for you.* Let us rejoice with David saying:/ *My flesh and my heart have grown faint;/ You are the God of my heart,/ and the God that is my portion forever./ Blessed be the Lord forever/ and all the people will say:/ Let it be; let it be./ Amen.*

– Saint Bonaventure

"*T*HIS IS LOVE, not that we…, but that he…" Such a recognition of the priority of God's love over ours is called faith. And faith means a readiness to receive the love of God as a gift, as one acknowledges God's deed of love, as one permits it to occur to oneself. Such acceptance, such recognition then becomes the innermost ground of the human responding love and becomes indeed the initiator of such love.…

From a Christian point of view faith cannot be simply a springboard for love (of one's neighbor) but only its inner form. To have seen this is to have discovered that faith (as a recognition and acceptance of love) originally is itself love, indeed is "love in its originating." Thus one can only grasp the Christian meaning of the statement "God is love" when one has seen its proof. That is to say: "God so loved the world that he gave his only-begotten Son [to represent us in our lostness]" (Jn 3:16) and: "He who did not spare his own Son but gave him up for us all [to represent us in our lostness], will he not also give us all things with him?" (Rom 8:32 RSV). In this proof we see not only that God has loved the world and men *divinely*, but that *he* (and not in the first place we!) in the same act has loved the world and men also *humanly*.

– Father Hans Urs von Balthasar

Ruth

RUTH IS A MOABITE WOMAN who has married into an Israelite family. In her mother-in-law, Naomi, she has come to know the God of Israel and embraced him as her own. When both women have lost their husbands, Ruth is set free from her family obligations by Naomi. Go back to your people, Naomi insists. But Ruth will not budge! "[W]herever you go I will go, wherever you lodge I will lodge, your people shall be my people, and your God my God" (Ru 1:16). Ruth has been captured by this new-found faith and insists on following Naomi to *her* homeland rather than returning to her kin.

She goes with Naomi to Bethlehem. And there, following the Lord takes on a new form: in order to support herself and Naomi, she goes out with the other poor to glean the few stalks of grain that fall to the ground as the wheat is gathered in the field. Staking everything on the God of Israel, she willingly becomes a pauper, a beggar— and he does not turn his back on her. With Naomi's help, Ruth appeals to Naomi's kinsmen, Boaz, who instantly recognizes her virtue and means to take her as a wife. No longer a beggar, Ruth finds a home among God's own.

– Lisa Lickona

To be human, "man's response to God by faith
must be free....
The act of faith is of its very nature a free act"
(DH 10; cf. CIC, can. 748 § 2). (CCC 160)

A THEOLOGICAL THREAD that runs through the writings of Saint Thomas Aquinas is the fact that man is made for God. In this life we search for the good God by choosing wisely of the good things of this world. So when the good, the true, or the beautiful is presented to us, we move toward it naturally and freely. No one forces us to choose things that we believe will make us happy. Because we were made for the truth, we make every effort to possess it. This desire to be happy is built into us by our creator.

This applies to the theological virtue of faith as well, and one author on the subject calls it "happiness of mind." The mind has a "desire" to know things. All we have to do is listen to three-year-olds to be reminded of this. They want to know how something works, when it works that way, and the biggest of all questions, why it works that way. We want to know all the same things about our life, God, eternity, and everything in between. This is freedom in action as we pursue the Lord as the happiness not just of our mind, but of our whole being.

– Father James M. Sullivan, O.P.

*T*HE SUBJECT MATTER that forms the essential content of revelation—that man has been elected to participate in the divine life; that that divine life has been offered to him, in fact, already given—this subject matter owes its reality to nothing but the fact that it is pronounced by God. It is real in that God reveals it…. The Incarnation of God and the revelation in Christ are one and the same reality. For the believer there is once more the experience that he, in accepting the message of the self-revealing God, actually partakes of the divine life therein announced. There is no other way in which he could partake of it save by belief. It is imparted to him…. Divine revelation is not an announcement of a report on reality but the "imparting" of reality itself. That imparting takes effect, however, only upon the believer.

Only now can we answer the question of whether it is "good" for man to believe. And the answer will have to run somewhat as follows: If God has really spoken, then it is not only good to believe him; rather, the act of believing generates those things that in fact are goodness and perfection for man. Receptively and trustfully hearing the truth, man gains a share not only in the "knowledge" of the divine Witness, but in his life itself.

– Josef Pieper

Hannah

IN HANNAH, the mother of the prophet Samuel, we see the tenacious faith of the Hebrew wife who bears the scorn of others in her barren state and yet turns again and again to the Lord, dependent on him alone for her consolation. When the priest Eli observes Hannah praying under her breath for a child, he assumes that she is drunk—again she is mocked in her moment of need! But Hannah braves his accusation: "It isn't that, my lord,…I am an unhappy woman…I was only pouring out my troubles to the LORD" (1 Sm 1:15). Hannah bares her soul, risks her heart in prayer; the Lord alone is her refuge. Like the priest, Eli, Hannah enters the holy place—the inner sanctuary of her soul—, and there she implores God, promising him her son, should she be blessed with one! Eli wisely recognizes Hannah's faith and blesses her with his priestly blessing.

When Hannah bears Samuel and then, at age three, brings him to Eli, her joy is complete. The sorrows of her soul are at once transformed into great joy! Like Mary's *Magnificat*, Hannah's exultant prayer is based on what she herself has seen, the miracle that has been worked in her own flesh: "[The LORD] raises the needy from the dust;/ from the ash heap he lifts up the poor" (1 Sm 2:8).

– Lisa Lickona

At the Manger All Are Fed

Love is an exchange of gifts. – Saint Ignatius of Loyola

MARY FEEDS THE FLESH OF GOD
with the goodness He has given her.
Israel's King
ingests
the pure, warm milk
of Providence.
The pulse of memory beats
beneath her royal robe,
for there is her treasure
to be pondered
pierced and offered
over and over
in time
and time again.

Body of Christ
built at the Virgin's breast,
do we drink with delight
or forgetfulness?

– Rita A. Simmonds

*"Simon, Simon, behold Satan has demanded
to sift all of you like wheat, but I have prayed that
your own faith may not fail." (Lk 22:31-32)*

ULTIMATELY, of course, Peter's "denial" only denied a truth *about himself*. There is admittedly a fine line between "*I* do not know him" and "I do not know *who he is*." Still, Peter recovers when he sees his actions against the truth he knows so deeply.

Theologians distinguish between *fides quae* and *fides qua*. The first refers to the objective, unchanging deposit of faith, the second to the subjective act of assent. One of the great consolations of Catholic life is the supreme confidence we have that the Church's objective faith will never fail—however great the crisis of personal conformity to that truth may be. This confidence is not given to other ecclesial communions; and it takes only a little looking to see that many sectors of Christendom have progressively debased and lost the faith.

The Church's infallibility is rooted in the infallibility of Jesus' own prayer, invested here in the person of Peter. It is a terrifying thing to be in Satan's sights—and the office of Peter certainly is. Yet however a pope may morally fail—and there have been spectacular cases—the common faith cannot be sifted. It stands like a rock, an unchanging norm against which we measure ourselves.

– Father J. Anthony Giambrone, O.P.

*T*HE PERFECTION OF CHARITY is essentially the same shape as the most elementary act of faith. Faith punctures the self-sufficiency of our world, so that there is room for God to be God. Perfect charity is when that puncture has become all-embracing, so that we are nothing but space for God to be God. All that we find in ourselves is God being all in all.

Then God is no longer an object to us, nor we to him. He is subject and object to himself. There is nothing outside his utter self-containment and self-reference.

But God's self-containment is also always a self-emptying. Pseudo-Dionysius says that love is always ecstatic in the strict sense, in that it displaces us from ourselves. Because we love, we are no longer the center of ourselves. So the Father does not contemplate himself in himself, he finds himself in his Son, who is his Word, his Image, his Expression. And the Son finds himself in the Father, and the Holy Spirit exists only as Gift. And in the same ecstasy God gives himself also to creatures, in a giving revealed most fully in the Incarnation. This giving is truly revelation: it shows us what God is in himself. And by the outpouring of the Holy Spirit, we too are drawn to be displaced from ourselves, so that we might live "no longer for ourselves but for him."

– Father Simon Tugwell, O.P.

Eli

How desperate we feel when our children take a self-destructive path and our counsel is of no avail.

Before Israel had king or Temple, there was a priest serving before the Lord of hosts at Shiloh. His two sons serve as priests too, but Eli in old age discovers they don't have faith in a living God who cares how we act. They exploit the people instead of serving them.

What darkness! His life's work turns to dust in his hands; he loses his sight. God curses his household. But faith can burn in the darkness: "He is the Lord. He will do what he judges best" (1 Sm 3:18). Imagine Beethoven, whose whole world is music, and his hearing fails. Yet from the abyss of silence comes the music of the Ninth Symphony. The Lord visits Eli in his darkness through Hannah. If God grants her a son, she will return him to the Lord for priestly service. Thus Eli receives a spiritual son, Samuel.

Is not life thus? A narrowing, a straitening, toward the grave—and then a ray of light in the darkness: Eli, this imperfect Simeon, is given a child. As we decline toward death, the glory of life departs. And yet, and yet— if our heart trembles for the presence of God, something slowly emerges on the other side of the field to greet us: God himself in his glorious mercy, there in the darkness, ready to receive us.

– J. David Franks

*"Faith is an entirely free gift that God makes to man….
To live, grow and persevere in the faith…we must beg
the Lord to increase our faith"*
(Cf. Mk 9:24; Lk 17:5; 22:32). (CCC 162)

SAINT PAUL REMINDS THE THESSALONIANS: "And for this reason we too give thanks to God unceasingly, that, in receiving the word of God from hearing us, you received not a human word but, as it truly is, the word of God, which is now at work in you who believe" (1 Thes 2:13). The only way to have the gift of faith is to receive it, and God offers this gift to us freely. Once we receive faith, however, it remains our task to nourish it and to protect it from all that could harm it. Along with the graces of the sacraments, we nourish faith most especially with the words of Sacred Scripture. In Saint Paul's words, the Word of God works in us. It works to perfect our faith, to strengthen us against doubt and any other sin against faith.

More importantly, the words of Sacred Scripture speak to us as one friend would speak to another. When we need encouragement, challenge, or comfort, the Word of God speaks to us. When we suffer from loss, sin, or weakness, the Word of God speaks to us. This is why Saint Paul gives thanks unceasingly: proof that the Word of God has already been at work in him.

– Father James M. Sullivan, O.P.

HRIST TOOK the yoke of the Law upon himself in that he fulfilled it perfectly and died for and through the Law. Just so did he free from the Law those who wished to receive life from him. But they can receive it only if they relinquish their own life. For those who are baptized in Christ are baptized in his death. They are submerged in his life in order to become members of his body and as such to suffer and to die with him but also to arise with him to eternal, divine life. This life will be ours in its fullness only on the day of glory.

But even now we have—"in the flesh"—a share therein insofar as we believe; believe that Christ died for us in order to give us life. It is this faith that unites us to him as the members are joined to the head and opens for us the stream of his life. And so faith in the Crucified—a living faith joined to loving surrender—is for us entrance into life and the beginning of future glory. The cross, therefore, is our only claim to glory.... He who has decided for Christ is dead to the world and the world to him. He carries in his body the marks of the Lord's wounds, is weak and despised by the people but is precisely therefore strong because the power of God is mighty in the weak.

– Saint Teresa Benedicta of the Cross

Samuel

THE LORD CALLS, "Samuel, Samuel!" Samuel answers, "Speak, for your servant is listening" (1 Sm 3:10). The arc of Samuel's prophetic career is marked from beginning to end by these words of youthful, ready obedience. After Moses, Samuel is the next great prophet called by God to communicate his Word in the world. Nurtured by the incandescent prayer life of his mother Hannah, and prepared for his mission by the wise priest Eli, Samuel goes forth to fortify the faith of his people.

But the people cry: "Appoint for us a king to govern us" (1 Sm 8:6 RSV). Displeased, Samuel prays. The LORD said: "Hearken to the voice of the people...they have rejected me from being king over them" (1 Sm 8:7 RSV). Starting here, at the transition from tribal confederacy to monarchy, every prophet from now on will stand in tireless confrontation with politics, trying to bend the ear of the king to listen to God. In tragic fashion, Saul, the first king, fails. Samuel then anoints David, "a man after [God's] own heart" (1 Sm 13:14), a man who so fully reconciles the religious and political realms in himself as to become the type of the Future King.

What stands out most about Samuel? His ears—always open to obedience (from *ob* + *audire*: to listen to). Ears that point to Abraham, to Mary: to the joyful obedience of faith.

– Andrew Matt

*F*AITH IS NOT ONLY the intellect's adherence to the truth revealed, but also a submission of the will and a gift of self to God revealing himself. It is a stance that involves one's entire existence. The Council also recalls that this faith requires "the grace of God to move [man] and assist him; he must have the interior helps of the Holy Spirit, who moves the heart and converts it to God, who opens the eyes of the mind and 'makes it easy for all to accept and believe the truth'" (*Dei Verbum*, n. 5).… Faith spurs us to true and deep consistency, which must be expressed in all aspects of a life modeled on that of Christ. As a fruit of grace, faith exercises an influence on events. The faith of the Canaanite woman was also bold and insistent. Jesus countered this woman, who had come to seek the cure of her daughter, with the Father's plan which restricted his mission to the lost sheep of the house of Israel. The Canaanite replied with the full force of her faith and obtained the miracle: "O woman! Great is your faith! Be it done for you as you desire" (Mt 15:28). The role of faith is to co-operate with this omnipotence… For Jesus, faith has a decisive importance for the purposes of salvation.

– Blessed John Paul II

David

How TO DO JUSTICE to Israel's greatest king who governs his people with justice in feats that an entire book of Scripture can scarcely outline? When we consider this larger-than-life shepherd-king, we think of his great deeds and his great sins. In a paean of praise, Sirach alludes to both: "With his every deed [David] offered thanks/ to God.... The LORD forgave him his sins/ and exalted his strength forever" (Sir 47:8, 11).

When the Ark of the Covenant is brought to Jerusalem amid great festivities, David dances before the Lord with abandon in a linen apron (cf. 2 Sm 6:14). Mixing sacred enthusiasm with obeisant humiliation—and perhaps offering contrition for Israel's sinfulness as well—he glorifies the Lord and estranges his wife in one seamless, shameless act (2 Sm 6). From barbs to stones: in the wake of Absalom's revolt, cursing Shimei has the grit to throw rocks at David and his officers for the bloodshed they caused in Saul's family (2 Sm 16). Refusing his bodyguards' request for revenge, David gladly accepts rocks and insults as just punishments from God. What dependence on the Lord! Whether in good times or bad, whether appearing as the most active of agents or passive of penitents, David interprets each moment as an opportunity to accept everything from God in faith as a priceless gift.

– Father Lawrence J. Donohoo

"Do not let your hearts be troubled.
You have faith in God; have faith also in me."
(Jn 14:1)

JOHN'S FIRST LETTER SAYS that if we disbelieve God's testimony, we make God himself a liar. What is God's testimony? "He has testified on behalf of his Son" (1 Jn 5:9). This testimony is no abstraction. It came as a clarion voice from the heavens, when the Son first stepped forth in mature manhood: "This is my beloved Son, with whom I am well pleased!" To have faith in God *is* to have faith in Jesus Christ.

It can be quite attractive, of course, to have God without Jesus. Believing that God is in control, that there is a divine plan, that something other than chaos steers the course of our lives is obviously deeply consoling. Believing that God concretely shows his "control" by abandoning his beloved ones to suffer is somewhat less compelling. Yet, here in his Last Supper discourse, facing his own execution, Jesus presents faith in him as the key to quiet our troubled hearts. He addresses our hearts because, like Thomas, we are all troubled that we do not know the way. But we do know where *Jesus* is going. He is returning to the Father. And he has prepared a place for us there. Thus, whoever faithfully follows Christ as his or her guide has found the Way to True Life.

– Father J. Anthony Giambrone, O.P.

*I*N THIS WORLD, the only way one can know God supernaturally is by faith. Reason can give us a certain, but natural, knowledge of his existence and of some of his attributes; but faith alone can tell us of the wonders of his love and his plans for us. Faith alone can put us in vital contact with him, for when we believe in God, we share his knowledge, we lean on him, and draw our strength from him…. The Church insists that reason authorizes faith, and so far from asking us to deny our reason, she teaches that faith insists on being founded on reason. Once, however, the reasonableness of believing our authority is established, that authority may ask us to go beyond our reason, but never to go against it…. "Faith," as Prat points out, "is not a pure intuition, a mystical tendency towards an object more suspected than known; it presupposes preaching; it is the yielding of the mind to divine testimony. Faith is opposed to sight, both as regards the object known and the manner of knowing; one is immediate and intuitive, the other takes place through an intermediate agent. Nevertheless, faith is not blind: it is ready to give a reason for itself and aspires always to more clearness."

– Dom M. Eugene Boylan, O. CIST. R.

FOR YEARS ON END/ I wandered through/
    Deserts hot,
Parched and alone.

For years on end/ I climbed cold/ Heights and
Measured step/ By step/ Abysses deep.

For years on end/ I walked in/ Loneliness too
Deep for words/ In search of you.

Then quite suddenly/ I came upon you
My All…my love/ Standing naked/ Against a
whipping post./ Clad only in the crimson
Cloak of blood and pain.

You smiled, and/ Bade me stand
Against the other/ Side,
Untied, held/ Only by the bonds/ Of love for you.

I did, and the/ Long Roman whips/ Cut me apart
And clad me in/ The crimson of/ My own blood and
pain/ Yet mingled with/ Some drops of yours.

Because of this/ I am still here/ At the same whipping
post/ Of yore./ You are not here./ The drops are
Changed into/ Ones of fear and hate/ Yet defenseless
I remain/ Because you still/ Mingle your blood with
mine/ Beloved.

> – Servant of God Catherine de Hueck Doherty

The Sign of Conversion

BETHLEHEM STAR
light years in wait,
releases good news
with celestial gait:
The Word that stirred Heaven
before time began,
is lauded by angels:
the Heart of God's plan.
The power of paradise,
traveling time,
alights on a stable
in silence sublime
that wise men may seek
ageless knowledge foreknown:
The star is the sign,
New Being
the goal.

— Rita A. Simmonds

Bathsheba

BATHSHEBA IS A LEGENDARY BEAUTY, married to King David's head soldier Uriah. David sees her bathing one day, falls madly in lust, has her brought to him, seduces her, and impregnates her. So David has Uriah sent to the front lines (to add insult to injury, he has Uriah himself bear the message to the general who would issue the order) where he will almost surely be killed.

Uriah is in fact killed in battle, and David takes Bathsheba as his wife. But God is angry. We know David says to Nathan, "I have sinned against the LORD" (2 Sm 12:13 RSV). We know Nathan answers: "The LORD…has put away your sin," but "the child that is born to you shall die" (2 Sm 12:13, 14 RSV). We know the child Bathsheba bears him does die. We know much about David and his ensuing repentance, but very little about Bathsheba. Does she mourn Uriah? Does she chafe against the bonds of forced matrimony? All we know about Bathsheba is that she eventually bears David another son, Solomon, and that she successfully finagles to have this son, rather than one of David's sons by his first wife, named David's chief heir.

We tend to hold Bathsheba's enticing beauty against her. But for all we know the most beautiful, the most secret thing about her, was her love for her son Solomon.

– Heather King

*W*E BELIEVE NOT IN PROPOSITIONS but in the reality which is expressed by the propositions; we believe, not in a creed, but through a creed.... It is possible to accept the formulas of the creeds and still to have a quite wrong idea of the nature of God and of his providence; it is possible to worship God and still to fall into a sort of practical idolatry. If you turn your religion into magic: if you expect an immediate and literal answer to all your prayers, if you expect the grace of God to do for you by miracle what only demands a little hard work, you are misunderstanding the faith.... If you allow yourself to accept the assumptions of a pagan environment as far as conduct is concerned, and keep your faith in abstraction from practical affairs, you are betraying it.... The truth is given us from without, yes; but it is something that we have to realize in actual experience: we have to translate the formulas of the creed into the stuff of life; we have to learn so to see the faith in all the everyday circumstances and events of life that it becomes not something we sometimes think of but something we always are.

– Father Gerald Vann, O.P.

*Faith makes us taste in advance
the light of the beatific vision....
Faith is already the beginning of eternal life.*
(*CCC 163*)

PERHAPS there is no greater mystery in the Christian life than the very gift that began that "Christian life" in the first place, namely, the gift of the theological virtue of faith. It is by this virtue that we come to know God as he is in himself. We are able to grow in knowledge and therefore in love for him. We thus begin our eternal life here on earth!

We then realize that the words of Saint John's Gospel are not an empty promise: "Truly, truly, I say to you, he who believes has eternal life" (Jn 6:47 RSV). Christ does not say "*will have* eternal life," nor does he say "*might have* eternal life." Christ definitively states that the believer *has* eternal life at that very moment of belief. This "eternal life" then is a reality in the present and not only some longed-for or long-off reward. In truth, the eternal reward of beatitude will be, according to our capacity, the full knowledge and love of God as he is. But this truth need not deny that we can have a share of that glory even now in the present. "So faith is already the beginning of eternal life."

– Father James M. Sullivan, O.P.

Nathan

As a "seer," or prophet, Nathan may have indirectly kept a journal of his own adventures of faith, for the Chronicler says that he is one of the biographers of King David, who is both his foil and protégé (1 Chr 29:29). Their lives are trebles and clefs in the song of Israel. Nathan does not tell where he is from, and his only concern is where faith will take him. Very simply, it takes him to dangerous places, for he challenges rulers and he even has the audacity to confront David with his crimes of adultery and murder. Nathan's loud "I accuse" rings through the centuries: "You are the man!" (2 Sm 12:7). He is so bold as to expose the attempt of Adonais to usurp the royal succession from David's son Solomon.

Strong faith frees him from self-consciousness and self-promotion, so that he might selflessly perform the good works without which faith is dead (Jas 2:17). While the details of his death are as obscure as those of his birth, we know that he envisions the glorious Temple in Jerusalem and prophesies that it will be built, not by David but by Solomon. It will shine in the sun as glittering proof that the faith of such a man as Nathan is strong as stone and in fact more enduring.

– Father George William Rutler

*F*AITH IS AN ACT OF CONFIDENCE, and therefore a product of the heart. It requires in him who accords it the same uprightness as in him who inspires it…. To confide is to give oneself; none give themselves but the magnanimous, or at least the generous. Not that faith excludes prudence, or that we must put our trust in the first word that falls from unknown lips, but prudence being satisfied, there is still necessary a generous effort to bring forth that difficult word: I believe….

Science is not the principle of human order; it is but one of its glorious ornaments, and if it oppress faith instead of sustaining it, it becomes the parricidal instrument of a ruin wherein man will acknowledge, too late, that he must believe in order to live a single day, even although it were needless to believe in order to live eternally. Human faith is the life of the natural man as divine faith is the life of the supernaturalized man, and these two men constituting but one, divine faith preserves human faith as human faith sustains divine faith, were it only in proving the synthesis which exists between the two orders whose distinct but harmonious elements compose our destiny.

– Father Henri-Dominique Lacordaire, O.P.

Jonathan

JONATHAN LOVED DAVID AS HIS OWN SOUL. He held friendship higher than clinging to the ambition of succeeding his father Saul, when the king's favor turned to David for confronting the Philistine leader, the giant Goliath. Later, when Saul seeks to kill David because enraged by his growing popularity, Jonathan is loyal to a covenant made with his friend. He warns David about the danger, even risking his own life. In this he shows that greater love Jesus speaks of at the Last Supper. When he falls in battle together with his father, David weeps for their loss in a famous song (cf. 2 Sm 1:19-27).

The friendship between these two is often cited as a model of love, deeper than mere sentiment or natural affection. Saint Aelred writes of it in his work on spiritual friendship. The writer C. S. Lewis states their love needn't have unseemly overtones. Rather, it indicates noble loyalty, a faithfulness possible when persons are reciprocally strengthened to pursue the highest ideals.

These heights are only reached through faith in God's design revealed by Jesus as the eternal communion of *agape* or unconditional love. Jonathan's life symbolizes this. To believe and live in this love is ultimately the fruit of sharing the Eucharist, faith's mystery bonding us to give ourselves for others.

– Father Michael L. Gaudoin-Parker

*F*AITH IS TO BELIEVE without understanding, without seeing…. You have been walking in the sunshine of your intellect. God has helped you and encouraged you to use it. Then, just like in the tropics where there is no twilight and day becomes night within minutes, so God plunges you into the night. He says, "Put your head in your heart and believe! For now there is no answer. I am the answer. You won't see me in the dark. You will have to follow me in faith, without knowing. Arise and believe!"

There is a tremendous secret in God's ways of doing things if we do follow him across that dark night of the tropics, of the soul. There will be a moment, maybe just before death, or in the midst of life, or maybe when we are at a very tender age. At this moment he will appear. He will just be there. What you knew by your own intellect has blended together with what was added to you because you believed and walked in the darkness of night. You have entered into the fullness of the kingdom of God even before your death. The kingdom of God is in your midst now.

– Servant of God Catherine de Hueck Doherty

"[Paul and Barnabas] strengthened the spirits of the disciples and exhorted them to persevere in the faith, saying, 'It is necessary for us to undergo many hardships to enter the kingdom of God.'" (Acts 14:22)

THE TWO MEN ARE LIKE GENERALS, strangers to fear, steeling their green recruits before a battle. Paul stirs Timothy with such words, "God did not give us a spirit of cowardice" (2 Tm 1:7). The great Apostle's Brag sings like a play of epic suffering: "Five times at the hands of the Jews, I received forty lashes minus one. Three times I was beaten with rods…" (2 Cor 11:24-25). Saint Catherine de' Ricci spoke of "holy rivalry" among the saints, and one can almost imagine here the fey mood of Beowulf and Breca egging each other on to show their hearty feats of one-upmanship.

Faith needs fuel if it is to stay alive; and the fuel God gives it is hope. Hope is the power of patient endurance, the engine that fires resolve. Hope swells the spirit, after faith has filled the mind; while sanctified intellect and passion bear fruit as saving deeds of charity. The demons have dead faith, because the demons have no hope. Nothing can drive them to suffer in heroic love. But the Christian is bold, a martyr who steps smilingly to meet his fate. In hope-filled faith he courageously lives a life of loving greatness.

– Father J. Anthony Giambrone, O.P.

THE KINGDOM OF GOD that our Lord came to establish upon earth was not merely the elaborate or simple knowledge of the ways of God; rather, it was the individual acceptance of truth simply as a means of life. God teaches me about himself so that, in the end I may be led to a closer union with him; it is he for whom I am created, not for faith, but for possession.

The kingdom of God, therefore, is something that the individual, from the age of reason to the end of life, must continually realize for himself. He must continually hammer away at the truths of faith, endeavoring to get more meaning out of them, to find in them the help and guidance that daily life continually demands. The whole series of mysteries will certainly be of no use to me in my endless advance toward God unless I try to make them my own by ceaselessly pondering over them. Of themselves, they are just the bare outlines of truths, yet it is not truths, but the facts that are contained in the truths, that are ultimately to influence my life....

Faith has to be regarded as the revelation to us of the meaning of life, the understanding of life, the effects of life. I shall never become interested in religion until I have come to see that I must make it personal to myself.

– Father Bede Jarrett, O.P.

Faith Is Acknowledging a Presence

MONSIGNOR LUIGI GIUSSANI describes faith as the acknowledgment of a Presence. The Christian faith is more than commemoration; "it means acknowledging the operative or operating presence of the Mystery, of the Father in our life. But the way in which the Father works is called Christ, and therefore the Church, and therefore communion among us." My faith is in Jesus Christ who is acting in my life through the members of his Church in the here and now. He is acting in my life whether or not I recognize him, but when I acknowledge his presence which chooses me now, then my awareness of myself and of the people and circumstances of my life begins to change radically. At this point faith becomes life.

Saint Paul bears witness to what Giussani shows to be the essence of faith. Paul's conversion occurs when he encounters the risen Christ directly, but how does his faith continue from there? He is put into relationship with other Christians, and Paul recognizes that it is through these disciples of Christ that God is present and operating in his life. Ananias baptizes him; Barnabas, Silas, Luke, and others travel with him; Lydia offers him hospitality. Paul's acknowledgment of Christ's continued presence will change the way he looks at even the most difficult of circumstances, recognizing God's operative hand in everything he faces. Paul doesn't merely suffer the shipwreck near Malta, he faithfully *lives* it as a God-given opportunity to proclaim Christ in a new place. His faith is his acknowledgment and ready response to Christ as the giver of this seeming disaster.

Paul sees himself in a new light as well. He knows, frail as he is, that he carries the treasure of God's presence in the earthen vessel of his humanity. He understood the great affection that the presbyters of Ephesus held for him was because he had become one with Christ, in loving Paul they were loving Jesus. His weaknesses don't lead Paul to doubt Christ's presence with and through him.

Benedict XVI has reminded us that the Church is called here and now to "reveal in the world, faithfully, although with shadows, the mystery of its Lord until, in the end, it shall be manifested in full light."

We await the fullness of the end, but we live now in the midst of internal and external shadows, and Christ enters reality as it is to be with us now. Let us live the faith of Saint Paul, Luigi Giussani, and Benedict XVI in acknowledging Christ's active presence in the fleshly, earthly, shadowy present where each of us is living now.

– Father Richard Veras

Abigail

ABIGAIL, "intelligent and attractive," is married to Nabal, who is rich but also "harsh and ungenerous" (1 Sm 25:3). When David is an exile, he camps near Nabal's flocks and protects them. Yet when he asks Nabal for supplies, he is rudely rebuffed ("'Who is David?'" [1 Sm 25:10]). Ever hot-blooded, David "girded on his sword" and prepared to wipe out all the men of Nabal's household.

When Abigail hears of it she hurries, laden with food, to meet David on the warpath. She bows low before him and begs that the guilt of her foolish husband be on her alone. David is moved and tells her, "Blessed be the LORD, the God of Israel, who sent you to meet me today. Blessed be your good judgment and blessed be you yourself, who this day have prevented me from shedding blood and from avenging myself personally" (1 Sm 25:32-33). When she relates to her husband how she had saved them, "he became like a stone" (1 Sm 25:37); ten days later he dies. And Abigail? Her humility and wisdom win her a royal admirer, and David soon weds her. Ever modest, she says, "Behold, your handmaid is a servant to wash the feet of the servants of my lord" (1 Sm 25:41 RSV). In this, she foreshadows another guiltless handmaid, Mary, who willingly endures the suffering that is her part in God's plan to save us fools and sinners.

– Angela Franks

We must turn to the witnesses of faith.
(CCC 165)

OUR OWN SUFFERING can often bring the full weight of doubt upon our faith. We can begin to question God's goodness and his love for us. At times of difficulty it is important to remember and to learn from the example of the saints. Reading any saint's biography reminds us of how much they suffered in their lives, and the fruit of that suffering, by God's grace, is always a stronger faith.

One saint who might slip by us, however, is the Blessed Mother. We mistakenly think that she was so perfect that she did not face doubts or uncertainties in her life or trials in the spiritual life. While her life was certainly different from ours because of her freedom from original sin, she did live in this world, and suffer here, with the eyes of faith. As the one who shared more perfectly than any other person in the sufferings of Christ, Mary shares in our sufferings as well. She helps us on our own pilgrimage so that we may join her in the blessedness of heaven, once our own "night of faith" is over.

– Father James M. Sullivan, O.P.

*F*AITH IS THE FOUNDATION of the Christian life. It is a virtue by which the human intelligence is so transformed that it is capable of recognizing the voice of God speaking through the prophets, the Church, the Scriptures and ultimately through Jesus Christ and his Holy Spirit. It believes the Word of God on the Word of God and rests on no other authority. It is given the child in baptism and to the adult in a conversion which baptism completes. Yet although faith transcends reason, it is reasonable, because, though its formal motive is solely the Word of God, yet its material conditions are the signs which God has given to make it humanly credible. These signs are both objective and subjective. The objective signs are the fulfillment of prophecies and miracles and the sign accessible to all is the moral miracle of the Church. The subjective signs are the Gospel's fulfillment of our deepest spiritual needs....

A faith that is firm and pure...is not blind or uncritical: rather, it is critical in the truest sense of the word; it discerns what is the Word of God from lesser truths: what is revealed from what is mere theological speculation or human opinion (especially one's own opinions about what is revealed).

– Father Benedict M. Ashley, O.P.

Elijah

THOUGH SCARCELY a handful of pages are needed to tell the story of this amazing man, so crowded with incident and importance is the telling that it fairly takes one's breath away. Only God could fashion a tale so fantastic, beginning with the name itself, which means "Yahweh is my God."

From the first moment of his appearance, Elijah speaks truth to power, bluntly informing the wretched Ahab that because of his wickedness and worship of Canaanite gods, "during these years there shall be no dew or rain except at my word" (1 Kgs 17:1). Speaking nine centuries before Christ, the voice of the prophet echoes along the corridors of our own age, rebuking the ungodly for their idolatries. "I have been most zealous for the LORD, the God of hosts" (1 Kgs 19:14), he warns, hurling thunderbolts against all who prefer darkness to light. Determined to purify God's people, Elijah will be fed by ravens, raise the dead to life, summon fire from the sky with which to destroy the altar of Baal, and, sheerest miracle of all, be swept "up to heaven in a whirlwind" (2 Kgs 2:11) after bestowing a double portion of his spirit upon his successor, Elisha. That he appears alongside Jesus and Moses in the Transfiguration lends an everlasting proof of a faith triumphant over adversity and death.

– Regis Martin

WE THANK YOU, Lord Jesus,/ because the Gospel of the Father's love,/ with which you came to save the world,/ has been proclaimed far and wide in America/ as a gift of the Holy Spirit/ that fills us with gladness./ We thank you for the gift of your Life,/ which you have given us by loving us to the end:/ your Life makes us children of God,/ brothers and sisters to each other./ Increase, O Lord, our faith and our love for you,/ present in all the tabernacles of the continent./ Grant us to be faithful witnesses/ to your Resurrection/ for the younger generation of Americans,/ so that, in knowing you, they may follow you....

May families always be united,/ as you and the Father are one,/ and may they be living witnesses/ to love, justice and solidarity;/ make them schools of respect,/ forgiveness and mutual help,/ so that the world may believe;/ help them to be the source of vocations/ to the priesthood and the consecrated life....

Protect your Church and the Successor of Peter,/ to whom you, Good Shepherd, have entrusted/ the task of feeding your flock./ Grant that the Church in America may flourish/ and grow richer in the fruits of holiness./ Teach us to love your Mother, Mary,/ as you loved her./ Give us strength to proclaim/ your word with courage/ in the work of the new evangelization,/ so that the world may know new hope./ Our Lady of Guadalupe, Mother of America,/ pray for us!

– Blessed John Paul II

*T*HE TRUTHS OF FAITH…surpass the scope of the human intellect; they cannot be measured by the human intellect's inherent criteria for evidence. In believing, therefore, the intellect, under the impulse of the will's command, effected by grace, assents to what exceeds its natural requirements and capacities, namely, the truthfulness of God revealing. According to the truth of the Catholic faith, Christ himself stands at the center of the entire revelatory process. Faith then comes from God, both as a free gift of grace that causes faith's required assent, and as a lavish outpouring or effusion of doctrine about those things that pertain to our salvation.

The New Testament clearly affirms that the human person discovers God in knowledge and love, and that the perfection of Christian existence achieves a consummation of this intentional union. In the Gospel of John, Jesus himself instructs us: "It is written in the prophets, 'And they shall all be taught by God.' Everyone who has heard and learned from the Father comes to me" (Jn 6:45).… "That person who considers maturely and without qualification the first and final cause of the entire universe, namely God, is to be called supremely wise; hence wisdom," says Aquinas, "appears in Saint Augustine as knowledge of divine things."

– Father Romanus Cessario, O.P.

The Widow of Zarephath

THE WIDOW with whom Elijah stays demonstrates the lengths to which our Father will go to give us life. The widow faces death not once but twice: the first time, when Elijah meets her and asks her to share some of her last food before she starves; and the second, when her son dies of illness. In the first instance, she has only a "handful of flour" and "a little oil," but by the Lord's power "the jar of flour did not go empty, nor the jug of oil run dry" (1 Kgs 17:12, 16). This marvel foreshadows Jesus' feeding of the five thousand with five loaves and two fish: in both cases, the Father takes what little we have and multiplies it beyond our ability to imagine. We need only return to him what he has already given us, and he will work wonders with us.

In another anticipation of the New Testament, the widow's son is taken from her—except in the case of that other widow, Mary, her Son is willingly given back to the Father, while the widow of Zarephath cries out to Elijah: "Why have you done this to me, O man of God?" (1 Kgs 17:18). Both women's sons are raised from the dead: the one to die again, but the Other to eternal life, which he freely shares with us. If we give him our lives, our little handfuls of self, he will in return give us everlasting life and happiness.

– Angela Franks

*"Through him we have received the grace of apostleship,
to bring about the obedience of faith, for the sake
of his name, among all the Gentiles." (Rom 1:5)*

MAN IS A MASTER, but not of himself. It is by obedience alone that we find peace in our hearts. If we must thus obey, three laws contend for our service. The "law of sin" wars within our members and subjects our will to do what it does not want (Rom 7:19-25). It is a slave revolt and lawless law of violence. It foments the passions and so topples the hierarchy which justly sets mind over flesh, enthroning base instincts by disordered force and clinging to rule like a despot. The Law of Moses, in contrast, proscribes a peaceful order, where the lower rightly serves the higher. But this Law is a dead letter. It has no power to end the rogue rule of sin now tyrannizing in our hearts. The third law surpasses them both, for it carries both peace and power. It is the "law of the spirit of life in Christ Jesus" (Rom 8:2). God's Spirit has more force than mere violence—a force found in the "obedience of faith." The tranquil obedience of faith is born of God's peaceful power of persuasion, when by grace our mind is freely charmed into full submission. When we consent to the testimony of God, we suffer no debasement. The highest within us freely serves the Most High.

– Father J. Anthony Giambrone, O.P.

Litany of Faith
Based on the Letters of Saint Paul

℟ *Lord, keep us steadfast in the faith.*

◀ We have been justified by faith. ℟
◀ All depends on faith; everything is grace. ℟
◀ Faith in the heart leads to justification. ℟
◀ Faith comes through hearing. ℟
◀ Faith is to be used as our rule of life. ℟
◀ The strong in faith should be patient with the weak. ℟
◀ Our faith rests on the power of God. ℟
◀ We walk by faith, not by sight. ℟
◀ We live a life of faith in the Son of God. ℟
◀ Nothing counts for anything but faith that expresses itself through love. ℟
◀ The fruit of the Spirit is generosity and faith. ℟
◀ May Christ dwell in our hearts through faith. ℟
◀ There is one Lord, one faith, one baptism. ℟
◀ We hold faith up before us as our shield. ℟
◀ The justice we possess comes through faith in Christ. ℟
◀ We must hold fast to faith, firmly grounded and steadfast in it. ℟
◀ We are to be growing ever stronger in faith. ℟
◀ We put on faith and love as a breastplate. ℟
◀ The Lord who keeps faith will guard us against the evil one. ℟
◀ We must fight the good fight of faith. ℟
◀ We must guard the rich deposit of faith. ℟
◀ Faith in Jesus Christ leads to salvation. ℟
◀ We are to be servants of God for the sake of the faith. ℟
◀ We are called to share the faith with others. ℟

– Father Peter John Cameron, O.P.

Obadiah, Messenger for Elijah

OF THE ELEVEN OBADIAHS who appear in the Old Testament, perhaps the most intriguing is the master of the palace under the weak and wicked King Ahab. Here is a man caught between a rock and a hard place—or rather, between a prophet and king—or better yet, between life and conscience. Described as one who was "a zealous follower of the LORD" (1 Kgs 18:4), Obadiah risks death from the depraved Jezebel by hiding in two caves one hundred prophets whom she tried to murder.

While in search of water during a punitive drought, Obadiah meets Elijah, and is ordered by the great prophet to fetch his master. Fearing for his life, Obadiah protests that Elijah, a celebrated escape artist, will flee the king and so inflame his wrath that the messenger will serve as scapegoat. But the prophet swears that he will stand still. Relying on Elijah's word, Obadiah tracks down the king and arranges a meeting. Their encounter stands as one of the great prophet-king confrontations of Scripture, culminating in the decisive showdown on Mount Carmel between Elijah and the four hundred.

Obadiah teaches us that great acts of faith can spring up even in corrupt circumstances. It is possible to be in the employ of wicked masters if one ultimately is working behind the scenes as a trusting and trustworthy servant of the Lord.

– Father Lawrence J. Donohoo

*I cannot believe without being carried by
the faith of others, and by my faith
I help support others in the faith. (CCC 166)*

WE REALIZE EVERY SUNDAY that our Profession of Faith would not be possible if it were not for the many generations of believers who have preceded us. It is rooted in the faith first entrusted to the Apostles, handed down through the bishops of the Church to our very own day. Saint Irenaeus of Lyons († 202) offers insight into the reality of faith: "We guard with care the faith that we have received from the Church, for without ceasing…this deposit of great price, as if in an excellent vessel, is constantly being renewed and causes the very vessel that contains it to be renewed."

We are also particularly indebted to those who stand with us to make the Profession of Faith. Together we are there to worship God and by that act are strengthened by being united in that act. We profess our faith together so that we may live together as well. We profess our faith together so that together we may live the fulfillment of that faith in heaven.

– Father James M. Sullivan, O.P.

THE CATHOLIC MAKES A SURRENDER. But, paradoxically, this surrender frees him to walk familiarly into the hidden life of God. Faith removes the barriers of the natural order which shield, from the world and man, the inner life of the Godhead....

The barriers of nature crumble before the power of a simple act of faith, revealing a completely new and transcendent aspect of the Author of nature. Faith reveals not only many naturally attainable truths; far more importantly, a vast new order of truth rising completely above the natural capacities of the human mind appears before the believer. By faith the veil is drawn back to disclose what theologians call the supernatural order of life and truth in God. Faith brings into the focus of man's intelligence "the unfathomable riches of Christ"....

Faith...opens our minds to gaze on the ineffable supernatural mysteries of God.

This...is that singular gift of God for which [Hebrews] gives the profound and meaningful definition: faith is *"the substance of things to be hoped for, the evidence of things that are not seen"* (Heb 11:1). It is faith which implants in man the first beginnings ("the substance") of his eternal happiness ("of things to be hoped for"), and makes him absolutely certain of the hidden mysteries and glories of God ("the evidence of things that are not seen").

– Father Francis L. B. Cunningham, O.P.

123

Elisha

BY EXTENDING forward in time the mission and charism of his mentor Elijah, even as now the bishops carry on the charism of the Apostles in the Church, Elisha prefigures the mission of Christ and his Church. Contrary to the notion of Old Testament prophets receiving their calling alone in the silence of night (1 Sm 3:1-20) or in front of a bush on a lonely mountainside (Ex 3:1-2), Elisha's calling is something that resembles a laying on of hands, as in a priestly ordination. The fearsome prophet Elijah, passing by and inspired by God, "came upon Elisha, son of Shaphat,... and threw his cloak over him" (1 Kgs 19:19). Thus Elisha's vocation is intimately entwined with that of his mentor. When it comes time for Elijah to leave this earth, and for Elisha to carry on, Elisha asks for Elijah's intercession with God in order to "receive a double portion of your spirit" (2 Kgs 2:9). Finally, the doom that Elijah had foretold for King Ahab (1 Kgs 20:42) and his wife Jezebel is fulfilled through Elisha's ministry.

The relationship between Elijah and Elisha foreshadows for us the relationship that the Lord Jesus establishes in a greater way with his Apostles.

– Father Vincent Nagle, F.S.C.B.

*T*HE FORMAL OBJECT OF FAITH is the reason or motive that moves man to assent to the material object. The material object answers the question, "What is believed?" But the formal object provides the answer for *why* man believes. Man assents to all the truths contained in God's supernatural revelation "because of the authority of God himself who reveals them, who can neither deceive nor be deceived." The reason, and the only reason, for man's acceptance of supernatural truth is the authority of God himself. If God speaks to man, there can be no doubt as to the truth of his message. His knowledge is infinite; his veracity beyond question. And since God *has* spoken, the case is closed.

To anticipate, once again, the ever recurring objection—yes, it is true that the Catholic believes only what his Church proposes for his belief. Ecclesiastical authority, however, while determining the form in which the articles of faith will be proposed, does not *reveal* the truths which are to be believed. God alone reveals; the Church simply points out—and infallibly so—precisely what has been revealed by God....

"When you heard and received from us the word of God, you welcomed it not as the word of men, but, as it truly is, the word of God, who works in you who have believed" (1 Thes 2:13).

– Father Francis L.B. Cunningham, O.P.

Tobit

A GOOD STAGE MUSICAL involves a story with twists and turns, characters who intrigue, and a good tune you leave the theater humming. If the story of Tobit were a musical, it would meet all those requirements and more.

Taking place in Nineveh, the story has at its center a devout and wealthy Israelite named Tobit. He suffers several misfortunes, including blindness. Distraught by these problems, he prays for death. Tobit's prayer is not answered. Instead, what happens next involves a woman married seven times, his son's journey to find a cure for his father's blindness, a romance between the much married woman and Tobit's son, an attack by a large fish, and an angel named Raphael. At the end, grateful that he can now see, Tobit sings a song of praise. In it is the realization that difficulties and setbacks do not mean God has lost control of the world. Tobit sings that these are the moments when God is very near. He learns that spiritual blindness is cured by prayer, fasting, and charity. Tobit's story reminds us that our lives may be messy and filled with people and situations we don't understand. Those are the places, he sings, where God will meet us.

– Monsignor Gregory E. S. Malovetz

"I am not ashamed of the gospel...
For in it is revealed the righteousness of God
from faith to faith; as it is written,
'The one who is righteous by faith will live.'"
(Rom 1:16a-17)

IF WE LIVE BY FAITH, then faith has an animating power. It bears its own principle like a soul. Natural life is not generated from inanimate matter, nor does supernatural faith arise from any power in creation. Faith is transcendent, like the living spirit God breathed into Adam's clay.

Faith is a divine, self-attesting reality. It stands as its own premise and serves as its own end. Paul does not say "from *evidence* to faith," nor does he say "from faith to *higher knowledge*." No, the righteousness of God, he says, is revealed "from faith to faith." This means that faith itself proposes the grounds of its own assent. And faith also ratifies what is premised on belief. If this is a circle, it is not vicious. It is the eternal shape of the heavens.

To know God by this miracle of transcendent life implies a radical elevation. It means our mortal clay has been attuned to the incorporeal Word. It means we comprehend God's private language, the language the Trinity speaks. By faith we enter God's circumincession as eavesdroppers. "My sheep hear my voice," says the Lord (Jn 10:27). To hear the Lord's immutable voice speaking in the Word made flesh *is* eternal life. Such faith lifts our minds to abide in that place where God's Truth radiates in unchanging splendor.

– Father J. Anthony Giambrone, O.P.

Queen Come Forth

*"Behold, this child is destined for the fall
and rise of many in Israel."* (Lk 2:34)

A QUEEN
forever fruitful,
a kingdom
come forth,
Simeon sees
salvation
and sword.
He speaks
what a mother's heart
already knows.
The child
she lets go
is light,
light that will carry
flesh that will fall.
The prophet holds
what the queen brings forth,
and she will rule
with open eyes
the fall and the rise.

– Rita A. Simmonds

*T*HE MATERIAL OBJECT OF FAITH is the truth or body of truths, accepted by the believer. In the case of the supernatural act of faith, the material object is the content of God's supernatural revelation....

It is the plan of God that his message be communicated to individual men, not by the inner promptings of the Holy Spirit…but "through the hands of the Apostles." Divine revelation is, therefore, a *public* matter. God has determined from all eternity that his "good news," the Gospel, would be broadcast to the world through the tangible medium of his visible Church whose Head is Jesus Christ. "All power in heaven and earth has been given to me. Go, therefore, and make disciples of all nations…, teaching them to observe all that I have commanded you" (Mt 28:18-19). It follows, then, that when the Church speaks, Christ speaks; and when Christ speaks, the Father speaks: "The Word that you have heard is not mine, but the Father's who sent me" (Jn 14:24); "My teaching is not my own, but his who sent me" (Jn 7:16). To guarantee that his message will be public and open to all men—not the plaything of individual vagaries or personal feelings, not the football of miscreants and malcontents, not the private province or production of an elite—Christ established an infallible witness and objective proponent of his truth.

– Father Francis L. B. Cunningham, O.P.

Judith

IN THE FACE of the vast army of Nebuchadnezzar, come to lay all of Israel low, it is Judith alone who has not despaired of God's help. The Assyrian army has cut off Israel's water supply. The people, desperate, appeal to their leaders, who promise to give God five more days to save them before they surrender. Judith alone of the Israelites has not despaired of God being God, of his power being greater even than the might of the army or the threatening storm cloud, with its promise of rain. And it is precisely Judith's fidelity that makes her God's chosen instrument for the downfall of Nebuchadnezzar's army.

Beautiful as she is pure, Judith adorns herself in gold and silver and boldly makes her way to the army encampment. Beguiled by her beauty, Holofernes, Nebuchadnezzar's great captain, throws a banquet, hoping to seduce her. But Judith, lovely Judith, beheads him with his own sword as he swoons, drunk on wine. Confusion falls upon the Assyrians, who flee before the emboldened Israelites. And Judith is praised in words that will one day be spoken of another woman, in whom beauty, purity, and fidelity are one: "You are the glory of Jerusalem,/ the surpassing joy of Israel;/ you are the splendid boast of our people!" (Jdt 15:9).

– Lisa Lickona

It is the Church that believes first, and so bears,
nourishes and sustains my faith.
(*CCC 168*)

SAINT PETER MARTYR, one of the earliest canonized members of the Dominican Order, was slain in 1252 near Milan, Italy. He was a tremendous preacher and model of virtue, and he reveals both of these things in the last words of his life. They were not spoken words or preached words, but rather words written with his own blood, as he lay mortally wounded on the side of the road. In red letters, he traced this line into the ground: *Credo in unum Deum.* "I believe in one God." His last sermon was just as powerful as any of his others. It was more succinct, no doubt, but no less filled with truth. The words in fact were so powerful that they effected the conversion of the man who killed him. Repenting of his sin, the assassin would later enter the Dominican Order and himself take up the role that he had tried to strike down in Peter Martyr.

Our own "I believe" has the same power to convert our own hearts and those of others by our Christian example, for the truths of our faith are not only worth dying for, they are worth living for as well.

– Father James M. Sullivan, O.P.

*G*OD HIMSELF, the first and primary eternally true being, is the principal object of divine faith. The divine essence as it is in itself—not as known through its effects—certainly exists as the first of all truths, and it is the Godhead *in itself,* in its supernatural being, which is the primary object of our faith; this truth, then, transcends all our natural powers of knowledge. All other truths which are revealed by God are the object of belief because of their connection with this first truth, and they are assented to by reason of that first truth. "From this point of view," writes Saint Thomas, "the object of faith is in some way the First Truth, insofar as nothing falls under faith at all except in relation to God; so also the object of the art of medicine is health, since nothing is considered by it except by reason of its relation to health."

– Father Francis L. B. Cunningham, O.P.

Esther

IN ESTHER'S TIME, the Jews live under the reign of the Persian king Ahasuerus. The king's chancellor, Haman, has plotted against the Jews, having issued an edict for their destruction. But Esther, a Jewess, has found favor with the king and wears the crown of queen. Certain that Esther can help, Mordecai, her cousin and guardian, asks her to go to the king to seek a reversal of the edict. Esther at first resists Mordecai's suggestion—reminding him that anyone who enters the king's presence without having first been summoned is liable to execution. But Mordecai insists that Esther intervene: "Who knows," he concludes, "but that it was for a time like this that you obtained the royal dignity?" (Est 4:14).

Esther's faith is tested in this stark moment, when she can either go forward to meet possible execution or back to her baubles and her ladies-in-waiting. No one knows that she is a Jew, and she could take refuge in her anonymity. But instead, she falls prostrate before the Lord. What else can she do, but place her destiny in his hands? After three days, she rises and goes to the king without hesitation. And her faith is richly rewarded—Ahasuerus hears her plea, Haman, the enemy of the Jews, is destroyed, and the edict is lifted.

– Lisa Lickona

LORD, I believe in you: increase my faith./ I trust in you: strengthen my trust./ I love you: let me love you more and more./ I am sorry for my sins: deepen my sorrow./ I worship you as my first beginning,/ I long for you as my last end,/ I praise you as my constant helper,/ And call on you as my loving protector./ Guide me by your wisdom,/ Correct me with your justice,/ Comfort me with your mercy,/ Protect me with your power./ I offer you, Lord, my thoughts: to be fixed on you;/ My words: to have you for their theme;/ My actions: to reflect my love for you;/ My sufferings: to be endured for your greater glory./ I want to do what you ask of me:/ In the way you ask,/ For as long as you ask,/ Because you ask it./ Lord, enlighten my understanding,/ Strengthen my will,/ Purify my heart,/ and make me holy./ Help me to repent of my past sins/ And to resist temptation in the future./ Help me to rise above my human weaknesses/ And to grow stronger as a Christian./ Let me love you, my Lord and my God,/ And see myself as I really am:/ A pilgrim in this world,/ A Christian called to respect and love/ All whose lives I touch,/ Those under my authority,/ My friends and my enemies.

– From the Universal Prayer attributed to Pope Clement XI

*I*T IS THE WILL that moves the intellect to give its assent where direct proof is wanting. Belief—the act of faith—is an operation elicited by the intellect, but imperated, or commanded, by the will…. Clearly we can see that no *one believes unless he wills freely to believe.…*

The will is free, but since it is engaged with a supernatural object its own activity is not enough, it must also be moved by God's grace.

Saint Thomas includes all these elements in his definition of the act of faith. Faith is *"the act of the intellect assenting to divine truth under the dominion of the will as moved by God's grace."*

From this analysis it is evident that faith, a supernatural act about a supernatural object, immeasurably transcends mere erudition about religious matters or persuasion about rational truths, as rationalists hold…. It is knowledge of mystery, imperfect and obscure but a real glimpse of eternity…. Faith for a Catholic is a firm judgment based on God's Word. And yet faith in this realistic Catholic sense is much more than a soberly intellectual conviction, though it always begins with that. A loving faith, energized by charity, overflows into good works, the keeping of God's law: "So faith too, unless it has works, is dead in itself" (Jas 2:17).

– Father Francis L. B. Cunningham, O.P.

Eleazar

WE HEAR the phrase "culture wars" often enough. To us it means disagreement over moral values, like the life of the unborn, authentic marriage, or respect for conscience. In the time of the Maccabees, the conflict was even more acute: it was a conflict between the sophisticated and elegant culture of the Greeks and the humble religious observance of the Jews.

The Greek culture, which gloried in its literature, philosophy, art, and sport, was very attractive to the Jews, and many Jews yielded and adapted. Under the tyrant Antiochus IV Epiphanes, the Jews were brutally forced to abandon the practice of the law. Circumcision and the observance of the Sabbath were prohibited, and those who disobeyed were executed. Jews were forced to sacrifice to Zeus and to eat pork.

Among those who resisted the Greeks was the ninety-year-old scribe Eleazar. The Greeks urged him to eat one mouthful of pork, or even to pretend to; they would give him acceptable meat. But he refused even the semblance of apostasy, of accommodation to the Greek culture. A moment came when faith in God's law had to say, "No!" Eleazar balanced a few more years of life against loyalty to God's law, and remained faithful to that law. His dreadful death bore witness to the beauty of unwavering faith.

– Father Joseph T. Lienhard, s.j.

*F*AITH IS MORE than a transitory act proceeding now and then under the intermittent influence of God's actual grace. The Scriptures speak of faith rather as a permanent disposition or quality that is requisite for salvation....

At the moment of his justification, when he is ingrafted into Christ, the sinner receives, along with sanctifying grace, "all these things infused simultaneously: faith, hope and charity."

In this sense, then, faith was defined by the Vatican Council as "a supernatural virtue whereby we believe," and by Saint Thomas as "a habit of the mind by means of which eternal life is begun in us, making the intellect assent to things that are not evident."

The virtue of faith is absolutely necessary in order that the intellect might attain to the heights of God's supernatural message. As the eye can establish visual contact with the colored objects surrounding it only by means of physical light, so the intellect—the eye of the mind—is able to contact the supernatural revelation of God only through the instrumentality of some "light" proportionate to the nature of that revelation. And this "light" is precisely the divinely infused, theological virtue of faith.

– Father Francis L. B. Cunningham, O.P.

The Mother with Seven Sons

IN THE SECOND CENTURY BEFORE CHRIST, a mother and her seven sons are ordered to eat pork in violation of Hebrew dietary laws. They refuse and are brought before the Greek king, who has the tongue of the son who has vocally defied the rule cut out, directs the soldiers to slice off his hands and feet, and while he is completely maimed but still breathing, orders him to be fried in a caldron. Each of the sons in turn suffers the same treatment; each, before dying, declares his fidelity to the God of Israel.

Flummoxed, the king appeals to the mother to save the last son by cajoling him, at least, into eating pork. Instead, she leans over and speaking in her native tongue, encourages him to die as nobly as his brothers had. Thus he is killed too; as is, last of all, the mother.

In *Guilt,* the British mystic and convert Caryll Houselander points out that non-believers will voluntarily suffer as long as the suffering "is for *some purpose,* used as a means to an end, but they abhor 'useless suffering.'" The person of faith, by contrast, will undergo "useless" suffering for fruits that are eternal. The believer knows that even higher than a child's life is the child's soul. Thus the follower of Christ, of whom this brave mother is a forerunner, will die for love.

– Heather King

Lenten Daily Penances

for Growing in Faith

◖ *On Sundays – Lectio Divina:* Devote a half hour or so each Sunday to reading Sacred Scripture in a prayerful manner. You might begin with one of the Gospels, or perhaps take up next Sunday's Bible readings.

◖ *On Mondays – Meditative Prayer:* Set aside time to pray by yourself and in silence. You might repeat peacefully the Jesus Prayer: "Lord Jesus Christ, Son of the living God, have mercy on me, a sinner."

◖ *On Tuesdays – Fasting:* Choose one day of the week each week—perhaps this day—to fast. Offer your mortification for specific intentions. Pray that your spiritual hunger will match your physical hunger.

◖ *On Wednesdays – Charitable Works of Mercy:* Use this day to go out of your way to care for the poor, the needy, and the lonely. Reflect on all the corporal and spiritual works of mercy, and commit to carrying out each of them during the season of Lent.

◖ *On Thursdays – Adoration of the Blessed Sacrament:* Make regular Eucharistic Adoration a priority of your Lenten observance. Bring all your prayer requests and the needs of your family and friends before the Lord's Eucharistic presence. Let him gaze at you in love.

◖ *On Fridays – Study of the Faith:* Build into your Lenten Fridays choice time to study the *Catechism of the Catholic Church.* Start with those areas of doctrine which you need to understand better.

◖ *On Saturdays – Confession and Mortification for Sins:* Let your Lent be marked by frequent confession. Resolve to give up certain pleasures and conveniences during Lent as a penance for sin.

– Father Peter John Cameron, O.P.

How to Grow in Faith

A PHYSICIST EXPERT in the self-assembling properties of metal alloys comments, "All we are able to do in science is disprove rather than fully prove. We can determine what is *not* by means of experiments, but we can never fully determine what is."

This physicist is free to prescribe the limits of his own method, but he would be too modest if he applied these limits to all our ways of knowing. Reason helps us grasp the universe and our place in it. But reason is not the exclusive remedy for human ignorance.

Faith is not the default leap to fill in the gaps left by the "disproving" activity of scientific inquiry. Faith is receptivity to the evidence proposed by one judged to be trustworthy. Faith is a habit of mind that engages objects which transcend scientific modes of explanation. Faith squarely faces the phenomena of nature around us—including human nature. Faith penetrates the real insofar as the real presents itself to us.

Persons of faith sell others and their faith short if they fail to pay attention to the results of scientific inquiry, or propose superficial answers to the problems that continue to occupy scientists.

Galileo became a celebrity in the cause of divorcing human reason from the claims of faith—in ways Galileo himself would have rejected. Yet the joint operations of reason and faith are not "self-assembling." The quest for data, the discipline of research, and the desire to understand the world are themselves spiritual impulses. But without humility and integrity on all sides, we can reduce the larger meaning of what we discover. We too easily settle for partial conclusions, especially when we become the object under scrutiny.

Richard Zaner suggests that T. S. Eliot's questions are still relevant today: Where is the knowledge we have lost in information, where the wisdom we have lost in knowledge?

Persons of faith have found wisdom, and hunger and thirst for more. We seek "after physics," and we want to know what precedes and follows physics. We want information we acquire to be transformed into knowledge, to be in the service of wisdom. The work of scientists stirs respect; it awakens wonder; it prompts new questions. When the horizon of truth we seek is engaged by our coordinated capacities of reason and faith, then we approach the goal toward which all good-willed labors lead: Jesus Christ, Wisdom Incarnate.

– Father William Joensen

*"Faith...is an encounter with the living God—
an encounter opening up new horizons
extending beyond the sphere of reason."*
– Pope Benedict XVI

Job

HE IS THE GOLDEN BOY, the star pupil, the teacher's favorite and a parent's dream. God asks the world if there is anyone as good and devoted as Job? The forces of evil respond, "Would Job be so faithful and devoted if his life were not so golden and the dreams became nightmares?" And so begin the many troubles of Job.

Held sacred by those who follow Christianity, Judaism, and Islam, this story is known even by those with no religious affiliation. Job's situation is made worse by three friends who ridicule him and insist these disasters are punishments from God. His patience tried, Job demands answers from God. What is startling is that there is no detailed explanation given. Job learns there may be no answers for why there is suffering, or why lovely people can't seem to catch a break in life. God explains that in the face of suffering, what gives hope is faith, not answers.

Job stands as a friend to all who suffer. He tells us it is understandable that we want to know why. The challenge is to believe God will give us the strength, even in the darkest hour, to stand firm.

– Monsignor Gregory E. S. Malovetz

"What occasion is there then for boasting?
It is ruled out. On what principle, that of works?
No, rather on the principle of faith.
For we consider that a person is justified by faith
apart from works of the law."
(Rom 3:27-28)

"BOASTING" IN SAINT PAUL must be decoded. It refers to a very specific attitude, not of self-reliance or self-salvation, but of religious ethnocentrism. It means vaunting Jewish privileges to the exclusionary disadvantage of all other peoples. "Works of the law" thus signifies for Paul not so much a doctrine of merit as a vision of God's saving favor strictly bound to the Law of Moses. Whenever the Apostle speaks against "works" we must thus know he is addressing the *Jewish Law*.

Catholics accordingly accept a doctrine of salvation *by grace alone*. But this is a very different thing from salvation *by faith alone*. By grace, there is no longer Gentile or Jew; God makes no distinction. Christians need not keep kosher or be circumcised to live in the Lord's covenant. We must, nonetheless, still perform works—not the Law of Moses, but the Law of Christ. Yet still we do not boast, for works (like faith) are ever born of grace. We are "created in Christ Jesus for the good works that *God has prepared in advance*" (Eph 2:10, emphasis added).

– Father J. Anthony Giambrone, O.P.

*F*AITH IS THAT SUPERNATURAL VIRTUE by which we conquer temptations. "By faith the saints conquered kingdoms, wrought justice, obtained promises, stopped the mouths of lions, quenched the violence of fire, recovered strength from weakness, became valiant in battle, and put to flight the armies of foreigners. Through faith women received their dead raised to life again. But without faith it is impossible to please God, for he who comes to God must believe that he exists and is a rewarder to them that seek him" (Heb 11:33). Through faith we overcome temptations. This is clear because every temptation is either from the devil, the world, or the flesh. The devil tempts us so that we might not obey God nor subject ourselves to him. This diabolical temptation is removed through faith, for through faith we know that God is the Lord of all and consequently we are obliged to obey him. "Be sober and watch, because your adversary the devil, as a roaring lion, [goes] about seeking whom he may devour" (1 Pt 5:8).

The world tempts us, either by seducing us with its vanities or by terrifying us with its misfortunes. But even these we can conquer through faith, which enables us to believe in another life superior to this and teaches us to believe that better things are awaiting us. Hence by faith, we conquer the vanities of this world and fear not its adversaries. "This is the victory which [overcomes] the world, your faith" (1 Jn 5:4).

The flesh tempts us by attracting us to the pleasures of present life, which pleasures, at most, are fast fleeting and perishable. But faith warns us that through these pleasures, if we cling to them improperly, we will lose eternal happiness.

– Saint Thomas Aquinas

Isaiah

AT A TIME OF MORAL DECLINE within Judah and political threats closing in from without, Isaiah is given the grace to see the Lord. He recognizes himself to be unworthy of the vision, but when a seraph cleans his lips and tells him his sin is removed, his trust in this forgiveness is so great that he immediately and confidently puts himself forward to go wherever God would send him. He has great faith that God's forgiveness is greater than man's sinfulness, and can propel him into any mission.

Isaiah is so often quoted in the New Testament because of his many promises of the coming of the Messiah. He is not shy about detailing the darkness that characterizes his time, but no amount of darkness discourages him from proclaiming that light that surely would come in the form of a child who would be called Immanuel (Is 7:14), "Mighty God," and "Prince of Peace" (Is 9:5). Isaiah tells us of the Lord's servant who has done no wrong but will bear our offenses and be pierced for them and die and then somehow live to see life and light (cf. Is 53).

Isaiah does not encounter Christ in the flesh, but he has unwavering faith in his coming.

– Father Richard Veras

We do not believe in formulas, but in those realities they express, which faith allows us to touch.

(CCC 170)

HEBREWS 11:1 teaches us that "Faith is the assurance of things hoped for, the conviction of things not seen." In order to hope in these things, and to be convinced of things not seen, we need a means to get there, to get to the end of our faith, which is God himself. Faith is the virtue that allows us to believe, and the formulas of faith that we profess are the means.

We have creedal statements that the Church has been professing for centuries: I believe in one God. I believe in the Holy Spirit. I believe in one, holy, catholic, and apostolic Church. These are not just words, as if they list off the ingredients of a random recipe that makes up a Catholic. These words have the power to unite us to God himself. Professing "I believe" with full assent of our intellect and our will makes the assurances and convictions of our faith more certain. The more often we make an act of faith, the more often we are built up in that faith, not by the power of repetition but rather by the power of petition: "I do believe, help my unbelief!" (Mk 9:24). We do not believe in formulas; we believe through them.

– Father James M. Sullivan, O.P.

*F*AITH BRINGS TO MAN the only full and true picture of reality. It features God as the rewarder of good and as the punisher of evil....

Faith also presents God as the only infinite good, the most desirable object to which man could aspire, the beneficent Father who lavishes unsurpassing love on his adopted children. When man is effectively and affectively united and subjected to God by means of grace and a faith animated by charity, servile fear gives place to filial fear. To the degree one grows in the love of God, to just such an extent his fear of eternal punishment gives place to the reverential fear of the child, who stands in horror of being separated from the tender love and care of his parents. Servile fear centers attention more and more on oneself; filial fear, on the contrary, directs one more and more to focus attention on God.

In addition to engendering salutary fear of God, faith is responsible for another effect, called by Saint Thomas "the purification of the heart." By raising the mind to supernatural truth, faith directly frees man from the defilement of error, while at the same time it provides a basis for moral purity. Even unformed faith guarantees intellectual purity, but when charity impregnates faith this purification is brought to its perfection by ridding the will of evil.

– Father Francis L. B. Cunningham, O.P.

Jeremiah

IN A LIFE OF AT LEAST EIGHTY YEARS, Jeremiah faithfully speaks God's wisdom in his native town of Anathoth northeast of Jerusalem, in the Holy City itself, and then in Maspath in Egypt when the Jews are driven out of their Land of Promise. At the same time in Athens, the philosopher Solon is teaching, but his wisdom does not claim the faith in God's providence that inspired Jeremiah. That faith mourns the sorrows of his people while envisioning a joyful renewal of life. Faith saves Jeremiah from bleak pessimism as it also saves him from the indignity of facile optimism.

In the Sistine Chapel, Michelangelo draws Jeremiah's face as that of a man who has never smiled, because he sees the tragedy of faithlessness all around him. Saint Jerome, so sensitive to literary style, remarks how abrupt and unadorned are the words of Jeremiah, but true pathos has no time for decoration. Jeremiah is among those whose mourning is blessed, as says the Messiah on the Mount. Jeremiah waits for that Messiah in faith. He cannot have known how accurately his own suffering, and that of his people facing captivity in Babylon, prefigure the Passion and cross, but his lamentations have become part of the Good Friday liturgy, sung three days before Christ wipes away many tears.

– Father George William Rutler

*I*DENTIFY YOUR FAITH with that of the Church without paying attention to the movements of your heart which seem contrary to it. For those feelings that arise in you are not what you believe, but the faith of the Church is what you believe, though you neither see it nor feel it. Accept these disturbances patiently, then, as a trial sent from God to purify your heart and confirm your faith. You should love and respect also all the laws and ordinances made by prelates and those that rule the Church concerning the faith, the sacraments, or the conduct of Christians. Assent to them humbly and sincerely. Even though you do not know their cause and some seem unreasonable to you, do not condemn or criticize them. Respect them all, though they concern you very little. Do not receive under color of greater holiness, as some foolish people do, any opinion, whether it comes from your own imagination or the teaching of other men, if it is contrary in any way to the law or teaching of the Church. And beyond this you should confidently believe that you are chosen by the mercy of God to be saved as one of his elect. Never depart from this hope whatever you see or hear, or whatever temptations come upon you.

– Father Walter Hilton

Lord, help me to conquer anger with gentleness,/ Greed by generosity,/ Apathy by fervor./ Help me to forget myself/ And reach out toward others./ Make me prudent in planning,/ Courageous in taking risks./ Make me patient in suffering, unassuming in prosperity./ Keep me, Lord, attentive at prayer,/ Temperate in food and drink,/ Diligent in my work,/ Firm in my good intentions./ Let my conscience be clear,/ My conduct without fault,/ My speech blameless,/ My life well-ordered./ Put me on guard against my human weaknesses./ Let me cherish your love for me,/ Keep your law,/ And come at last to your salvation./ Teach me to realize that this world is passing,/ That my true future is the happiness of heaven,/ That life on earth is short,/ And the life to come eternal./ Help me to prepare for death/ With a proper fear of judgment,/ But a greater trust in your goodness./ Lead me safely through death/ To the endless joy of heaven./ Grant this through Christ our Lord. Amen.

– From the Universal Prayer attributed to Pope Clement XI

Ezekiel

"SON OF MAN," said the Lord, "can these bones come to life?" (Ez 37:3).

The Lord had led the prophet Ezekiel into a broad plain filled with bones—dry and bleached in the unforgiving sun. "Son of man," said God, "these bones are the whole house of Israel" (Ez 37:11). For their sins, the people had been led captive into Babylon. Jerusalem, with its holy Temple, had been destroyed.

What life could now arise?

None that man can see. Years before, when Ezekiel was called to be a prophet, the Lord had given him a scroll to eat. On it was written, "Lamentation and wailing and woe!" (Ez 2:10). Yet when he ate the scroll, "it was as sweet as honey" (Ez 3:3). We recall the strange manna that lay upon the desert sands like flakes. When the people made it into bread, it tasted like wafers baked with honey. How strange that a prophecy of sorrow should be sweet and nourishing, like manna from heaven!

So it is with our faithful and holy God. Ezekiel understood this, even if his people didn't. He builds our faith as we walk through our own desolate valley. Can these bones come to life?

"Lord GOD," said Ezekiel, "you alone know that" (Ez 37:3).

– Anthony Esolen

The Stations of the Cross

Focusing on Faith

◀ *First Station: Jesus Is Condemned to Death*
May I always praise, honor, and glorify you, Lord.

◀ *Second Station: Jesus Takes up His Cross*
Help me to accept my suffering as redemptive.

◀ *Third Station: Jesus Falls the First Time*
I can face my falls because I am united with you.

◀ *Fourth Station: Jesus Meets His Mother*
Mary meets you as an icon of the Father's mercy.

◀ *Fifth Station: Simon Helps Carry the Cross*
Saying yes to your cross is a great Yes of faith.

◀ *Sixth Station: Jesus Meets Veronica*
Faith is meeting something—Someone—greater
than anything I can think up for myself.

◀ *Seventh Station: Jesus Falls a Second Time*
I fall like the seed that becomes the fertile harvest.

◀ *Eighth Station: Jesus Comforts the Women*
Despair does not win; your comfort brings life.

◀ *Ninth Station: Jesus Falls a Third Time*
I keep my focus only on your mercy and power.

◀ *Tenth Station: Jesus Is Stripped of His Garments*
May I be stripped of all my false attachments.

◀ *Eleventh Station: Jesus Is Nailed to the Cross*
Give me the faith to stand by your cross so that
all my sins may be nailed fast to it with it you.

◀ *Twelfth Station: Jesus Dies on the Cross*
By faith you carry us over the elements of death.

◀ *Thirteenth Station: Jesus' Body Is Taken Down*
I receive your body with the same reverence with
which I guard the great deposit of faith.

◀ *Fourteenth Station: Jesus Is Laid in the Tomb*
May I keep vigil at your tomb as at a tabernacle.

– Father Peter John Cameron, O.P.

"[Abraham] believed, hoping against hope,
that he would become 'the father of many nations.'…
He did not weaken in faith when he considered
his own body as [already] dead… He did not doubt God's
promise in unbelief; rather, he was empowered
by faith and gave glory to God."
(Rom 4:18-20)

PAUL REPEATEDLY brings Abraham forward to illustrate the sound, biblical doctrine of salvation by faith apart from the Law. Yet in trusting he is justified: "Abraham 'believed God, and it was credited to him as righteousness'" (Gal 3: 6; cf. Gn 15:6).

Abraham believes when the Lord calls him from his father's home. He believes when the Lord promises him a child. He believes, as well, on that terrible day when God requires Isaac, his only beloved son. This is truly "hoping against hope": accepting the Lord's promise of blessing as a certainty stronger than death, obeying God's command when it offers no prospect but mocking tragedy.

All faith must ultimately measure itself against this standard. Perhaps we should again "look to the rock from which [we] were hewn" (Is 51:1). Abraham's faith is a Christian faith forty generations before Christ is born. For Abraham believes that even should his "seed" fall to the ground and die, it will yet bear much fruit as a blessing to all the nations.

– Father J. Anthony Giambrone, O.P.

Daniel

APOCALYPSE NOW. Not malevolent fire from above; rather, the good news that the Kingdom of God comes on, that the Son of Man standing at the right hand of the Most High does not hold himself harmless above our sufferings. What rough beasts slouch across the stage of history, or mill around each of us in our den of despair? Jesus walks with us in the fiery furnace as enemies internal and external oppress us. The Christian has a future in hope, even when it seems there's no way out, because Jesus opens up the horizon of a resurrected life—by loving us to the end, faithfully, on the cross.

Daniel heralds this coming Son of Man as a prophet living in exile, so attuned to providence that he divines the future in dreams. Even as he serves in the royal household of the Babylonian Empire, contributing to ordering worldly realities wisely, he is faithful to all Israel's laws, a living sign of the sovereignty of the true God. Everyday faithfulness is the opening for the Kingdom to come to earth. The Son of Man strides into this opening—interrupting the proud power of this world, vindicating the powerless victim. Daniel is faithful within the Lord's faithfulness: "I worship not idols made with hands, but only the living God who made heaven and earth and has dominion over all mankind" (Dn 14:5).

– J. David Franks

*T*HE ACT OF FAITH, proceeding from a divinely implanted supernatural virtue and under the divinely instigated movement of actual grace, enables man to accept the only all-inclusive view of reality as it truly is. Men are brought into a universe that consists in much more than appears to earthly eyes, or that can be discerned by reason's natural capacities. A whole supernatural order of life and truth completes the picture of things as they really exist. And the only truly healthy mind is that which embraces both the natural and supernatural aspects of this real order. This can only be done through the supernatural virtue of faith: a gift supernatural in origin, in purpose, in manner of operation.

When God thus enables the mind of man to assent to his Word, then, and only then, does man begin to contact eternity. The "Credo" of the believer is the beginning of his salvation, truly eternal life begun. Thus is given meaning to the words of the Preface for the Mass of the dead: "For to those who believe in you, Lord, life is only changed, not taken away; and in exchange for the dissolution of this earthly dwelling place they receive an eternal home in heaven."

– Father Francis L. B. Cunningham, O.P.

The Church…faithfully guards "the faith
which was once for all delivered to the saints"
(1 Tim 3:15; Jude 3). (CCC 171)

W E PRAY "AMEN" repeatedly at church on Sunday, at home with family, and even in the car for those special moments. The Catechism teaches us that the root word for "Amen" is actually "to believe" (cf. CCC 1064). "Amen" is another way of saying, "I believe." The Church then teaches us by her example how best to guard "the faith which was once for all delivered to the saints": by simply professing the words "I believe" or "Amen."

This does not mean a simple saying of words, but rather a framing of our life with these words. "Amen" when suffering occurs in my life. "I believe" when a great blessing is bestowed upon me. We can actually be surrounded by many acts of faith throughout the day. Anytime we pray "Amen," we are adding our own "I believe" to whatever it is we have just prayed. When we offer prayers of petition, contrition, adoration, or thanksgiving, they are concluded with the best of all prayers: "Amen." "I believe in all that God has revealed to me to be true and I believe that his Church will lead me deeper into that truth."

– Father James M. Sullivan, O.P.

Susanna

T WO LECHEROUS ELDERLY VOYEURS conspire to surprise Susanna at her bath and rape her, but she screams and puts them off. They threaten blackmail, saying they will explain her screams by reporting that they had caught her in adultery. But she continues to spurn their advances, and they flee.

Brought before the townspeople, the crowd believes the elders and condemns her to death. But Susanna cries aloud: "O eternal God, you know what is hidden and are aware of all things before they come to be" (Dn 13:42).

The Lord hears her. The young Daniel steps out from the crowd, calls for a fair investigation, separates the elders, and asks each to name the kind of tree under which they had seen Susanna lying with a man. One answers a mastic and the other answers an oak: thus, they are shown to be liars and are put to death in Susanna's place.

Falsely accused, ready to die rather than compromise her integrity, a caller-upon God *in extremis*, Susanna is an early Christ figure.

As well, Susanna's purity evokes just the kind of bold, gallant, creative response in Daniel that does purity—and womanhood—proud.

– Heather King

*A*LTHOUGH FAITH IS FIRM and infallibly certain, since it is founded on the authority of God himself, it does not have the clarity and evidence of reason, for it treats of matters that surpass the powers of reason.... For that reason the Apostle says that faith is of those things that are not seen, that is, of those things which reason cannot comprehend but are known only through the revelation of God. But it is precisely the merit of faith that it commands reason to believe those things which reason itself cannot attain....

Saint John Chrysostom says that the servant of God must be so constant that even if there appear to be a contradiction in the things that God reveals, he must not on that account refuse to believe them....

The authority of God is a sufficient basis for our faith and we need not seek elsewhere for other reasons for believing.... When God speaks, we must humble ourselves and let down the wings of our intellects....

But no one should think that because the truths of faith surpass reason, we should on that account believe in them for any light or baseless motives. The divine truths which surpass our understanding are nevertheless compatible with reason. Moreover, there is all the more reason for believing when miracles have been performed to demonstrate the truth of the revelation.

– Venerable Louis of Granada

Hosea

IN TIMES OF TROUBLE, it is understandable that one might seek out a professional for guidance. Often, however, it is the one who has gone through a similar crisis who can offer wisdom from experience. It is the person at a Twelve Step meeting, telling her story, who gives others struggling a glimpse of hope.

The prophet Hosea is one of those people. Little is known of his life, although his writing reveals a deeply passionate and sensitive man. Hosea is commanded to marry a woman he will later discover is a prostitute. Rather than give up on her, Hosea remains faithful and waits for her return. His entire life becomes a parable for the Hebrew people. They had been unfaithful to God, turning to idolatry and making unholy alliances with foreign nations. Rather than give up on them, God remains faithful and waits for their return. Hosea strongly condemns Israel, but is equally strong in believing there is a way back. His experience tells them that it is only love that changes a human heart. Hosea wants those who have fallen along the way to believe they can begin again. Nothing they can ever do will make God love them less.

– Monsignor Gregory E. S. Malovetz

*S*OMETIMES THE VIRTUE OF FAITH is accompanied by charity and in that case it is called formed faith or living faith, because it receives life from charity, which is the soul of faith. At other times it is found to exist in a soul without charity and then it is called unformed or dead faith, not because it is not true faith, but because it lacks the vitality, perfection, and beauty which come to it when it is vivified by charity....

When faith is accompanied by charity it carries with it obedience to the divine commandments, for it is proper to a vital and formed faith to incline the Christian to live in accordance with the truths which faith proposes. Thus, when faith considers the words of the Savior: "Unless you shall do penance, you shall all likewise perish," it inspires us to do penance. When faith reminds us of the words of Christ: "Not every one that says to me, 'Lord, Lord,' shall enter into the kingdom of heaven, but he that does the will of my Father who is in heaven," it strives with all its power to fulfill the divine precepts. And when the Lord says: "Unless you be converted and become as little children, you shall not enter into the kingdom of heaven," the living faith of the Christian strives to imitate the humility and simplicity of the little ones.

– Venerable Louis of Granada

*"Faith comes from what is heard,
and what is heard comes through the word of Christ."*
(Rom 10:17)

"YOU MUST SEE IT TO BELIEVE IT." So the saying goes. Saint Paul has a different idea: "Faith comes from what is heard." Faith is in the ears, not the eyes; it is best had at *second-hand*, not by personal witnesses. The Fourth Gospel says that, entering the empty tomb, the Beloved Disciple at once "saw and believed"—but the risen Lord also says, "Blessed are those who have *not* seen and have believed."

The nature of faith explains this. "Faith is the realization of what is hoped for and evidence of things not seen" (Heb 11:1). What do we ultimately believe in? Things not seen. John found faith in the evidence of his unseen hope, a hint of Jesus' still hidden Resurrection. What did Thomas himself believe as he put his finger in the wounds? Not the flesh he touched. He accepted Jesus' unseen divinity: "My Lord and my God."

God is spirit. He dwells in unapproachable light. Hearing excels all senses because it comes nearest to the nature of God. Words are the wavelength of the mind, of intelligence and speech, and the greatest depth of self-disclosure. Christ came in 3-D Technicolor, but his true flesh talks to the soul. Faith is supernatural hearing, for it attunes us to the eternal Word who visibly speaks his Father's glory.

– Father J. Anthony Giambrone, O.P.

Joel

JOEL, one of the twelve minor prophets, announces the great theme of the coming of *the Lord's Day*. He presents the critical situation of his nation devastated by a scourge of locusts, compared to an invading army. He calls for faith in God's protection through history, urging all the people to pray that the disaster be averted. He reassures them that if they repent for their infidelity, blessings would follow. "I will pour out/ my spirit upon all mankind./ Your sons and daughters shall prophesy,/ your old men shall dream dreams,/ your young men shall see visions…/ Then everyone shall be rescued/ who calls on the name of the LORD" (Jl 3:1, 5).

Saint Peter recalls Joel's words in his sermon after Pentecost. He isn't raising false hopes. Since this prophecy has been fulfilled, he exhorts people from many nations gathered in Jerusalem to repent and be baptized to receive the Holy Spirit.

Like the first converts, by baptism we receive the new spiritual life of grace to look forward in faith to *the Lord's Day*. Deepening our faith-based hope, the Eucharist offers the pledge and already a foretaste of the great banquet when the Son of Man will come in glory. Joel long ago foretells this joyous feast: "On that day,/ the mountains shall drip new wine,/ and the hills shall flow with milk" (Jl 4:18).

– Father Michael L. Gaudoin-Parker

FAITH IS A MASTER and tutor that teaches us how to live. It is a candle that enlightens our understanding and gives us a knowledge of the truth. It is a physician that shows us the remedies by which we can cure the illness of our soul; a legislator that gives us laws of good living and guides our life by salutary precepts; an architect of the spiritual edifice that declares to the other laborers what each one must do in his particular capacity. Faith is the sun of our lives, brightening the darkness and showing us where and by what paths we should travel. It is the eyes by which the wise man directs the steps of his life. It is the commander-in-chief that marches in advance to point out the ambushes of the enemy and guide us by a safe path. It is the wings of prayer by which we soar to the presence of God and obtain from him that which we ask, as our Lord has told us: "All things whatsoever you ask when you pray, believe that you shall receive, and they shall come to you."…

Faith does not know what falsity is; it grasps that which reason itself cannot understand; it embraces obscure things and immense things; it understands the future and passes beyond the limits of human reason and the boundaries of experience; in its narrow breast it contains all eternity.

– Venerable Louis of Granada

*Faith is a personal adherence of the whole man
to God who reveals himself.*

(CCC 176)

THE THEOLOGICAL VIRTUE OF FAITH engages the very core of man. We claim that what makes us different from animals and the rest of creation is that we have the use of reason and that we have emotions. Philosophically (and even theologically), we can use the words "intellect" and "will" to describe these human attributes. In simpler terms, we think and we feel. To be human is to be a "feeling thinker." The virtue of faith then makes use of both our intellect and our will. Faith could not exist within us without both of these faculties. It is from this beginning of intellect and will that all human action flows.

We prove what we believe by what we choose to do. We give assent to God's revealed truth not only by the words we profess, but also by the actions we undertake. Thus we imitate God in a certain way because he not only told us that he loved us, but his Son died on the cross to prove it. His deeds and words are united in the death of his Son just as our deeds and words are united in the sacrifices we make to live our faith.

– Father James M. Sullivan, O.P.

Amos

A RESUMÉ can only give you a small glimpse into a person's abilities and talents. If he had to write a resume, Amos would have included shepherd, herdsman, and sycamore fig farmer. In considering him for the job of prophet, we might have discarded his resumé. But God sees something in him that will make Amos a compelling prophet.

Living in the eighth century BC, Amos' jobs have given him a keen glimpse into the disparity between the rich and the poor. God sends him to the northern kingdom of Israel where the increase of wealth is matched with a decline of religious faith and indifference to the poor. Amos, without any special training and relying only on the power of God, finds his voice. He is not the kind of prophet who uses poetic words and beautiful images. Amos is blunt as he insists those who follow God must be people of justice. Prayers and rituals are meaningless if they do not lead to service. It is believed that his career as prophet lasted less than a year, yet Amos' voice still challenges us today. No special skills are needed to work for justice, only a heart that sees God in every human need.

– Monsignor Gregory E. S. Malovetz

O GOD, I love thee, I love thee—
Not out of hope of heaven for me
Nor fearing not to love and be
In the everlasting burning.
Thou, thou, my Jesus, after me
Didst reach thine arms out dying,
For my sake sufferedst nails, and lance,
Mocked and marred countenance,
Sorrows passing number,
Sweat and care and cumber,
Yea and death, and this for me,
And thou couldst see me sinning:
Then I, why should not I love thee,
Jesu, so much in love with me?
Not for heaven's sake;
Not to be out of hell by loving thee;
Not for any gains I see;
But just the way that thou didst me
I do love and I will love thee:
What must I love thee, Lord, for then?
For being my King and God. Amen.

– Saint Francis Xavier

*F*AITH CONQUERS KINGDOMS, effects justice, obtains promises, stops the mouths of lions, quenches the violence of fire, escapes the edge of the sword, recovers strength from weakness, makes men valiant in battle, puts the enemy to flight, and restores to mothers their dead children.

Such is the faith, as Saint Paul reminds us, that the patriarchs had from the beginning of the world. By faith they regulated the steps of their life, trusting in the words and promises of God, believing in that which they could not see and hoping for that which they did not yet possess, going beyond the testimony of their human faculties and being governed by the light of the divine revelation. This is what Habakkuk meant when he said that the just man shall live in his faith. Thus, faith raises a man to a state far above that which is his by nature, for in receiving the enlightenment of the Holy Spirit, the Christian possesses something that is more than human and enters into the region of divine things.

– Venerable Louis of Granada

Jonah

JONAH MIGHT WELL COMPLAIN that people think of the whale more than of him. Jesus does not scorn the story himself: "Just as Jonah was in the belly of the whale three days and three nights, so will the Son of Man be in the heart of the earth three days and three nights" (Mt 12:40). What that scene with the whale looks like is left to the imagination, but we know that Jonah and the Ninevites to whom he preaches, are humans like us. While Jonah's faith impels him to convert others, he is incredulous at its power. He has not envisioned the possibility that his faith might actually bring others to faith.

Great things will be accomplished by faith so long as it is faith in God and not in ourselves. To keep faith is virtuous, but it is not a thing to be kept to oneself, like a firefly that soon fades in a sealed jar. The way to keep faith is to spread it. Jonah does that to his own astonishment, and this is credited by "the Author and Finisher of our faith" when he tells those who ask for a miracle to bolster their trust in God: "At the judgment, the men of Nineveh will arise with this generation and condemn it, because they repented at the preaching of Jonah; and there is something greater than Jonah here" (Mt 12:41; Lk 11:32).

– Father George William Rutler

*S*INCE THE BLESSINGS OF FAITH are so great and numerous, it follows that one of the principal efforts of the good Christian should be to strive as much as possible to perfect and intensify his faith. Faith, like hope and charity and all the other infused virtues, grows by meritorious acts. Moreover, charity and the gift of understanding greatly perfect the virtue of faith, and as a Christian is moved more and more by the gift of understanding, the clarity of his faith is proportionately increased. Sometimes this clarity reaches such a point that the soul feels that it no longer sees by faith but by some light that is much brighter than faith. Such is not the case in reality, however, but faith itself has been greatly illumined by the gift of understanding.

Conversely, the gift of understanding is greatly aided by the truths of faith, and as the Christian humbly studies the truths of faith, he disposes himself for an increase in the light of faith and the gift of understanding. The more he penetrates these mysteries, the more firmly he believes them and the more he is moved to live a life that is conformable to the truths he believes.

– Venerable Louis of Granada

The Sins That Erode Faith

THE CHURCH gives the following instruction for the worldwide celebration of the Year of Faith: "Bishops are invited to organize penitential celebrations…in which all can ask for God's forgiveness, especially for sins against faith" (CDF "Note," III, 7). Why should we examine our consciences about the sins against faith? The answer is simple: so that we can love God and neighbor rightly. Unaided by the gift of divine truth, there is no guarantee that loving will make us happy.

The *Catechism of the Catholic Church* (2088-2089) enumerates the sins that one may commit against faith. What might these sins entail? Here are some examples: Voluntary doubt sins against faith. A doubt is voluntary when we choose to indulge the doubt instead of to resolve it. Doubt should be distinguished from difficulty. The person who faces difficulties with one or another Catholic truth says, "I don't get this." The solution for difficulties begins with study and sound education. The one who *chooses* to remain doubtful about the Catholic faith withholds assenting to truth. This sinful choice erodes the personal adherence to God that faith requires of the believer.

The general sin against the virtue of faith is called infidelity (with resonances that evoke marital infidelity) or incredulity. God intends that his gift of divine truth should reach the whole world. To miss this gift places the human person in an imperfect situation with respect to God. In the present life, this imperfect situation includes non-belief, that is, the state of those who have never heard Catholic truth preached. In addition, unbelief characterizes those who withhold assent to the preaching of Catholic truth, while disbelief remains the sin of those who dissent from or reject Catholic truth. When these sins generate an obstinate or contumacious spirit, they attain a special gravity.

Things can get worse. A baptized person who remains obstinate in refusing to believe what is held by Catholic and divine faith commits the sin of heresy. On the other hand, apostasy arises when a person repudiates completely the Christian faith. Schism results from refusing submission to the pope or communion with the members of the Church subject to him.

Hopefully none of us have committed these worst of offenses against the gift of faith. However, all of us should examine our conscience to see whether we regularly take every means to grow in our understanding of the Catholic faith.

– **Father Romanus Cessario, O.P.**

"The New Evangelization begins in the confessional."
– Pope Benedict XVI

Micah

FOR A MINOR PROPHET allotted a scant seven pages to exercise his art, the fact of Micah's eloquence is arresting. Drawn from such sincerity and depth of faith as to lay bare the very mind and heart of God, he mediates both judgment and hope from above. "For see, the LORD comes forth from his place,/ he descends and treads upon the heights of the earth" (Mi 1:3). Woe to the wicked, then, whose idols God will lay waste. Because of their transgressions, "Zion shall be plowed like a field,/ and Jerusalem reduced to rubble" (Mi 3:12). Yet the springs of hope shall not run dry; a holy remnant will be found amid the ravaged land.

But where exactly will this promised deliverance come from? Here the prophet strikes the great chord announcing an entirely unexpected event. From Bethlehem, God tells him, "shall come forth for me/ one who is to be ruler in Israel;/ Whose origin is from of old,/ from ancient times" (Mi 5:1). What a nice touch that the name Micah—it means "Who is like Yahweh?"—suggests a God so full of surprises that even poor, unprepossessing Bethlehem shall be given pride of place in the birth of a Savior.

– Regis Martin

*"For since in the wisdom of God
the world did not come to know God through wisdom,
it was the will of God through the foolishness
of the proclamation to save those who have faith."*
(1 Cor 1:21)

WISDOM IS IN THE MIND and the mind is made to see order. When the mind is alive it sees the way things are. If it looks deeper, it can see not only how things are but how they have to be.

It is this need of the mind to see how things have to be that disqualifies it from having the final word about God. There is no "have to be" in God as Creator. He didn't have to make anything. He was and is perfectly complete and happy in himself. His creation is both wonderful and totally unnecessary.

Neither is there a "have to be" with respect to us. God didn't have to make us. Having made us, he did not have to make us to share his life and his friendship for ever. Having made us for his friendship, he did not have to die on a cross to restore that friendship when it was foolishly lost.

It pleased God to restore that friendship through dying in an act of love that seemed excessive and foolish and that certainly did not have to be, but in which we are invited to share by the foolishness and freedom of belief.

– Father John Dominic Corbett, O.P.

In order to believe,
man needs the interior helps of the Holy Spirit.
(CCC 179)

As a THEOLOGICAL VIRTUE, faith has as its ultimate goal to "adapt man's faculties for participation in the divine nature" (CCC 1812). This means that each of us needs to be "re-shaped" in conformity to what we now profess by our faith. This process of "re-shaping" is achieved only by our firm adherence to the truths of the faith. It is not obvious to all why Mother Teresa would spend her life in service of the poor; yet it is completely obvious to those who believe in Christ. Faith sheds light on all aspects of our life, not just the religious ones. Faith speaks words then that need to be spoken not only in the pulpit, but in the bank, in the coffee shop, and in the bedroom as well.

This work of adapting us for heaven and for the "participation in the divine nature" is accomplished only by the power of the Holy Spirit and the working of his gifts within us. If our faculties are going to be reshaped, then they need the assistance of a greater power than our own. Sometimes all we need to do to have this power is simply to ask for it.

– Father James M. Sullivan, O.P.

Nahum

THE BOOK OF THE PROPHET NAHUM is a book of contrasts. On the surface, Nahum throbs with hatred for Assyria and hope for the destruction of the city of Nineveh (which fell in 612 BC). Beneath the surface, the prophet's message is rooted in his sense of justice, and in his faith.

Nahum portrays a terrible battle: "The crack of the whip, the rumbling sound of wheels;/ horses a-gallop, chariots bounding,/ Cavalry charging,/ The flame of the sword, the flash of the spear" (Na 3:2–3). We cannot deny the existence of suffering and evil, symbolized in the raging battle. But our faith looks higher. Our trust is not in chariots and swords, but in God the Lord. "The LORD is good,/ a refuge on the day of distress," Nahum sings (Na 1:7).

Nahum also uses images that later prophets will borrow. The bearer of good news will advance over the mountains and announce peace (Na 2:1). Even more, the Lord will restore the vineyard of Jacob and the vineyard of Israel. The enemy had trampled down the vines, but God will restore them (Na 2:3). Vineyards, and the wine they produced, were precious symbols of prosperity and security—and of salvation. Much later, the wine of the vineyard will mean far more: it will mean the blood of the Redeemer himself.

– Father Joseph T. Lienhard, S.J.

*I*T IS WELL TO OBSERVE at this point that there are two kinds of faith: supernatural faith, which the Holy Spirit infuses into souls, and human faith, which is the belief we give to human witnesses. In infused faith there is no measure or mean,… for just as there is no limit or measure to the love of God, neither is there any limit or measure to our belief in God. The more we love him and the more we believe in him, the more perfect will be our charity and our faith. But there is a measure or medium in human faith, as in all other acquired virtues, and it is discovered by the virtue of prudence.… The two extremes of credulity and incredulity are both vices because it is a vice to believe anything too readily and on light grounds and it is a vice to refuse to believe when prudence dictates that a thing is worthy of credence.…

When writing to the Hebrews, Saint Paul warned them to take care not to foster the vice of incredulity because God had sworn that the incredulous would not enter the kingdom of heaven. In order to strengthen our faith, God permitted Thomas to fall into the sin of incredulity, although Thomas should have believed the other Apostles because they were worthy witnesses and Thomas himself had known about the resurrection of Lazarus from the dead through the power of Christ.

– Venerable Louis of Granada

Habakkuk

THE PROPHET HABAKKUK presents us with a figure of a prophet who goes somewhat in the opposite direction of most other prophets. Whereas the others tend to bring the word of the Lord—full of caring comfort or dire warning—from God to his people, Habakkuk brings the trembling hearts of the people to their God. "How long, O LORD?" he asks. "I cry out to you, 'Violence!'/ but you do not intervene" (Hb 1:2). In anguish he places before his Creator the existential threat mounting against the children of Abraham, pointing out the "unruly people,/ That marches the breadth of the land/ to take dwellings not his own/…like the eagle hastening to devour" (Hb 1:6, 8).

Habakkuk shows us how a true relationship with God does not consist simply of passively ceding to his inscrutable will, but also risking our own desires, doubts, and fears in our dialogue with him. The Lord answers his prophet saying, "If [the vision] delays, wait for it,/ it will surely come" (Hb 2:3). In his waiting, Habakkuk remembers how great the Lord is, and faithful: "You come forth to save your people" (Hb 3:13). This prophet teaches us to approach the Lord full of entreaty and memory.

– Father Vincent Nagle, F.S.C.B.

*T*HE RATIONAL SOUL HAS TWO FACULTIES, the intellect and will, and God desires that both of them should be used in his service. In this way the whole man can become reformed and perfect. In the first place, God desires that man's intellect should be truly enlightened and instructed so that it will have a clear knowledge of who God is. Then it will gradually grow in the knowledge of God's being, power, goodness, justice, mercy, and knowledge. It will likewise understand all that God has done and still does for man. And when he has attained the knowledge of these things, the Christian will know how to adore God as he ought, how to recommend himself to God, how to trust in God, how to follow God's instructions, and how to thank God for everything.

God does not want man to construct a false god in his heart, nor to conceive of God other than he really is. For if a man were to have an erroneous concept of God, he would not be able to adore the true God, but he would adore the false notion of God that he has in his intellect. Neither would he be able to attribute the works of creation to the true God, but to the false notion of God by which he has been deceived. Therefore, he who lacks a true knowledge of God is in great danger of going astray and missing the path that leads to salvation.

– Venerable Louis of Granada

"Stand firm in the faith, be courageous, be strong."
(1 Cor 16:13)

STANDING FIRM means staking out a claim and then resisting the resistance to the claim. Standing firm means resisting the mere wear and tear of time, resisting the spiritual entropy that erases boundaries and blurs vision and turns confident conviction into a conjecture barely spoken and hardly dared. Standing firm in the faith means speaking out for the faith, for a faith that will not speak is a faith that is ceding ground and in flight from that to which it had once surrendered in joy.

Courage in this matter presupposes vulnerability. There is no need to be brave if one cannot be hurt. The ways we might be hurt vary. In some parts of the Third World, active faith means physical persecution. In the secularized West, active faith might involve marginalization and ridicule. In all parts of the world, faith requires such commitment that our very selves are bound up in its profession. If we were to let the faith slip from our minds and hearts, we would lose the very reason for our being and be unable ever truly to be glad again.

Our persistent belief finds its strength in the power, strength, and weakness of the Crucified.

– Father John Dominic Corbett, O.P.

Jesus, lover of my soul,
Let me to thy bosom fly,
While the nearer waters roll,
While the tempest still is high.
Hide me, O my Savior, hide,
Till the storm of life is past;
Safe into the haven guide;
Oh, receive my soul at last.

Other refuge have I none,
Hangs my helpless soul on thee;
Leave, ah! leave me not alone,
Still support and comfort me.
All my trust on thee is stayed,
All my help from thee I bring;
Cover my defenseless head
With the shadow of thy wing.

Thou, O Christ, art all I want,
More than all in thee I find;
Raise the fallen, cheer the faint,
Heal the sick, and lead the blind.
Just and holy is thy Name,
Source of all true righteousness;
Thou art evermore the same,
Thou art full of truth and grace.

– A hymn by Charles Wesley

*T*HE MARIAN or Catholic fundamental act is beyond understanding and not understanding. When you say Yes to God unconditionally, you have no idea how far this Yes is going to take you. Certainly farther than you can guess and calculate beforehand, certainly as far as participation in failure and derision, cross and God forsakenness—but just how far and in what form? At the same time, this Yes is the sole, nonnegotiable prerequisite of all Christian understanding, of all theology and ecclesial wisdom. You cannot understand a Lord *in* whom "all the promises of God find their *Yes*" (2 Cor 1:20) *alongside of* this Yes. Christian truth is esoteric in the sense that it can be discerned only from within, in being carried out in faith and action, not from outside, from a box seat in the theater. Nor by a partial identification (with the reservations that implies), but only out of a total, universal, and, therefore, catholic identification with God's ways in the flesh.

– Father Hans Urs von Balthasar

Faith can…try to examine the circumstances
of Jesus' death…the better to understand
the meaning of the Redemption.
(CCC 573)

GOD REVEALED HIS LOVE and what we need to know for salvation in the context of complex interactions among Jesus, his disciples, the Pharisees, Sadducees, crowds, and Roman authorities. Charged with assuring that such an important message be accurately communicated, we might think it necessary to control the environment. Obviously, God did not reveal his love in a classroom but in the midst of the interactions between Jesus and those around him. This invites us to re-read the scriptural witness to Christ's death with faith-filled, prayerful attention. The goal is not to satisfy curiosity, even less to assign blame to those who crucified Jesus. It is, rather, to grasp the depths of his redeeming love as this love is revealed in every detail of Jesus' words, actions, sufferings, and even his silences throughout the Passion.

The meaning of redemption is love, and the goal of faith is to understand it more and more fully. Especially on Passion Sunday and throughout Holy Week, faith seeks to know better the love of the One who loved us first.

– Douglas Bushman

Zephaniah

ZEPHANIAH lives at a time when the faith of many of God's chosen people is waning. They are turning to the false gods of foreigners, as if the one true God who has called them through Abraham and freed them through Moses is just one among many.

In his prophesying, Zephaniah notes an interesting corollary between humility and faith. Those who doubt God and forget him are proud and shameless people who exalt themselves and accept no correction. They profane what is holy because they have no respect for it. To have faith in the Lord requires humility, because this faith tells me that I am not the center of reality, I depend upon another. False gods are an imaginary projection of human beings. In truth, however, human beings are creatures who are continually created and generated by God.

God wants us to humble ourselves, not to degrade us, but so that he can exalt us. To be humble is to recognize the truth that God is the source of our existence, our sustenance, and our dignity. This faithful recognition opens us to the revelation that God is a God of love, whom Zephaniah vividly describes as singing with joy over his people whom he wants to gather to himself.

– Father Richard Veras

Holy Thursday Vigil

(Based on John 14-17)

The night before you died, Lord Jesus, you asked us not to let our hearts be troubled. You commanded us to have faith in God and faith in you. Renew and deepen our faith in you. For you are the way, and the truth, and the life. No one comes to the Father but through you. You promise that the person who has faith in you will do the works you do, and greater far than these. Whatever we ask in your name you tell us you will do. Help us to be obedient to your commandments, for the one who obeys the commandments we have from you is the one who loves you. Make us ever true to your Word. We see you as one who has life, and through you we will have life. Whoever loves you will be loved by your Father. You and your Father will come and make your dwelling in those who believe. You are the vine, we are the branches. Let us live on in you. For apart from you we can do nothing. You call us—not slaves, but—your friends. There is no greater love than to lay down one's life for one's friends. It was not we who chose you; it was you who chose us to go forth and bear fruit. You have told us all this to keep our faith from being shaken. Eternal life is to know the only true God and you, Jesus Christ, whom the Father has sent. Your Word is truth. Consecrate us by means of truth. May we all be one, even as you are one with the Father. May our unity be complete so that the world may come to believe that the Father sent you and that you are the Savior of the world.

– Father Peter John Cameron, O.P.

The Seven Last Words

from the Perspective of Faith

(*"Father, forgive them."* Lord Jesus, your dying wish for my forgiveness reveals the depths of your love. Deepen my belief in your love, and give me the faith that moves me to rise above all my sins.

(*"...with me in Paradise."* Lord Jesus, even when I see the worst in me, my longing is for you. Faith is recognizing that I need to be given something. Please give me what I do not deserve—paradise with you.

(*"Behold your Mother."* Lord Jesus, the gift of your Mother enables me to look at everything with our Lady's own eyes of faith. Fill me with the same trust and confidence with which Mary stands at your cross.

(*"My God, why have you forsaken me?"* Lord Jesus, even in this plea you reveal that you are not alone, for you call out to your Father. Bless me with a faith that keeps me certain and close to you in my times of suffering.

(*"I thirst."* Lord Jesus, you thirst for me to receive the love that pours forth from your pierced side. Always renew in me the work of faith: believing that there is nothing higher or greater than this absolute love.

(*"It is finished."* Lord Jesus, until the last moment of your life you fulfilled your Father's will to love those he had given. Give me the obedience of faith to spend my life in devoted service to God.

(*"...I commend my spirit."* Lord Jesus, you handed yourself over to the Father in a perfect gift of self. Bless me with a faith that liberates me from my preoccupation with self and that makes my life one of loving self-surrender to you. I want to live for you.

– Father Peter John Cameron, O.P.

Haggai

THE JEWS have returned to Jerusalem from captivity. The glorious Temple of Solomon is no more. The people were slow to rebuild it, in part because they wanted to keep their wealth, but in part also because they were disheartened. What could match the old Temple?

Here strides forth the priest and prophet Haggai. He doesn't say, "What difference does a mere building make?" Instead he cries out, "Take courage, all you people of the land,/ says the LORD, and work!" (Hg 2:4). For the Lord is with them. It must have seemed incredible, as they surveyed the rubble and the broken walls. But Haggai proclaims that the new Temple will be more glorious than the old. So the Lord speaks through him: "One moment yet, a little while,/ and I will shake the heavens and the earth,/ the sea and the dry land" (Hg 2:6). What will happen then? "The treasures of all the nations will come in,/ and I will fill this house with glory,/ says the LORD of hosts" (Hg 2:7). But the older translations say that *the desire of the nations* will come; and that refers to the Messiah.

Either way, Haggai is a prophet of faith. The nations will bring their wealth to Israel, but Israel brings her wealth to all the nations. She brings to them the One they all desire: the One who makes his home among them; the One who brings them home.

– Anthony Esolen

Women's Witness

WE WENT
to anoint
the body
of our Lord.
We should've known
his tomb would be
empty,
death could not
bind.
It was not
in his composition
to decompose
but to rise
with flesh still torn
that dark and early
Easter morn.

– Rita A. Simmonds

Zechariah

IN THE FIRST EIGHT CHAPTERS of the book bearing his name, Zechariah, the eleventh minor prophet, encourages his people on their return from seventy years of captivity in Babylon to rebuild the Temple of Jerusalem lying in ruins.

His deeper concern is to stir up faith in the future coming of the Messiah. He states that by obeying God people can look forward to the coming of "the man whose name is the Branch" who "shall build the temple of the LORD" (Zec 6:12 RSV). He is pointing here to David's human and divine descendant, whose universal Messianic kingdom will bring justice, peace, and wellbeing. People of other nations will then be drawn to it, saying: "Come! let us go to implore the favor of the LORD" (Zec 8:21).

However, for chastising his people's faithlessness in turning to idol worship, he is killed. Recalling this atrocity, Jesus rebukes the religious leaders for being no better than their ancestors, whose crimes stretched "from the righteous blood of Abel to the blood of Zechariah" (Mt 23:35).

Jesus endures the same fate for pointing to true worship as being not merely formalistic ritual with external pomp, but an obedience of faith in which people relate to God and one another through participating in his Body as a spiritual Temple of precious living stones.

– Father Michael L. Gaudoin-Parker

*W*E...POSSESS [A NATURAL LIGHT], and it leads us to the place where the light of faith begins, to that point where, as Pascal says, "reason's last step is the recognition that there are an infinite number of things which are beyond it." This light of faith comes directly from God and shapes our supernatural existence. It gives our actions, which appear to resemble those of other people, an end that the actions of others do not have, and it gives an incomparable value to ourselves and to souls. Our bodily and rational lives differ in no way from those of the other members of the human race, but there is something "beyond," not, as all too many people imagine, antagonistic to this life. There is a higher life, which permeates our entire selves, transforming them, giving them motives for action, supernatural like itself, and fashioning our outer lives into the likeness of our innermost being, so as to create an harmonious unity....

Shining on humble as well as powerful minds, it reaches the soul within and gives it a motive for living and acting, the meaning of suffering, an explanation of death, as well as revealing to it the beauty and usefulness of our activity in this world and its supernatural fruitfulness....

This is the life of faith, understood not as passive acquiescence on the part of the mind, but as an active acceptance, a lively assimilation of truths that surpass the mind and which constant experience, suggested and directed by grace, impresses upon us.

– Servant of God Elisabeth Leseur

Malachi

LIKE THE WIZARD OF OZ speaking behind a curtain, the prophet Malachi is a voice without a face. The Hebrew people return from the Babylonian exile in jubilation. Filled with enthusiasm, they rebuild the city and their lives. A hundred years later, however, boredom has set in. Jerusalem is no Emerald City but a place where worship has become mechanical, relationships have deteriorated, and faith in God is low. Worse still, the religious leaders of the day do not inspire the people. They have become lax in their duty and complacent in addressing the moral decline of the day. The name Malachi means "my messenger." Because the prophet's words are strong against the religious leaders and rulers, he keeps his identity a secret. Malachi speaks of a future moment when God will come to restore justice and peace for all people. In order to prepare for that day, he calls people to repent and renew their commitment to live their faith authentically.

In our own time, Malachi still speaks. His message is that life is not always enthusiasm and jubilation. There are many days of boredom and "going through the motions." Those too can be days of a new beginning.

– Monsignor Gregory E. S. Malovetz

*I*N REVEALING TO US his intimate life and the great mysteries of grace and glory, God enables us to see things from his point of view, as he himself sees them. The assent to the truths of faith is of itself most firm and certain because it is based on the authority of God revealing. The revealed truths remain for us obscure and non-evident, however, and hence the will must intervene, under the motion of grace, to impose upon the intellect that firm assent not by reason of intrinsic evidence, which is lacking to us concerning those truths, but simply by reason of the infallible authority of God, who can neither deceive nor be deceived. In this sense the act of faith is free, supernatural and meritorious.

Faith is incompatible with intellectual or sensible vision. Of itself it is of those things which are not seen. Therefore, faith disappears in heaven and is replaced by the face-to-face vision. Nevertheless, faith is the first of the Christian virtues so far as it is the positive foundation of all the others, although charity is more excellent than faith and all the other infused virtues, inasmuch as it bespeaks a relation to God in a more perfect manner and is the form of all other virtues. Without charity, no virtue can be perfect.

– Antonio Royo, O.P., & Jordan Aumann, O.P.

Mary

MARY NEEDS NO INTRODUCTION. She carries us in her womb.

One morning last Advent I was trudging to the grocery store. My heart was heavy. A friend's mother had just died, another friend was suffering from depression, a shooter had randomly opened fire earlier in the week near my neighborhood in L.A. I kept gazing hopefully at the faces of the people I passed: no response. "Hi there," I kept saying: no response. The sky was gloomy, trash littered the streets, and everyone I met looked hung-over.

Headed down a steep hill, I passed a wiry man in his mid-twenties who was headed up. Just as we passed, he looked me full in the face, smiled, and said "Good morning!" "Morning!" I smiled back, and out of nowhere came the thought: "Hail Mary, full of grace! The Lord is with thee. Blessed art thou among women, and blessed is the fruit of thy womb, Jesus…"

Never had I recognized so clearly that we are all—man, woman, and child—Mary. Never had I felt so keenly the joy of Elizabeth as she saw Mary approaching over "the hill country." Never had I seen that Christ is born, over and over again, within each of us—every time we acknowledge each other as human beings; every time we greet the morning.

– Heather King

"We walk by faith, not by sight."
(2 Cor 5:7)

FAITH MAKES US WALK BLIND. How so?

Walking is a biblical way of describing lifestyle. Faith entails a lifestyle that ignores some things that are so evident to most people that not to see them is to be counted blind. Imagine a recent widow receiving news that her child in the womb is marked with Down syndrome. She rejoices. She speaks so hopefully of her life and of the future life of her child that the doctor wonders if she is in full contact with reality. She is. Because she walks by faith and not by sight she knows that somehow God will supply her needs, and this faith makes her blind, blessedly blind, to the doctor's estimate of their chances and to his suggested remedy to her plight.

Or imagine a young man in the seminary. He is bright, has good social skills, and a very marketable degree in finance. His friends think he belongs on Wall Street. So did he until recently when he started attending Mass more regularly, and then somehow knew that he needed to walk down another road following Jesus as his priest. His friends can't see it. He is only just beginning to.

– Father John Dominic Corbett, O.P.

*J*UST AS THE BELIEVER is choked by the salt water of doubt constantly washed into his mouth by the ocean of uncertainty, so the nonbeliever is troubled by doubts about his unbelief, about the real totality of the world he has made up his mind to explain as a self-contained whole....

Anyone who makes up his mind to evade the uncertainty of belief will have to experience the uncertainty of unbelief, which can never finally eliminate for certain the possibility that belief may after all be the truth. It is not until belief is rejected that its unrejectability becomes evident....

Both the believer and the unbeliever share, each in his own way, doubt *and* belief, if they do not hide from themselves and from the truth of their being. Neither can quite escape either doubt or belief; for the one, faith is present *against* doubt; for the other, *through* doubt and in the *form* of doubt. It is the basic pattern of man's destiny only to be allowed to find the finality of his existence in this unceasing rivalry between doubt and belief, temptation and certainty. Perhaps in precisely this way doubt, which saves both sides from being shut up in their own worlds, could become the avenue of communication. It prevents both from enjoying complete self-satisfaction; it opens up the believer to the doubter and the doubter to the believer.

– Pope Benedict XVI

Word Made Flesh

A SPLIT SECOND
an instant
the flash of an angel's wing—
God uncloaked
and carried
to a tiny place
the most miniscule,
far away
within
invisible,
the most invisibly visible place
the space inside
the Virgin betrothed,
the space of eternal growth.
The heard Word
allowed
to be brought forth
from there
the place of the pact
between Heaven and humankind.
The whole world changed
in an instant
imperceptibly
radically
different
and from that moment on
Eternity came
and has forever stayed
maternally entwined
in time.

– Rita A. Simmonds

Faith is necessary for salvation.
(CCC 183)

IMAGINE AN ATHLETE who had won great awards for his physical stamina, and then after winning those awards never exercised or kept in shape. What would happen to his great stamina? It would, of course, weaken and the awards would then become fewer. The same is true for our growth in faith. It is within the sacred confines of our own consciences (that "inner sanctuary" within each man where decisions are made and activities are chosen) that we assent to the truth as revealed in our Catholic Faith. We have a duty, then, to keep our consciences clear so that the truth may take a firm hold of us. As the Catechism reminds us: "The education of conscience is indispensable for human beings who are subjected to negative influences and tempted by sin to prefer their own judgment and to reject authoritative teachings" (CCC 1783).

At times we can get "lazy," just like that athlete who gave up his rigorous routine of exercise. Christ, being the great teacher that he is, calls us to continual training. However, his training does not leave us exhausted and worn out, but rather aching to know and love him even more.

– Father James M. Sullivan, O.P.

Joseph, Mary's Husband

WHAT AN ASTONISHMENT IT IS that in giving us the life of so towering a figure as Saint Joseph, none of the Gospels reveal that he ever uttered a single word. Silence is surely his most salient characteristic. That and a profound humility of heart, which moved him again and again into the darkness of a faith unknown to other men. "The only wisdom we can hope to acquire," writes T. S. Eliot, "is the wisdom of humility: humility is endless."

Unlike Mary, whose spoken *Fiat* gave God permission to become man, at the time of Joseph's own Annunciation he remains mute, choosing instead *to do* all that the angel tells him. Joseph performs, he does not pronounce. And so hitching his wagon to the woman clothed with the sun, Joseph assumes guardianship of God's own Son. That custody of the perfect Child and his sinless Mother should be entrusted to a mere mortal—one the awful weight of whose responsibility only humility can carry—is at the heart of the mystery of his vocation. With an identity rooted in the mission he is asked to perform, the life of Joseph radiates out to the very ends of the earth, making him Patron of the Church his Child suffered to redeem.

– Regis Martin

O MY GOD, I firmly believe that you are one God in three divine Persons, Father, Son, and Holy Spirit. I believe that your divine Son became man, and died for our sins and that He will come to judge the living and the dead. I believe these and all the truths which the Holy Catholic Church teaches because you have revealed them, who can neither deceive nor be deceived.

DOMINE DEUS, firma fide credo et confiteor omnia et singula quæ sancta ecclesia Catholica proponit, quia tu, Deus, ea omnia revelasti, qui es æterna veritas et sapientia quæ nec fallere nec falli potest. In hac fide vivere et mori statuo.

– Act of Faith

*F*AITH RENDERS US open to the power of God. Accordingly, it is the liberation of our most intimate self, the redemption of our heart. It is as if God pulls aside a bolt in our deepest self and a door opens. Through this opening he can flow into the deepest dimensions of our self and pull it along in the loving grip and restorative power of his omnipotence. This resembles the much grander and more spectacular manner in which, on Easter morning, Jesus was raised from the dead by the overwhelming power of the glory of the Father. On a different scale but along the same lines, the coming of faith is such an event, one that seizes not only our minds but our entire human existence. From this experience we emerge very small and lost, small to ourselves, before others and before God, but not at all crushed. On the contrary, we are lifted up by this boundless confidence in him who "by the power at work within us is able to accomplish abundantly far more than all we can ask or imagine" (Eph 3:20 NRSV), and ready therefore for the miracles the Lord Jesus would again seek to accomplish through our faith even today. Beyond doubt, God is unceasingly at work in the Church and in the world. Only our faith can discern these continuing miracles and ultimately play its own role in them.

– Father André Louf, o.c.s.o.

The Magi

CHRISTIANS have long meditated joyfully upon the Three Wise Men. We give them names: Gaspar, Melchior, and Balthasar. We imagine them as representing the three great races of man. We paint their camels laden with goods, and we see in the three gifts the secret of the Eucharist itself, as Christ is at once "king and God and sacrifice." It's as if the Magi knew from before their journey exactly whom they were seeking, and why, and so they went forth in their glorious caravans.

But maybe theirs was a braver act of faith than we suppose. Imagine the bitter cold as they cross the mountains of Persia, a thousand miles away. Imagine the wealth they must sacrifice, just to pay the innkeepers and feed the camels and put up their servants. Imagine days of hunger and thirst, and sleepless nights. What did they have left when they arrived in Bethlehem, other than the precious gifts? And what were they following? A light in the heavens, a promise, or the memory of a promise, heard from the Jews who had been scattered across their alien lands.

On the wing of that promise they came from afar. We who have been given far more—when shall we too set out?

– Anthony Esolen

*F*AITH IS THE BEGINNING, the foundation and the root of justification, and without faith it is impossible to please God and to be numbered among his sons. It is the beginning because it establishes the first contact between ourselves and God, the Author of the supernatural order. The first thing is to believe in God. It is the foundation, inasmuch as all the other virtues, including charity, presuppose faith, and are established upon it as an edifice on its foundation. Without faith it is impossible to hope or to love. It is the root, because in it, when informed by charity, all the other virtues live. When informed by charity, faith produces, among other things, two great effects in the soul: the filial fear of God which helps the soul keep itself from sin, and the purification of the heart which raises it to the heights and cleanses it of its affection for earthly things.

– Antonio Royo, O.P., & Jordan Aumann, O.P.

The Relationship between Faith and Reason

THE YEAR OF FAITH to which the Holy Father Pope Benedict XVI and the bishops are calling us is not an exercise in piety and spirituality. Rather it is a time to reflect on the most crucial question confronting the Church in modern times: Is it really possible to be a Catholic today? This question inevitably raises the issue of the relation between faith and reason.

Growing up in a totally Catholic environment, I never experienced a conflict between my Catholic identity and my enthusiasm for scientific research. After graduation I was hired by a government-run laboratory and given the opportunity to continue my studies. At the lab there were a number of young scientists whom I admired very much.

I confronted the issue for the first time while working as a scientist when one of my co-workers asked me: "Tell me, how can you be such a good scientific researcher Monday through Saturday, but on Sunday you affirm that a man who died almost two thousand years ago is now alive and somehow present, literally alive in your Sunday religious rituals? Are there two personalities in you? Surely you don't believe in the bodily presence of Jesus today? It must be a metaphorical way of thinking and talking, isn't it?"

This question is more urgent today than it was fifty years ago because secularism—which is the dominant way of thinking in the secular world today—has succeeded in relegating faith to the world of subjectivity and metaphor.

Faith talk is a way of communicating values by which we should live.

Pope Benedict XVI believes there is no more important issue today than the relation between faith and reason because Christianity survives or falls depending on how it replies to this question. For the Holy Father reason is the instrument that allows us to build a bridge between Christianity and the world. Reason is our capacity to know the truth and orient our lives to it. Although supra-rational, Christianity presupposes reason and is, in fact, the synthesis between faith and reason.

Faith is an undeserved and unearned gift. It is the capacity to recognize Christ's presence with us today, victorious over sin and death. Faith and reason cannot be separated lest faith become a paralyzing and/or intolerant fundamentalism that will ultimately succumb to secularism and its denial of our capacity for certainty, leaving us exposed to the violence of ideologies, whose power will sooner or later strike against the freedom of scientific research.

– Monsignor Lorenzo Albacete

Zechariah, Elizabeth's Husband

THE ANGEL GABRIEL'S PROPHECY that Zechariah doubted concerns not only John the Baptist's conception and birth, but also his career as an ascetic prophet filled with the Holy Spirit who would return many to the Lord. Zechariah's punishment was then to last until the fulfillment of this prophecy some thirty years later. But God finds a way to shorten this sentence when Zechariah "discovers" another way to express his developed faith and new-found obedience to the angel. He writes on the tablet: "John is his name" (Lk 1:63).

Using his nine months of punishment most productively, Zechariah slowly labors to give birth to words of faith, hope, and love that will culminate in the great *Benedictus*, thereby bequeathing to the Church this hymn that she has made her Gospel of morning prayer. In its clarion call of salvation that doubles as Zechariah's act of contrition, we hear in this soaring hymn of faith a retracing of God's saving love and fidelity to the covenant. Here we see most clearly that human faith is a response to the divine fidelity first shown us: we can rely on the Lord because he is faithful to us. With the past now secure in divine love, Zechariah the prophet and father of the future prophet strains in his last verses to secure a future of hope and proclaim the best is yet to come.

– Father Lawrence J. Donohoo

*T*HROUGH OUR CHRISTIAN FAITH, we believe that certain things are true, and we believe them because of words spoken by someone. We believe certain truths and we believe in a certain speaker. Christian faith is a virtue, an abiding habit or disposition to believe the things in question and to believe in the person in question. Occasionally we move beyond the disposition and explicitly express our belief in the truths and the person, and when we do so we perform an act of faith. The act of faith is often performed in public, as we declare our belief before others by our speech or by our significant actions, but the act of faith can also be performed in solitude before the God in whom we believe. Indeed, even when we perform an act of faith in public before other men, what makes it an act of faith, an act of theological virtue, is the fact that we are also expressing it before and toward the God in whom we believe. The Christian act of faith always remains an assent and a submission to the Word of God and to the God who has spoken the Word; it is never merely a report to other men of convictions that we hold.

– Monsignor Robert Sokolowski

*"Faith is a foretaste of the knowledge
that will make us blessed in the life to come"*
(St. Thomas Aquinas, Comp. theol. 1, 2).
(CCC 184)

SAINT THOMAS AQUINAS uses the example of sight to give us insight into the theological virtue of faith. He says that faith enables us to "see" God in the way our vision enables us to see color. By every other sense we have, we can learn about our surroundings: the shape of things, the texture of things, their relative distance from us. What we could not know without sight is the particular color of something. Likewise, faith enables us to see the "color" of God. We can perceive his brilliance and radiance with the eyes of our faith. And just as it is with seeing color in the world, the more light we have in faith the truer the "color" of God appears. This is why God continually reveals himself to us through the Church; we are enlightened by Sacred Scripture, Sacred Tradition, and the Magisterium. Each of these sheds light on the mysteries of God so that we can comprehend them all the better. This knowledge of divine realities that we come to by faith here on earth will be the foundation for our happiness in heaven. God has begun to reveal to us in this life all that he will fulfill in the next.

– Father James M. Sullivan, O.P.

*T*HE WORD *FAITH* SIGNIFIES…*an assent of the mind to truth*, which assent, however, is based upon *trust*. To believe any one, we must have confidence in him.

In the *Old* Testament, faith is presented as a necessary virtue, on which depends the salvation or the ruin of the nation: "Believe in the Lord your God, and you shall be secure." "If you will not believe, you shall not continue." This faith is an assent given to the Word of God, but accompanied by trust, self-abandonment, and love.

In the *New* Testament, faith is so essential that to believe means to profess Christianity, and not to believe is not to be a Christian: *"He that believes and is baptized shall be saved: but he that believes not shall be condemned."* Faith means the acceptance of the Gospel preached by Jesus Christ and his Apostles; therefore, it presupposes preaching: *"Faith, then, comes by hearing."* This faith, then, is not an intuition of the heart, nor a direct vision…it is the acceptance of divine testimony, free and enlightened, since man, on the one hand, can refuse belief, and on the other, he does not arrive at belief without reasons, without an intimate conviction that God has really spoken. This faith is associated with hope and is perfected by charity.

– Father Adolphe Tanquerey, s.s.

John the Baptist

FAITH IS A GIFT, and it is given in abundance to the cousin of Jesus, for he greets his Lord while still in the womb of his mother Elizabeth. Unlike other saints, he and the Mother of our Lord have feasts celebrating their earthly birthdays. His sturdy faith leads to his execution by Herod, a man so morally weak that he even lacks faith in himself. In his insecurity, Herod is reduced to letting his courtiers shape his decisions. Jesus sizes him up as "that fox." In contrast, he paints an indelible picture of his cousin: not a moral weathervane, not a man soft or delicate: "No one is greater than John" (Lk 7:28).

Then our Lord comments on the perils of rationalizing instead of trusting in God, for that kind of twisted reasoning is what happens when the intellect in not strengthened by faith. The same people who label John a fanatical hermit, accuse the Lord of Life of living life on the fast track. Faithlessness also leads to superstition. Herod, haunted by the integrity of John, fears that Jesus might be John's ghost. John is no ghost, but as a solid man of solid faith he changes lives beyond number. Later on, in far away Ephesus in Turkey, the Apostles come across people who Apollos and others have already baptized in the manner that John has taught them.

– Father George William Rutler

*F*AITH IS *A THEOLOGICAL VIRTUE that inclines the mind under the influence of the will and of grace, to yield a firm assent to revealed truths, because of the authority of God.*

Faith is before all else an act of the *intellect,* since it is a question of knowing the truth. But, since this truth is not self-evident our assent cannot be effected without the action of the *will,* bidding the mind study the reasons for believing, and, when these are convincing, giving a further command to assent. Because it is question of a supernatural act, *grace* must intervene to enlighten the mind, and to aid the will. It is in this way that faith becomes a *free, supernatural* and *meritorious* act.

The *material object* or the subject matter of our faith is the sum-total of revealed truths, both those that reason alone could not possibly discover, and those others which reason could come to know, but which faith makes better known.

All these truths refer to God and to Jesus Christ. They refer to *God* with regard to the oneness of his nature and his Trinity of Persons, our first beginning and our last end.

– Father Adolphe Tanquerey, s.s.

Simeon

He is an old man and has come to know what is in men's hearts. In his own heart there is an entreaty for the "consolation of Israel" (Lk 2:25) and the God-given certainty that, before he dies, he will see with his own eyes and recognize the Savior destined to bring this consolation. Perhaps he has already heard the stories surrounding this baby's birth and is on the lookout for him. The signs are few, but enough. This is the One. And he prophesies: This baby is a "revelation to the Gentiles" (Lk 2:32). But more than that, knowing the connivance of man with his own enslavement, and aware of the prophecy of the Suffering Servant (Is 53), he says that this child is destined to be "a sign that will be contradicted" (Lk 2:34). And finally, gazing into the eyes of that mother, he understands that she cannot be separated from the mission of this Savior, and so, as if in warning, says "a sword will pierce through your soul also" (Lk 2:35 RSV).

Simeon's wisdom shows us that salvation cannot be had apart from justice, and therefore consolation must be accompanied by suffering. And he who would join himself to the Savior, must, in gratitude, enter into his Passion.

– Father Vincent Nagle, F.S.C.B.

O LORD, you are my Lord and my God, yet I have never seen you. You have created and redeemed me, and have conferred on me all my goods, yet I know you not. I was created in order that I might know you, but I have not yet attained the goal of my creation. I confess, O Lord, and give you thanks, that you have created me in your image, so that I might be mindful of you and contemplate you and love you. I seek not to understand in order that I may believe; rather, I believe in order that I may understand.

– Prayer of Saint Anselm of Canterbury

HE FORMAL OBJECT or what is generally called the *motive* of our faith is *divine authority* made known through revelation and imparting to us some of the secrets of God. Thus, faith is a virtue entirely supernatural, both as to its object and its motive; it puts us in communion with the divine thought.

Ofttimes revealed truth is authentically proposed to us by the *Church* which Jesus Christ instituted as the official interpreter of his teaching; this teaching is then termed a doctrine *of Catholic faith*. If there has been no authentic definition of the Church regarding revealed truth, the said teaching is simply called a doctrine of *divine faith*.

There is nothing more firm than the assent of faith. Having full confidence in the divine authority much more than in our own lights, we believe revealed truth with our whole soul. We do so with a far greater sense of security, inasmuch as divine grace comes to facilitate and strengthen our assent. And so it happens that the assent given by faith to revealed truth is more prompt and more firm than that given to natural truth....

Faith thus understood cannot but have an important share in our sanctification. By bringing us into communion with divine thought it becomes the *foundation* of our supernatural life and *unites* us *to God* in a most intimate way.

– Father Adolphe Tanquerey, s.s.

> *"I live, no longer I, but Christ lives in me;*
> *insofar as I now live in the flesh, I live by faith in the Son*
> *of God who has loved me and given himself up for me."*
> *(Gal 2:20)*

SAINT PAUL is surely one of the most singular personalities in the New Testament. Fiery, opinionated, pleading, jealous and making jealous for Christ's sake, his life offered up again and again for his people's sake, Saint Paul could never be taken for anyone else.

Yet Saint Paul could only be "himself," could only live his own life, by forgetting all about his own life and by handing his own life over every day to his Savior. In doing so, he found a principle of life in him that led him where it, and not he, would go. Christ, in calling Paul, implanted his own image in him, laid claim to him, and lived through him so that when the people of Corinth or the people of Athens or the people of Rome heard Paul preach, they also heard the Lord Jesus preach.

We are terrified of drawing near to God because we are sure that, in one way or another, he will put us to death. And we are right, but not in the way we think. Christ wants to live in us so that we can finally become the people he already knows us to be.

– Father John Dominic Corbett, O.P.

Anna

CONSTANCY. Prayer. Perseverance. These are the hall-marks of the faith of Anna, the prophetess who encounters Mary and Joseph as they present the infant Jesus in the Temple. Like Simeon, with whom she "shares a scene," her entire life has been given over to prayerful waiting for the Promised One of Israel. Since the end of her brief marriage, Anna has been in the Temple, worshiping "night and day with fasting and prayer" (Lk 2:37). Now, with the Chosen One suddenly before her, life, at the age of eighty-four, is about to change dramatically!

We are told that "she gave thanks to God and spoke about the child to all who were awaiting the redemption of Jerusalem" (Lk 2:38). To her earlier contemplative character we now add a joyous sharing, a bubbling effusiveness. She goes from being the woman who prays all the time to the one who talks all the time, sharing with the other faithful the miracle of the scene she has just witnessed: the purity of the mother, the uprightness of the father, but, most of all, the prophetic words of Simeon, who proclaims the truth about this Child, "a light for revelation to the Gentiles,/ and the glory for your people Israel" (Lk 2:32).

– Lisa Lickona

*The Church also wanted
to gather the essential elements of her faith
into organic and articulated summaries,
intended especially for candidates for Baptism.*
(CCC 186)

"Is it your will that your child should be baptized in the faith of the Church, which we have all professed with you?" The priest or deacon asks this question of the parents of the child to be baptized just before water is poured over the baby's head. The sacrament of baptism is that privileged moment in the life of each believer when the gift of faith is first given. It is a moment most of us are not ever aware of, almost as if to remind us of the primacy of God's movement in the working of faith. Our own faith, however, is indispensable for our growth in holiness and for the sanctification of our lives. "If your own faith makes you ready to accept this responsibility, renew now the vows of your own baptism." The Creed sums up our faith, but it does not exhaust it. It begins our faith, but it is not the completion of it. "What do you ask of God's Church for your child?" The Rite of Baptism provides some possible answers, the best of which is: eternal life.

– Father James M. Sullivan, o.p.

*F*AITH IS THE *BEGINNING* OF JUSTIFICATION, because it is the mysterious means used by God to initiate us into his life, to make us know him as he knows himself. On our part, it is the first supernatural disposition for justification, without which we can neither hope nor love. It is, so to speak, the taking possession of God and of divine things. In order to lay hold upon the supernatural and live by it, we must first of all come to the knowledge of it: *"Nothing can be willed that is not foreknown."* Now, we arrive at a knowledge of the supernatural through faith, a new light added to reason, which enables us to look into a new world, the supernatural world. It is like a telescope that enables us to discover far-off things invisible to the naked eye. Still, this is but an imperfect comparison, for a telescope is an outward instrument, while faith penetrates into the recesses of the mind and sharpens its power of perception as well as its field of vision.

Faith is likewise the *foundation* of the spiritual life.… Now, the deeper the foundations, the higher the edifice may rise without danger to its stability. Hence, it is important to strengthen the faith of devout souls… so that upon this solid foundation may rise the temple of Christian perfection.

– Father Adolphe Tanquerey, s.s.

Peter

"DEPART FROM ME, Lord, for I am a sinful man," said Peter, after the miraculous haul of fish (Lk 5:8). Yet the same Peter, in his boat one night on the Sea of Galilee, sees Jesus walking toward them upon the water, and cries, "Lord, if it is you, command me to come to you" (Mt 14:28).

That is stunning. It's one thing to believe that Jesus can do all things. It requires far deeper faith to trust that, in Jesus, we ourselves can do all things. For we have a more direct knowledge of our frailty than we have of Christ's strength. So, for me, the most impressive manifestation of Peter's faith comes when he dares to put it into action. Sometime after Pentecost, he and John meet a man crippled from birth, begging for alms. Says Peter, "I have neither silver nor gold, but what I do have I give you: in the name of Jesus Christ the Nazorean, rise and walk" (Acts 3:6).

How does Peter know what will happen? But after the Resurrection—after he had witnessed Christ's glory—what is the cure of a lame man? Let us then not merely believe. Let us be bold, as Peter was.

– Anthony Esolen

May Devotions to Our Lady

◀ *On Sundays:* O Mary, the Immaculate Conception, you are the New Eve. All that Adam and Eve longed for—and tried to steal from God—you give to us as the Mother of God. May we share in your holiness by our union with you.

◀ *On Mondays:* At your nativity, O Blessed Virgin, the way by which earth will be united to heaven is born. By the grace of your birth, we are led away from our slavery, and are blessed with holy joy.

◀ *On Tuesdays:* May we live every day, O Blessed Virgin Mary, the miracle of the Annunciation. United with you, may our life be a constant Yes to the presence of the Word made flesh. May we turn with our yearning to the humanity of God.

◀ *On Wednesdays:* O Mother of God, may we experience through you all the graces of the Visitation: you bring Jesus close to us; we rejoice with new life; your *Magnificat* becomes our hope.

◀ *On Thursdays:* O Blessed Mother, God chose you to offer his fatherly love more generously to the world. You are the Mother of the Life by which we live—Jesus. He leads us to you. Through your maternal mediation, all things are made new.

◀ *On Fridays:* Our Lady of Sorrows, your presence at the cross instills a grace that displaces horror. Your faith contains a light greater than any darkness in my heart. Be with me in my Calvary.

◀ *On Saturdays:* O Blessed Lady assumed into heaven, give me the ability to await God's future and to abandon myself to the Lord's promises.

– Father Peter John Cameron, O.P.

*M*ARY WILL SHARE her faith with you. Her faith on earth was stronger than that of all the patriarchs, prophets, apostles and saints. Now that she is reigning in heaven she no longer has this faith since she sees everything clearly in his by the light of glory.... Therefore, the more you gain the friendship of this noble Queen and faithful Virgin, the more you will be inspired by faith in your daily life. It will cause you to depend less upon sensible and extraordinary feelings. For it is a lively faith animated by love enabling you to do everything from no other motive than that of pure love. It is a firm faith, unshakeable as a rock, prompting you to remain firm and steadfast in the midst of storms and tempests. It is an active and probing faith which like some mysterious pass-key admits you into the mysteries of Jesus Christ and of man's final destiny and into the very heart of God himself. It is a courageous faith which inspires you to undertake and carry out without hesitation great things for God and the salvation of souls. Lastly, this faith will be your flaming torch, your very life with God, your secret fund of divine Wisdom, and an all-powerful weapon for you to enlighten those who sit in darkness and the shadow of death.

– Saint Louis de Montfort

Andrew

SAINT ANDREW, a quiet, self-effacing Apostle, excels at making connections. He is a master mediator who brings others to Jesus and Jesus to others. Recognizing at once that the Stranger from Nazareth fits the description of the Messiah, he introduces him to his brother Peter (Jn 1:41). In the wilderness where souls are replete but bodies are hungry, Andrew negotiates between divine power and human need by noticing a boy with a sack of food. A few days before Christ's Passion and Death, Andrew presents some interested Greeks to Jesus. They come from the nations, whom Jesus excluded from his initial proclamation of the kingdom (Mt 15:24). In all three instances, Andrew is remarkably successful: Peter becomes the Church's rock, the boy is the grocer for the loaves and fishes, the Greeks learn that the impending sacrifice of Jesus will draw *everyone* to himself (Jn 12:32).

Andrew's remarkable agility in bringing people to Christ rests upon a faith in One who always accomplishes something far mightier than the disciple imagines. Our faith in divine grace assures us that often we need only to get things started. When we introduce someone to Christ, we should expect the unexpected—that Jesus will take them much further than we would have ever thought, and perhaps ourselves along as well.

– Father Lawrence J. Donohoo

*F*AITH IS THE *ROOT* OF SANCTITY. Roots seek in the soil for the chemicals necessary to nutrition and growth in a tree; so, faith sinking its roots into the furthest recesses of the soul, and feeding there on divine truths, furnishes perfection with a rich, life-giving sap. Roots, if deep, lend solidity to the tree they sustain; so the soul, imbedded in faith, withstands spiritual storms. Hence, deep faith is of capital importance in order to attain a high degree of perfection.

Faith *unites* us to *God*, and makes us share in his thought and in his life. This is God's own knowledge of himself given in some measure to man. "By it," says Mgr. Gay, "the light of God becomes our light; his wisdom our wisdom; his knowledge our knowledge; his Spirit our spirit; his life our life."

It unites our intellect directly to the divine wisdom; but, since the act of faith cannot be performed without the action of the will, this faculty also has a share in the results produced in our soul by faith. One may say, therefore, that faith is a source of *light* to the mind, a source of *strength* and *comfort* to the will, a source of *merit* to the entire soul.

– Father Adolphe Tanquerey, s.s.

"For by grace you have been saved through faith,
and this is not from you; it is the gift of God."
(Eph 2:8)

FAITH ISN'T A MATTER of a human being's deciding, but of God giving. It is not first of all a human act that pleases God, but a divine act in us to which we give consent. It is God's act of sharing his own knowledge with us of who he is and what he does. This act saves us because it is in this act that we surrender ourselves to God and allow his love for us to penetrate our resistant souls. It isn't primarily about believing unproven propositions. It's about believing a person, entrusting oneself to that person, and as a consequence believing that person.

There are two appropriate responses to that gift. The first is humility. We think of knowledge as a form of mastery and then (unconsciously) apply that to faith and somehow imagine that faith gives us power even with respect to God. In fact knowledge is as much receptivity as activity, and the faith we have received is a gift not an accomplishment.

The second response should be gratitude. We have received glad tidings concerning our salvation. God has shone us his true face in his Christ. Let us receive him with gratitude.

– Father John Dominic Corbett, O.P.

John the Evangelist

SAINT JOHN THE APOSTLE leaves us a Gospel, often called the spiritual Gospel. The original ending of John's Gospel is an invitation to faith: John says that he wrote what he did "that you may [come to] believe that Jesus is the Messiah, the Son of God" (Jn 20:31).

Of the many beautiful passages in Saint John's Gospel, two stand out. The Prologue, the opening chapter, is a great hymn about God the Word: he was in the beginning, he was with God, and he was God. And the Word became flesh and dwelt among us. Here, John lays the foundation for the two great doctrines of our Christian faith: the Trinity, and the Person of Christ, true God and true man.

Then, near the end of the Gospel, John presents a very different scene, a moment of beautiful tenderness. As he is dying on the cross, Jesus entrusts his Mother to John's care. "Woman, behold, your son," Jesus says to Mary. And to John: "Behold, your mother." Saint John comments, "And from that hour, the disciple took her into his home" (Jn 19:26–27). As he is about to leave the world, Jesus entrusts his Mother and the beloved disciple to each other. John is to take the place of Jesus, as a sign of the Church, and Mary stands for all believers, the Mother of the Church. In his Gospel, John has taught us the fullness of our Christian faith.

– Father Joseph T. Lienhard, S.J.

The first "profession of faith" is made during Baptism.
The symbol of faith
is first and foremost the baptismal creed.
(CCC 189)

GROWING UP IN A FAMILY, one gradually learns about his parents and their love. Similarly, faith grows by continually discovering the meaning of the baptismal gift of new life and God's love revealed by Christ. "We have come to know and to believe in the love God has for us" (1 Jn 4:16). Knowing better the baptismal profession of faith means knowing better the God who fully revealed his love for us in Jesus Christ. This means believing that the Father sent his Son to love us "to the end" (Jn 13:1), and that together they send the Holy Spirit of love to dwell in our hearts (Rom 5:5). The Father's love is seen in creation, his plan of redemption, and sending his Son to save us. The Son's love is revealed in the forgiving mercy, teaching, miracles, Passion, Death, Resurrection, and Ascension of Christ. The Spirit's love sanctifies us, dwells in our hearts, and moves us to confess Jesus Christ as Lord (1 Cor 12:3), to call God our Father (Rom 8:15), and to know him as Lord and Giver of life. As faith's understanding of God's love grows, the "Yes" of faith becomes ever more mature.

– Douglas Bushman

*F*AITH IS A LIGHT which illumines our intellect, and differentiates the Christian from the philosopher, as reason distinguishes a human being from an animal. There is in us a threefold knowledge: *sense* knowledge, attained through the senses; *rational* knowledge, acquired through the intellect; and *spiritual* or *supernatural* knowledge, obtained through faith. The last is by far superior to the other two.

It widens the scope of our knowledge of God and the things of God. Reason tells us little of God's nature and of his inner life, while faith teaches us that he is a living God; that from all eternity he has begotten a Son, and that from the mutual love of the Father and the Son proceeds a Third Person, the Holy Spirit; that the Son became man for our salvation and that those who believe in him become the adopted sons of God; that the Holy Spirit comes to dwell in our souls, to sanctify them and to endow them with a supernatural organism which enables us to perform acts that are Godlike and meritorious. This is but a portion of what has been revealed, to us.

It gives us a *deeper insight* into the truths already known by reason. Thus the moral precepts of the Gospel are far more definite, far more perfect than those of mere natural ethics.

– Father Adolphe Tanquerey, s.s.

James the Apostle

JAMES, the son of Zebedee (Mt 10:2), is one of the disciples whom Jesus prefers. The Lord repeatedly singles him out, together with Peter and James' brother John, to witness special occasions such as Jesus' Transfiguration on Mount Tabor (Mt 17:1-2) and his agony in the garden (Mt 26:37).

Why does Christ have this preference for James? Maybe it is his fierceness and his ambition. He is fierce when he and his brother want "to call down fire from heaven to consume" the inhabitants of a village that refuses to welcome the Lord (Lk 9:54). Perhaps for this reason, the Lord names them "sons of thunder" (Mk 3:17). He is ambitious when he and his brother try to get the Lord to make a commitment to appointing them as his lieutenants when he reigns in glory (Mk 10:37). Jesus likes James' passion. Perhaps it is James whom Jesus has in mind when telling the parable of the dishonest servant whose master "commends him" for his initiative (cf. Lk 16:8).

The Lord rewards James' ambition by letting him become the first of the Apostles to be martyred (Acts 12:2). Jesus' preference for this fierce and ambitious man teaches us to not be afraid of coming to Jesus with all our humanity.

– Father Vincent Nagle, F.S.C.B.

*T*HAT OUR FAITH is a source of strength is well brought out in the Epistle to the Hebrews.

Faith provides us with *deep convictions* which greatly strengthen our will: It shows us what God has done and what he incessantly does in our behalf, how he lives and acts in our soul to sanctify it, how Jesus incorporates us into himself and makes us share in his own life then, having our eyes directed towards the author of our faith, who preferred the cross and humiliation to joy and success, "who having joy set before him, endured the cross, despising the shame," we feel ourselves strong enough to carry our cross courageously after Jesus.

Faith ever keeps before our eyes the *eternal reward* that will be the rich fruit of the sufferings of a moment: "That which is at present momentary and light of our tribulation works for us above measure exceedingly an eternal weight of glory." Then, with Saint Paul, we say: "I reckon that the sufferings of this time are not worthy to he compared with the glory to come," and like him we rejoice, even in the midst of tribulations, for each of these, if patiently borne, will earn for us a further degree of God's vision and of God's love.

– Father Adolphe Tanquerey, s.s.

GRANT, O merciful God, that I may ardently desire, carefully examine, truly know, and perfectly fulfill those things that are pleasing to you, to the praise and glory of your holy name. Direct my course, O my God, that I may do what you require me to do. Show me the way and grant that I may follow it as is necessary and profitable to my soul.

Grant to me, O Lord my God, that I may not be found wanting in prosperity; that I may not be lifted up by one nor cast down by the other. May I find joy in nothing but what leads to you; sorrow in nothing but what leads away from you. May I seek to please no one, nor fear to displease any. May I fear only you. May I despise all transitory things, O Lord, and treasure all things that are eternal. Let me loathe all delights without you, nor desire anything apart from you. Let me find pleasure in all toil that is for you; and weariness in all rest where you are not.

– Saint Thomas Aquinas

Philip

We know nothing about Philip apart from his contacts with others. He is a follower of others from the start, and is never "his own man." He follows John the Baptist until John points to the Lamb of God who says, "Follow me." Next, he brings Nathanael to Jesus, and toward the end of those three years, he tells Andrew that foreign visitors to Jerusalem want to see Jesus, and both tell our Lord.

Perhaps it is a certain shyness and innocence about his personality that makes him the one to whom Jesus asks the leading question about how to feed a crowd of thousands. Later, Philip simply asks Jesus what he might not have asked had he been more complicated: "Master, show us the Father, and that will be enough for us" (Jn 14:8). That candor is the opposite of cynicism, and privileges him to hear the immortal words, "Whoever has seen me has seen the Father" (Jn 14:9). Philip's faith brings others to Jesus, just as Jesus brings Philip to the Father. The Apostle's name gets tucked into the middle of the lists of the Twelve, never first but never last, either (Mt 10:2-4; Mk 3: 14-19; Lk 6: 13-16). His bones now lie in the Church of the Twelve Holy Apostles in Rome, a reminder of the great things faith will do to anyone who helps others to see Jesus.

– Father George William Rutler

*F*AITH IS A *SOURCE OF MANIFOLD MERIT*: the *act of faith* itself is *highly meritorious*, for it subjects to divine authority the best that is in us, our intellect and our will. This faith has all the more merit since in our times it is made the object of more numerous attacks, and since those who make open profession of their faith are, in certain countries, exposed to ridicule and persecution.

Furthermore, it is faith that *renders meritorious our other acts*, since they cannot become so without a supernatural motive and the help of grace but faith by directing the soul towards God and towards Jesus Christ enables us to act in all things with supernatural intentions. Likewise, by disclosing to us our own weakness and God's power, faith makes us pray ardently to obtain his grace....

Since faith is at once a *gift of God* and a *free assent* of the mind to revealed truth, it is evident that in order to grow in faith, we must rely on *prayer* and our own *personal efforts*. Under this twofold influence, faith will become more enlightened, simple, strong, and active.

– Father Adolphe Tanquerey, s.s.

*"Preserve the unity of the spirit
through the bond of peace...
one Lord, one faith, one baptism."*
(Eph 4:3-5)

WHAT DOES SAINT PAUL MEAN when he exhorts us to preserve the unity of the spirit? What does he mean by the spirit? He must mean something different from the Holy Spirit himself. After all, the Holy Spirit cannot be "preserved" in unity since he is the very source of all unity in the Church and in the world.

Spirit is about communication. It is particularly about the communication of identity. The spirit of a group is that group's identity as it is communicated to others. So, in this sense, the Ephesians' "spirit" is their capacity to communicate with God on God's level. This capacity can only be the result of a divine gift. It is no wonder Saint Paul refers to this type of communication as consisting not in discursive reason but rather in "sighs too deep for words."

How could anyone preserve such a gift as this? It is accomplished through the bond of peace, that is to say, through the covenant bond of love which joins believers together in the one Lord Jesus Christ. Our very capacity to communicate with God as Church is effected by the way we are neighbor and friend to one another.

– Father John Dominic Corbett, O.P.

The Implication of Faith
in One God

W E BELIEVE in one transcendent God who creates and sustains everything that exists. I am awestruck when I really dwell on the greatness of God, a greatness that bursts all categories of wonder and amazement. The True God is *beyond all things*. He is the Source of the whole universe and everything in it. Not only did he create the universe "in the beginning." He is, right this moment, the Reason why anything exists at all, and why each thing exists in its individuality.

He is so necessary, and at the same time so mysterious. Both the fragility and the tenacity of created things—and especially created persons—point to him. The memory of our youngest child, Josefina, who was born prematurely, is a special reminder of this fact for me. This tiny being, clinging to life, with all of the attention of science and technology focused upon her; she was a new "someone" who had appeared in the world. It is simply not possible to imagine that a reality so small and endangered, yet at the same time so worthy of love, could be caused by anything that we can measure or conceive.

Also, whenever I truly reflect on the mystery of God, I am filled with a spirit of thanksgiving. As a created person, I cannot help asking fundamental questions, such as, "Why am I here? Where am I going?" And then there is the urgent question: "Am I, ultimately, *alone*?" Faith in God responds to these questions. I exist because there is a Someone who *gives* me my being, a Someone who wants me and who loves me. The created person is true to himself when he lives in gratitude to God for his whole being.

And this faith is a source of profound trust in God in every circumstance. I have had to deal with significant illness in my own life. I quickly become discouraged as soon as I forget that I am created and loved by Someone who is Infinite Goodness. No matter how sick or confused I may feel, God's love is still the truth of my life. Indeed, my own suffering has taught me compassion for others, and although it has restricted my life in some ways (e.g., by taking me away from my career as a full time teacher), it also continues to deepen my awareness of the possibilities for love where I am, working at home and being with my children. God indeed is Good. I must trust in him.

– John Janaro

"Faith liberates reason from its blind spots and therefore helps it to be ever more fully itself."
– Pope Benedict XVI

Nathanael (Bartholomew)

THE GOSPELS VARY in relating how Jesus gathers his disciples. The point they agree on is that these men come to believe in him. This precious gift of faith comes not only by hearing about Jesus, but also by first-hand experience of him. Nathanael does not believe in Jesus immediately, but only after dialogue at two levels, human and divine.

First, Nathanael, named Bartholomew in the Synoptic Gospels, hears Philip speak of having found the chosen Messiah, "Jesus…from Nazareth" (Jn 1:45). But he is unconvinced, skeptical: "Nazareth? Can anything good come from Nazareth?" Philip replies: "Come and see" (Jn 1:46).

Taking up the invitation, his doubts vanish. He becomes amazed when Jesus, who knows everyone's heart, addresses him as a "true Israelite," one awaiting the fulfillment of God's promise. This draws from him a confession of faith: "Rabbi, you are the Son of God; you are the King of Israel" (Jn 1:49).

Perhaps his faith is deepened by the "sign" Jesus gives at Cana, Nathanael's hometown. Later, when seeing the risen Lord (cf. Jn 21:2), he is confirmed in faith.

His seeking of truth is an example of waiting to be divinely awakened. Vigilance is a hallmark of Christian faith. It is worthwhile for it entails already a sense of having found God.

– Father Michael L. Gaudoin-Parker

A Meditation for
Eucharistic Adoration

O Bread of Life, at the multiplication of the loaves you asked your disciples, "Do you want to leave me too?" Like the faithful Saint Peter, we stay with you. For unless we eat your Body and drink your Blood, we will have no life within us. The Eucharist is the sum and summary of our faith. In the Sacrament of the Altar, you meet us as our companion. You walk beside us as our strength, as our food for the journey. As you hand yourself over to the Father in the Eucharist, you reveal the true meaning of sacrifice: to become totally receptive to God by letting ourselves be completely taken over by him. In the offering of your Body and Blood, you give life to humanity through your flesh. You show us the bond you long to establish with us. You will us to become the Body of Christ, and to lead us to your Father. The communion of the Eucharist is the ultimate goal of every human desire. We are made for your Real Presence in the Eucharist. Its power is the principle of new life within us. The Eucharist is an act of thanksgiving for the radical newness offered to us at every celebration of the Eucharist. Our worship of the Eucharist transforms every aspect of life. Eucharistic adoration transfigures us to reflect your image, beloved Son of God. For we are called to be bread broken for the life of the world.

– Father Peter John Cameron, O.P.

Pine

THE BREATH that blows
to shake this crooked evergreen
is the same breath that stirred
the embers of human souls
when fiery tongues fell
from the sky.

O tilted tree,
do you know
the life that slips like a thread
through the eye of every needle
of your existence,
vibrating your limbs
with every stitch,
sewing the scent of pine
into the pockets of air
that carry your treasures
like quiet money—
a gift for all who wonder
about the wind
and
pine?

– Rita A. Simmonds

Thomas

W E ALL KNOW why Thomas is dubbed "doubting," but nobody knows why he's nicknamed Didymus (Jn 11:16; 20:24; 21:2), "twin" in Greek. Thomas only speaks three times, all in John's Gospel. These words, plus the curious fact that his name is last recorded side-by-side with Simon Peter (Jn 21:2), reveal that Thomas is Peter's "twin" brother in the faith.

Thomas' first words resound with readiness to stand by Jesus: "Let us also go to die with him" (Jn 11:16). Such a courageous, generous affirmation reminds us of Peter: "Lord, I am prepared to go to prison and to die with you" (Lk 22: 33). At the Last Supper, Thomas asks an honest, if obtuse, question: "Master, we do not know where you are going; how can we know the way?" (Jn 14:5). Blustery Peter is no stranger to muddle-headed remarks (Mt 15:15-16, 17:4; Jn 13:9). Finally, Thomas utters his famous doubt. With perhaps a touch of post-Resurrection humor, Jesus responds, "Put your finger here" (Jn 20:27). As Benedict XVI notes, "Thomas reacts with the most splendid profession of faith in the whole of the New Testament: 'My Lord and my God!'" (Jn 20:28). Peter's twin profession: "You are the Messiah, the Son of the living God" (Mt 16:16).

Thomas' Petrine faith shows us that every doubt, even denial, can lead us back to what is most certain: Christ's mercy.

– Andrew Matt

Our profession of faith begins with God.
(CCC 198)

WHERE DID I COME FROM? Where am I going? Without an answer, we are like ships without rudders. With an answer we know the meaning and purpose of life. Faith provides the answer. By faith we know that "God is love" (1 Jn 4:8). We are not alone. Our God who made us also watches over us. Love is our beginning and end; we were created out of love and for love. If God is the beginning and end of all things, and if God is love, then love is the meaning of everything that exists. We believe that "all things work for good for those who love God, who are called according to his purpose" (Rom 8:28). We also believe that nothing "will be able to separate us from the love of God in Christ Jesus our Lord" (Rom 8:39). Note the "all things" and "nothing" in these sentences. Faith welcomes this as good news. By faith we discover that in Jesus Christ God has revealed that love is the meaning of all things, even suffering and death. This gives rise to that uniquely Christian joy that bears witness to the presence of God's love in our world.

– Douglas Bushman

*W*E ARE IN POSSESSION OF TRUTH, and we are sure of our title; this is enough for us. Besides, we have seen that our faith rests upon solid grounds; again, this suffices, for we cannot be every day raising doubts over things already proved. In the affairs of every-day life, we do not stop when such doubts, such inane ideas, cross our mind, but we go on, and certitude reasserts itself. Lastly, others more intelligent than ourselves believe these truths, and are persuaded that they are well proved; therefore, I submit to their judgment which is far wiser than that of those extremists who take a malicious delight in attracting notice by undermining all the bases of certitude. To these commonsense reasons we should add prayer: "I believe Lord, help thou my unbelief."

If the *temptations* are *well defined*, bearing on some particular doctrine, we hold firmly to our belief since we are in possession of the truth. But we seize the first opportunity to clear up the difficulty, either by personal study, if we have the intelligence and the documents required, or by consulting some learned man who may help us to solve the problem more easily. If we add prayer to this earnest and loyal research, a solution, as a rule, will not be long in coming.

– Father Adolphe Tanquerey, s.s.

Matthew (Levi) the Evangelist

THE CALLING OF SAINT MATTHEW, as painted by Caravaggio, is displayed in a church in Rome. In order to view the painting, one must put coins in a timer that illuminates the painting. There is something ironic about needing coins to see clearly the moment Jesus beckons the tax collector to follow him. That moment, however, pictures for us the theme of Matthew's Gospel.

Tax collectors, seen as collaborators with Rome, were despised and considered outcasts. They would be on no list of potential disciples. A central theme of this Gospel is the universality of the call. Imagining Jesus as the new Moses, Matthew records stories of Jesus leading people out of the dark and into the light. Going up on a mountain to preach the beatitudes, Jesus offers a new law that promises God's love not just to a chosen few, but to all. It all starts in that moment at the table. In the painting, Matthew points to himself, as if he cannot believe Jesus would call him. Yet that is the witness of Matthew and the meaning of his Gospel. Unlikely as it seems, Jesus is calling each of us into the light. No coins are needed. Only a willingness to get up and follow.

– Monsignor Gregory E. S. Malovetz

*"In all circumstances, hold faith as a shield,
to quench all [the] flaming arrows of the evil one."*
(Eph 6:16)

SPARKS ARE HAZARDOUS for forests particularly in very dry weather. One spark from a campfire might drift lazily through the air, settle on a stretch of parched grass, and then very quickly start a conflagration. One spark could devastate a whole forest.

Certain thoughts are dangerous for human hearts. Malicious thoughts, fearful thoughts, envious thoughts, lustful thoughts are not only wrong in themselves. They are dangerous as well. Why? They are dangerous because of the dry and parched conditions of our hearts. It doesn't take much for these thoughts, drifting lazily through the air, to settle on one or another damaged dimension of our being and to inflame envy for our neighbor's possessions and talents, jealousy for her relationships, or hatred for his very person.

Faith protects us against this. The waters of the Spirit run freely in a heart renewed by faith, and the sparks of hell can start no conflagration here. But faith is virtue as well as gift, and that means that the believer must exercise her faith in rejecting thoughts of malice, envy, and hate, and in doing so comes by degrees to know who our God truly is and what he is truly like.

– Father John Dominic Corbett, O.P.

DVANCED SOULS PRACTICE NOT ONLY FAITH, but the *spirit of faith:* *"The just man lives by faith."*

They read the Gospel with loving attention, happy to follow Jesus step by step, to relish his maxims, to contemplate his examples in order to imitate them. Jesus becomes the center of their thoughts: they seek him in their readings and in their labor, desiring to know him better so that they may love him more.

They accustom themselves to see all things, to judge all things from the point of view of faith. They see the hand of the Creator in all *his works,* and they hear all creatures repeat the refrain: "He made us, and not we ourselves." Hence, it is God whom they admire everywhere. The *persons* that surround them are to them so many images of God, children of the same heavenly Father, brethren in Christ Jesus. Events, which at times are so baffling to unbelievers, are interpreted by them in the light of the great principle that all is ordained in behalf of the elect, and that good and evil are dispensed with a view to our salvation and perfection.

– Father Adolphe Tanquerey, s.s.

James, Son of Alphaeus

OF ALL THE ODDITIES OF GOD, his choosing the Jew must surely rank pretty near the top. What was he thinking? But odder still, perhaps, was the choice of those twelve Jews whom God's Son recruited for apostolic service. Could a more motley crowd be found anywhere on earth? Especially number nine, whom we know as James, son of Alphaeus.

Leaving aside the utter obscurity in which he lived and died, what else do we know about him? Only that Jesus Christ expressly called him to be among his closest disciples. What more do we need to know?

Nothing is accidental with God. Nor is it his practice to instrumentalize those whom he invites to serve. If the Gospels put him in ninth place, leaving him seemingly in the shade, there must be a lesson in such anonymity that you and I need to learn. Could it be that this obscure son of Alphaeus, whom the tradition speaks of as James the Lesser, went on to achieve, by dint of his very dimness, things far greater than anything the world could offer? In choosing those who are not, so as to confound those who are, God is saying that it isn't finally about us at all. The wonders of holiness are wrought by God. And in that place beyond the stars we call heaven, it will be the least and the last who make the biggest splash.

– Regis Martin

GRANT TO ME, O my God, that I may turn my heart to you always, and grieve for my failings with a firm purpose of amendment. Make me, O Lord, obedient without opposition; poor without repining; chaste without blemish; patient without murmur; humble without pretense; merry without riotousness; serious without heaviness; cheerful without frivolity; God-fearing without abjectness; truthful without duplicity; doing good without presumption; correcting my neighbor without pride; edifying him by word and example without hypocrisy.

Grant to me, O Lord God, a vigilant heart that no subtle speculation may ever lead me from you; a nobleness that no unworthy affection may draw from you; a rectitude that no evil purpose may turn from you. Grant me a steadfastness which no tribulation may shatter; a freedom that no violent affection may overthrow. Give me, O Lord my God, a mind to know you, diligence to seek you, wisdom to find you. Give me a way of life pleasing to you, perseverance to trust and await you, and finally faith to embrace you.

Grant that my punishment may be averted through penance here; your benefits used in this life through your grace; that your joys may be enjoyed in heaven in glory. Who lives and reigns, one God forever and ever. Amen.

– Saint Thomas Aquinas

*A*BOVE ALL, advanced souls strive to *be led* in all things according to the principles of faith. Their *judgments* are based upon the maxims of the Gospel, not upon those of the world; their words are inspired by the Christian spirit, not by the spirit of the world, for they conform their words to their judgments and thus triumph over human respect; their *actions* become more and more Christlike for they delight in considering Our Lord as their model, and thus escape being carried away by the examples of worldlings. In short, they live a life of faith.

They strive, finally, to spread round about them *this faith* that is in them: through their *prayers*, asking God to send apostolic workers to labor for the evangelization of infidels and heretics: "Pray ye therefore the Lord of the harvest, that he may send forth laborers into his harvest"; through their *example*, discharging so well their duties of state, that those who witness their life may feel drawn to imitate them; through their *words,* declaring in all simplicity but without any human respect, that they find in their faith *power* to do good, and comfort in the midst of their trials; through their *works,* doing their share by their generous offerings, their sacrifices, and their personal efforts for the moral and religious instruction and education of the neighbor.

– Father Adolphe Tanquerey, s.s.

Thaddeus
(Jude the Brother of James)

Saint Jude, one of the Twelve, is also called Thaddeus, meaning the Magnanimous. How appropriate for the patron saint of lost causes! Thaddeus expands our hearts by interceding to give us hope in the most forlorn and straitened spaces of our lives. Faith is most faith when it must hope against hope, when we must act within the hopelessness of life's all-too-apparent futility: the wounds of love, suffering, depression, death—vanity of vanities. When the walls close in, we have the Judas who does not betray.

At the Last Supper, Jesus speaks of his going away. How appropriate that it's Thaddeus who asks, "Master, [then] what happened that you will reveal yourself to us and not to the world?" (Jn 14:22). What is more hopeless than the sighing desire to be with Jesus though he will cross the barrier of death? Jesus answers by speaking of the mysterious intimacy of Trinitarian indwelling, the very substance of our faith, which we now enjoy through baptism and the Eucharist. Though he is in heaven, lost to the sight of the world, we see Jesus through the eyes of a love that believes and hopes.

Jude's whole mission is to vindicate this final testament of Jesus: to lead us from the hopelessness of foaming with futile desires like wild waves (Jude 13), into the life of a love stronger than death.

– J. David Franks

Faith in God leads us to turn to him alone
as our first origin and our ultimate goal,
and neither to prefer anything to him
nor to substitute anything for him.
(CCC 229)

IF WE GIVE OUR FREEDOM TO GOD we shall remain free. If we prefer anything to God we shall lose our freedom and fall into slavery of some kind. Knowing this, God forbids us to acknowledge other gods. The Bible calls this God's jealousy, because he prefers our happiness to everything else. This is why Christian faith is exclusive. There is only one God, one Lord, one Creator, one Redeemer. Throughout the Bible God asks: "Has any other god done for you what I have done?" No other god is Creator. No other god took notice of Israel in slavery and set them free. No other god became man and died to set us free from sin. We owe everything—our existence, our freedom, our hope—to God. To believe this in faith means to prefer God to all else: riches, fame, power, pleasure. To prefer him to all things is to refuse to get distracted, to cling to what gives ultimate meaning and purpose to life. In this way faith fulfills the commandment not to have other gods besides him. Even more, by faith we prefer God to life itself: His "love is better than life" (Ps 63:4).

– Douglas Bushman

*N*OTHING RINGS MORE TRUE to men and women aware of themselves than the consciousness of their need; for this reason, nothing expresses what we are better than crying out, the cry of the needy person to the only One who can respond to this need....

The affection for your own humanity is the opposite of egotism, because affection for yourself..., rather than being an avid affirmation of what you think or feel, is instead wonder at something you find in yourself and that you didn't give yourself. In affection for yourself... there is the affirmation of the surprise at not being made by yourself... This affection for yourself leads to "the seriousness of gaze at our own needs. [...] In fact, we are bound to feel the exigencies or needs" (L. Giussani).

In order to have this true affection for yourself you need poverty of spirit. "Affection for yourself demands poverty. This is why Christ said, 'Blessed are the poor in spirit,'...because it's not attachment to something we ourselves have defined, but to something that defines us; the acknowledgment of something that defines us, without our having been able to intervene to determine the question. Thus, the need for love or the need for personal fulfillment or the need for companionship is, without equal, something greater and deeper to hear and heed with seriousness."

– Father Julián Carrón

Simon the Cananean
(the Zealot)

IN HIS 2006 AUDIENCES in which he teaches on the Apostles, Benedict XVI notes that we have little information on Simon the Zealot, and then the pope goes on to offer a profound reflection on the little that we do know.

In the Gospels, Simon is called the Cananean and the "zealot." These titles indicate that Simon is zealous regarding his Judaism. He takes his belonging to the Chosen People and the heritage given them by God very seriously.

What is amazing is that a man like this follows Jesus side by side with a man like Matthew, who as a tax collector has betrayed his heritage and his people.

What does this say about Simon's faith? His faith in Jesus begins in his recognition that Jesus, a carpenter from Nazareth, is sent by God. As with Simon Peter and the other Apostles, his faith gradually grows into his certainty that Jesus is, in fact, God himself. Simon's unity with Matthew as an Apostle shows us that his faith in Jesus encompasses and embraces everything. Matthew's previous transgressions do not cause Simon any hesitation. Simon's friendship with Matthew arises from the fact that Matthew is chosen by Christ, and this chosenness is the new foundation of the new men that both Simon and Matthew have become through their faith in Jesus.

– Father Richard Veras

God's Passion

GOD IS
always
was
yet becomes
as small as a speck
in a womb,
as a crumb
on a plate
placed
on the tip
of a tongue,
unleavened and raised
between fingers and thumbs,
lifted, beheld
manna become
Man
taken in hand
to be eaten,
absorbed
forgotten
remembered, re-offered, re-stored,
all whim and all wisdom
eternal
in fashion:
God's Gift
of Himself
in the Flesh
is all passion.

– Rita A. Simmonds

"Conduct yourselves in a way worthy of the gospel
of Christ…standing firm in one spirit, with one mind
struggling together for the faith of the gospel."
(Phil 1:27)

"LORD, I am not worthy that you should enter under my roof, but only say the word and my soul shall be healed." So we pray before the reception of each Holy Communion. What do we mean when we pray that we are not worthy? Do we mean that we have not earned by our own moral standing the right to such sacramental and personal intimacy with Christ. The answer to that question is yes, obviously. But we also mean something more. While we cry we are not worthy we nonetheless cry out for his personal visitation of our souls in this sacrament.

When we are told to conduct ourselves in a way worthy of the Gospel of Christ, we are not being asked to do what only Christ can do or to earn what only Christ can earn. We are told to live in such a way that our very lives call out for the visitation of the Son of God as their only fitting completion. Doing this personally brings personal sanctity. Doing this collectively gives the Bridal Church her voice as she cries out not only, "Lord, I am not worthy" but also and finally, "Come, Lord Jesus."

– Father John Dominic Corbett, O.P.

Nicodemus

Had his life ended the night he stole away to hear Jesus tell him that unless a man be born again he cannot enter God's kingdom, Nicodemus would have gone to his grave full of wonderment at the prospect of an old man having to "reenter his mother's womb" (Jn 3:4).

But he does not die. Instead, this wise and good man, this brave and noble member of the Sanhedrin, is fated not merely to be the recipient of words unmatched in human history—that God, for instance, "so loved the world that he gave his only Son, so that everyone who believes in him might not perish but might have eternal life" (Jn 3:16)—but of the Word himself, who in the sleep of death is entrusted to Nicodemus for burial in the garden alongside Golgotha. Only a faith as adamantine as the rock surrounding the tomb of the Lord could account for the actions of such a man. Who, in his only other recorded appearance, reminds the Pharisees determined on doing violence to Jesus, that the law condemns no man "before it first hears him and finds out what he is doing" (Jn 7:51). Perhaps it had crossed his mind that, if they too were to see and hear, they also would believe?

– Regis Martin

TEACH ME, my Lord, to be sweet and gentle in all the events of life: in disappointments, in the thoughtlessness of others, in the insincerity of those I trusted, in the unfaithfulness of those on whom I relied. Let me put myself aside, to think of the happiness of others, to hide my little pains and heartaches, so that I may be the only one to suffer them. Teach me to profit by the suffering that comes across my path. Let me so use it that it may mellow me, not harden nor embitter me; that it may make me patient, not irritable, that it may make me broad in my forgiveness, not narrow, haughty and overbearing. May no one be less good for having come within my influence. No one less pure, less noble for having been a fellow traveler in our journey toward eternal life. As I go my rounds from one distraction to another, let me whisper, from time to time, a word of love to you. May our life be lived in the supernatural, full of power for good, and strong in its purpose of sanctity. Amen.

– From *Manual of Prayers*,
Pontifical North American College

*D*EEP WITHIN EVERY HUMAN HEART...there lurks a sly, unrecognized cunning, all too well skilled in self-deception and evasion. This is the total adversary of belief. It is the cunning of pride, of self-possession, of self-sufficiency. To live fully out of our inheritance, to live solely by the faith of the Son of God, to live the life of Jesus—all this may sound beautiful (and beautiful it indeed is, beyond our wildest dreams), but in practice it strikes a deadly blow at human pride. This is why so many, face to face *in reality* with the self-dispossession that life in Jesus calls for, walk no more with him—not in the sense of complete desertion and denial of belief, but rather because they have said "No" to *his* cross, however many other crosses they may be carrying supposedly in his name.

Each of us has the choice either to live by faith or to live by "flesh." To live by "flesh" is to live within the limits of our own potential, within the limits of our own perception and understanding, according to how things seem and feel, according to our natural *experience*.... We cannot rid ourselves of this deeply rooted pride and self-possession by our own strength. Only the Holy Spirit of the Crucified and Risen One can effect it, and this he is indeed always trying to do. But we must recognize his work, and respond "Amen."

– Sister Ruth Burrows, O.C.D.

Jairus

IF JAIRUS LIVED IN OUR TIME, we could imagine him staring at a computer screen. Like so many parents of a child with a life-threatening illness, he might surf the Internet looking for answers, for a direction, for a reason to have hope. Before this moment of crisis, we have no idea of Jairus' opinion of Jesus. Like other religious leaders he may have viewed Jesus skeptically. His story must have touched the early Church deeply. It is found in three of the Gospels, although with some changes in each. At the heart of the story is a father who recognizes he cannot change this situation. All he can do is turn to God.

There is something touching about the version in which Jairus falls at the feet of Jesus (cf. Lk 8:40-56). It tells us that healing begins when we surrender anger, control, and fear to Jesus. As Jesus walks with Jairus to his home, we are reminded that Jesus is making this journey with us. The miracle of the story may be that Jairus' daughter is healed. But the greater miracle may be found in Jairus' realization that no matter how our life unfolds, God's grace will help us find the way.

– Monsignor Gregory E. S. Malovetz

> *The mystery of the Most Holy Trinity*
> *is the central mystery of Christian faith and life.*
> *It is…the source of all the other mysteries of faith,*
> *the light that enlightens them.*
> *(CCC 234)*

THE FATHER, SON, AND HOLY SPIRIT are a mystery of "consubstantial communion." Created in God's own image, man is made for communion with God and with others. Sin is the rejection of God's love and loss of communion with him. Christ came to forgive sins and to restore us to communion with God. The Church is the communion of saints; her mission is to draw all people into communion with God. The sacraments confer grace so that we can participate in the mystery of Trinitarian communion. Conscience hears God's voice calling us to communion in our actions. The commandments are God's wisdom regarding the actions that are conducive to this communion and are its fruits. Every moral virtue makes it possible for man to act in communion with God. Prayer is conscious communion with God in faith, hope, and charity. Heaven is eternal communion with God; hell is self-exclusion from this communion. In this way we perceive the integral unity of all that the Church teaches as a mystery of communion.

– Douglas Bushman

*F*AITH ISN'T OPTIONAL; reaching the point of acknowledging him is indispensable, because it is there, in the acknowledgment of Christ, where you can find the answer to this endless need, to this expectant awaiting of the infinite.

The only thing we need is "yourself"; no other thing is enough for this need of ours…. The fact that the Infinite exists, that God exists is what makes the heart glad, because there is an answer to our desire.

So when we speak of faith, we're speaking of…the answer to this. But in order…to be able to understand the difference between faith and any other thing, this kind of humanity is required. Otherwise, we can speak about faith without…needing faith, because we don't have within the urgency for this you, this "you yourself,"…because we can fill our life with so many useless things, or not have the courage to have this seriousness with our needs, thinking already in advance that there are no answers.

"Poor people in terms of the heart…went to listen to [Jesus] because 'no man has ever spoken like this man!'–that is, because they felt animated, touched in their affection; they felt renewed in the affection for themselves, their humanity… They were people who hungered and thirsted…. What do hunger and thirst mean?… Desiring that your own humanity be fulfilled" (L. Giussani).

– Father Julián Carrón

The Boy with the Loaves and Fish

Sometimes at the beach, the lifeguard will blow the whistle, and from the chair hold up a lost child. People pause and look up, and think how relieved the parents will be in seeing their child. Apart from the Resurrection, the only miracle found in all four of the Gospels is the feeding of the five thousand. In John's version of the story (Jn 6:1-14), the disciples spot a boy with a few loaves and fish. He doesn't have a name and we are not told his age. In a crowd numbering five thousand, one wonders where the boy's family is. And we do not even know if he gives over the loaves and fish without a fight.

John holds this young boy up for us in the midst of a sea of hungry people. In the time of Jesus, children were viewed as insignificant and would not have been counted among the five thousand. Yet in this moment, Jesus reveals that he sees no insignificant people. Every person is valued and has some gift, no matter how small, that can feed the hungers of the human family. When placed in the hands of Jesus those gifts become a miracle.

– Monsignor Gregory E. S. Malovetz

*Y*OU WOULD NEED some kind of total anesthesia in order entirely to lose your sense of attachment to yourself. The type of society we live in can achieve this…, but not permanently… Even…extremely widespread total anesthetics have a limit,…and so suffering and the wound are unavoidable. This lets grace enter, through this suffering and this wound.…

If you were able to create…beautiful things, you wouldn't need Christ present who draws all of you to him. This is why the Lord answers you, continuing to make beautiful things…happen anew before your eyes, so that sometimes you'll let yourself be drawn to him, and be so happy that it'll overcome even your shame… What a method, what tenderness of the Mystery, who… stoops down over us to draw us to the knowledge of him through what he makes happen in reality!…

He invites us to fix our eyes on his presence.…

All the complications begin when…simplicity of heart is missing,…because even if I could do things in exactly the right way, the problem of faith would remain intact, because I wouldn't have begun to respond to the challenge of facts that call me to another thing. This is why so often our insistence on exactness is our alibi ("I'm not adequate,…I'm not worthy…") to avoid accepting the challenge that the presence of Christ before our eyes hurls at us. This is immorality.

– Father Julián Carrón

"Persevere in the faith, firmly grounded, stable, and not shifting from the hope of the gospel that you heard."
(Col 1:23)

I MIGHT BE FACED with the prospect of a difficult exam, predict that I will fail it, and still study hard intending to pass it. There is a difference between predicting and intending.

We can intend to persevere in the faith. What we can't do is guarantee that we *will* persevere in the faith. Our free will is of all our faculties the most securely within our own power, and yet we cannot guarantee what final use of it we will make.

Paul tells us to persevere in the faith. Is he telling us to do something beyond our power? Yes, in a way. But pay attention to the words "firmly grounded, stable, and not shifting." They call to mind the Lord's Sermon on the Mount in which he tells his disciples that it is the man who *does* the will of his heavenly Father who will be firmly grounded. The rains came and the winds blew and the house did not come down. It persevered.

Even though we cannot guarantee our own perseverance in the faith until death, we can obey God's will each day. In doing this we have the strong hope that we will abide in him until the end.

– Father John Dominic Corbett, O.P.

Zacchaeus

ZACCHAEUS is a brilliantly clear witness that our Christian faith is not, at its core, a faith in doctrines or laws or ethical systems, but rather faith in a person, Jesus Christ.

The first stirrings of faith in Zacchaeus are what give him the energy to set aside his dignity and climb a tree to see Jesus. What he has heard about this carpenter-turned-rabbi leads him to believe that this man may very well be from God. It is Jesus' loving gaze upon Zacchaeus and his invitation to come down from the tree and welcome the Nazarene into his home which stirs into flame the faith that has already been born in the heart of the chief tax collector of Jericho.

Jesus' presence in his house moves Zacchaeus to repent of his sins and to offer generous restoration. Jesus responds to the dramatic change in Zacchaeus by saying, "Today, salvation has come to this house." Salvation is Jesus himself, and salvation meets its goal that day in Zacchaeus' faith-filled heart.

Zacchaeus' paradigmatic conversion communicates to us in action what Pope Benedict XVI communicates in his words in *Porta Fidei*: *"Belief in Jesus Christ, then, is the way to arrive definitively at salvation."*

– Father Richard Veras

*T*HOSE WHO DON'T PERCEIVE…this need that you haven't given yourself but that must be acknowledged…don't feel the urge to reach faith; they can stop halfway down the road; they can halt at the sign. This is why Fr. Giussani affirmed that without this [perception of need], the Christian event isn't possible—that is, it's impossible for the event to take possession of us, to truly happen in us.

Therefore, he underlines that affection for oneself "leads us to rediscover the constitutive exigencies, the original needs, their nakedness and vastness." He insists, "The poor in spirit are those who have nothing, except one thing, through which and by which they are made: an endless aspiration…a boundless expectant awaiting…" The originality of man is the expectant awaiting of the infinite: man entirely outstretched, intent on something… Here is true liberation: you feel such a gaze upon yourself, in this immensity of your own humanity. "Seriousness in affection for yourself is the perception of your own boundless need. It's boundless precisely because the 'I' doesn't prefix any image of things that are needed: The I 'is' need!"…"affection for the human— …attachment full of esteem and compassion, of mercy, for oneself,…that attachment that your mother had for you, especially when you were little."

– Father Julián Carrón

Faith and the Joyful Mysteries
of the Rosary

❨ *The Annunciation* – The Blessed Virgin Mary received the Word of God in deep humility and obedience. May I share in our Lady's faith so as to be ever open to the will of God and to the re-creation brought forth by his holy Word. Come, Holy Spirit—come through Mary into my life to perfect and sanctify it.

❨ *The Visitation* – Faith is the lifelong companion that makes it possible to perceive the marvels God works for us. Mary comes as a companion to Elizabeth so that together they may revel in God's marvels in their midst. May my life of faith make me attentive to the Mystery that comes to visit and stay with me in love.

❨ *The Nativity of Jesus* – In the Incarnation, the Son of God takes on our human weakness so as to transform it. Faith is acknowledging an exceptional Presence that has the power to change my life. May I always adore this Presence-with-us and adhere to it, affirming at every moment the Truth Jesus reveals.

❨ *The Presentation* – In the mystery of the Presentation, the newborn Jesus is offered in the Temple to the Father. May I always live by faith, handing myself over to God each moment in acts of self-sacrificing love. I come to possess the certitude I seek in life through my constant self-abandonment to Love.

❨ *The Finding in the Temple* – The temporary "loss" of Jesus shows how lost we would be without Christ in our life. I find Jesus through prayer, devotion to the Word of God, adoration of the Blessed Sacrament, and charitable works of mercy. May I always keep my eyes fixed on Jesus Christ, and find him always close.

– Father Peter John Cameron, O.P.

Faith and Prayer

STRIKE OPEN almost any copy of the Bible to mid-point and there one finds the Psalter, songs of praise, prayers. In a very material way this seems to suggest that the reading of Scripture, a faith experience, culminates in prayer—a marriage of faith and prayer. The fact is that faith without prayer is mute, and prayer without faith is void and aimless. Faith and prayer—the one implies and demands the other.

Our faith forthrightly requires that we pray: "Then he told them a parable about the necessity for them to pray always without becoming weary" (Lk 18:1). Note that there is in these words a subtle hint that prayer is not always a sheer joy. Otherwise no one would be tempted to become weary. Elsewhere Jesus implies that even the faith of the Old Law finds prayer imperative. "Jesus said to [the devil] in reply: 'It is written [in the Old Testament]:/ "You shall worship the Lord, your God,/ and him alone shall you serve"'" (Lk 4:8).

In any attempt to address God, faith is utterly required because God is who he is—he cannot be seen, heard, or touched as one can touch a human being or feel a breeze. It is only by faith that we can perceive him and address him.

The interplay between prayer and faith is intriguing. The broader and deeper one's faith, the richer one's prayer. Obviously one can have a more gratifying conversation with a well-known friend than with a virtual stranger. On the other hand, the more often one visits God in prayer, the more solid one's faith in him becomes.

Curiously, although prayer makes sense only when it springs from a vibrant faith, faith on the other hand can survive only when supported by prayer. Prayer is the flowering forth of faith. It is a logical, even necessary follow-up to faith. By faith one becomes aware of God, by prayer one connects with the God one has found by faith. The sheer hugeness of God, as discerned by faith, demands that he be acknowledged—prayer is that acknowledgment.

When all is said and done—there must be at least some tiny flicker of faith to warrant a prayer. You cannot have the one without the other. Prayer sits in tandem with faith. One does not ring a doorbell unless one believes there is someone inside who will answer.

– Monsignor James Turro

"Faith, before being a religious belief,
is a way of seeing reality, a way of thinking,
an interior sensitivity that enriches
the human person as such."
– Pope Benedict XVI

Father of the Possessed Boy

DEMONS HATE CHILDREN. Children are too-obvious reminders that we are always dependent, especially on God, and it was for "autonomy" that the demons rebelled. A demon has tormented this boy for years, sadistically casting him into fire and water. The boy's father is desperate. Is there anything like the pain of a father who cannot protect his children?

Jesus happens upon this father and son after the Transfiguration, in which the Father glorifies his Son as the faithful emissary of his saving will. Descending Tabor, Jesus sets his face like flint, totally trusting his Father, as he heads into the outer dark, to enter into all sin and suffering and godforsakenness on the cross. He's the eternal Son, the eternal Child, of the Father: children are ever the gateway to the kingdom. There's nothing darker in a dark world than the suffering of children. King Jesus rides on into that night, bearing the Father's light.

And Jesus finds the father of this boy here, crying out, "I do believe; help my unbelief!" (Mk 9:24). He believes, yet we can never trust God enough. How could we, if faith is our response to the Father's goodness to us, which has no limit? And nothing challenges faith more than the suffering of children. Jesus heals the son. He is faithful to the end, engendering ever greater faith in us.

– J. David Franks

Only faith can embrace the mysterious ways
of God's almighty power....
The Virgin Mary is the supreme model of this faith.
(CCC 273)

God calls us to communion with him, to be holy as he is holy. Without faith we would dismiss this as unrealistic. Surely God knows how weak we are. Only by the power of faith can we take his call seriously. Faith confirms simultaneously that: (1) God does call us to holiness; (2) this call is beyond us, we cannot respond to this call without his help; (3) he comes to help us in the power of his mercy.

We see this in Saint Peter. Peter could not follow Christ to the cross, but by the transforming power of God's mercy he did follow Christ in martyrdom.

We see it in Mary. God called her to be a Virgin Mother. Realizing she could not fulfill her vocation on her own she asked: "How shall this be?" Overshadowed by the Holy Spirit she conceived Jesus while remaining a Virgin. Mary teaches us that to live in faith is to turn to God every day to ask: "How shall I do your will?" By confronting what is impossible for us, we come to believe that nothing is impossible with God.

– Douglas Bushman

*F*AITH SIGNIFIES A BELIEF in things we have not seen and for which we do not know the reason of their being. It is impossible to live without some kind of faith....

Granting that man cannot live without some kind of faith, let us now proceed to treat in particular of Christian faith. In the first place, we should observe that there are two kinds of faith: acquired and infused. Acquired faith is that which is obtained through the repetition of many acts of belief....

Infused faith is that which is bestowed on the soul of the Christian by the Holy Spirit. It is infused into the soul at the moment of baptism, together with sanctifying grace and all the other virtues that flow from grace. It is a special supernatural light which illumines the intellect of the Christian and efficaciously inclines him to believe all that God has revealed and the Church teaches, without seeing the reasons for the truths proposed for belief. Indeed, whatever the intellect is able to accomplish in regard to divine truth, the light of faith is able to accomplish in a more eminent manner. This is manifested in the constancy of the martyrs, especially the women and children who were so firm in their belief that they willingly suffered death for their faith.

– Venerable Louis of Granada

Mary Magdalene

MARY MAGDALENE enjoys a special closeness to Christ. She is mentioned in all four of the Gospels.

She is one of the Galilean women who follow Jesus as he journeys from one town and village to another, proclaiming the Kingdom of God. She witnesses the crucifixion. She sits opposite the sepulcher and sees where he is laid. She brings spices to anoint him. She sees the empty tomb and runs to tell the others. She stands outside the empty tomb and weeps. She sees two angels in white.

Perhaps most movingly, "When he had risen, early on the first day of the week, he appeared first to Mary Magdalene, out of whom he had driven seven demons" (Mk 16:9).

When seven demons have gone out of you, you tend to be very aware that at any moment seven, or ten, or a hundred more, could take their place. You tend to want to stay very close to Christ.

To drive out seven demons costs. To sacrifice for people tends to make us love them all the more. So maybe one of the things Mary Magdalene tells us is that the more demons Christ has driven out, the more he wants to stay close to us, too.

– Heather King

"As you received Christ Jesus the Lord,
walk in him, rooted in him and built upon him,
and established in the faith."
(Col 2: 6-7)

"WALK IN HIM," we are told. What does that mean? "Walking" is about lifestyle. I think it means that our style of life is to reflect his. It means we are to be at home in him and that, being so at home, we are to behave as if conforming our ways to his were the most natural thing in the world.

We are to be "rooted in him." Roots are living things. So to be rooted in him is to draw our principle of life from him. It is to wither from lack of conscious contact with him.

On the other hand, to be "built upon" him suggests that growth in him is not something that happens automatically. A house does not build itself but only happens as a result of human choice and execution. Holiness is not an accident but happens because human beings decide that their free choices, organically related, are governed by the pattern of his own self-giving.

Finally, to be "established" in him suggests that because of him our lives have a kind of official and divine significance, that they have this permanently, and that they have this in plain view, open to the entire world to see.

– Father John Dominic Corbett, O.P.

*T*HE DYNAMIC OF FAITH is the same as the dynamic of reality, brought to the greatest power, because not only do I find before me reality, something real, but such an exceptional reality that the whole journey of knowledge is launched much more easily. But the dynamic is literally the same. So faith doesn't initiate from a suggestion, a sentiment, an imagination; everything begins in the face of an event that happens and that provokes reason more than all the others. At the beginning…there is…a given that sets itself forward and demands an explanation, that engages reason like nothing else, because nothing else mobilizes, jolts humanity like this thing.

A faith without reason, that has nothing to do with knowledge, isn't a faith grounded in certainty that Christ exists.… The problem of faith doesn't regard what we don't see, but what we *do* see. At the beginning of faith there isn't a subjective initiative, a sentiment, a decision, an imagination, but a fact: "Being Christian is not the result of an ethical choice or a lofty idea, but the encounter with an event, a Person, which gives life a new horizon" (*Deus Caritas Est* 1). Faith doesn't start from within, but from without, from the happening of something that strikes and provokes the subject in his fundamental dimensions: reason, heart, freedom, and affection.

– Father Julián Carrón

Joanna

LUKE, the Evangelist who tells us so much about Mary, does not neglect the other women who follow Jesus. In chapter 7, he gives us the woman who anoints Jesus' feet, a story that climaxes with the heart-stopping pronouncement: "So I tell you, her many sins have been forgiven; hence, she has shown great love" (Lk 7:47). Luke then describes other women who "had been cured of evil spirits and infirmities" (Lk 8:2): Mary Magdalene, Susanna, and "Joanna, the wife of Herod's steward Chuza" (Lk 8:3). Joanna's wealth and social standing would have been considerable, yet she puts all that aside to follow Jesus as he goes about "preaching and proclaiming the good news of the kingdom of God" (Lk 8:1).

That kingdom she and the other women experience in their very being. The Kingdom of God is where God rules. Joanna, like all of us before baptism, was first ruled by sin, but after her encounter with Christ, she lives out the early Christian confession: "Jesus Christ is Lord!" One way she does this is by providing for Jesus and the Twelve. Another way is by not flinching after the cross but rather going with her friends to the tomb on Easter Sunday, only to find it empty. Faithful Joanna's joy: she who first tastes the kingdom in Jesus' healing touch now sees that kingdom reign over death itself.

– Angela Franks

*W*HY CAN'T FAITH BE OPTIONAL? Precisely for this reason: because the originality of man is the expectant awaiting for the infinite....

The attraction Jesus exercised on others, that is, the attraction he awakens in us when we encounter him, was due to the fact that the ultimate point of reference wasn't him, but the Father; he attracted to himself in order to lead to the Father, to open us wide to the Mystery, the only One able to correspond. We find ourselves with this unique correspondence of the faith precisely because we encounter something real and present that satisfies us because within there is Something that opens us wide to the infinite, and we find a correspondence that we call impossible.

It is he who fulfills the nature of my "I," which is desire for the infinite.... The only thing that corresponds is a real and mysterious you. The object of faith is this real and mysterious you. This is what we're invited to... Something less than this wouldn't make faith so reasonable as to take up the whole "I" and demand the whole "I," because never, as in this relationship with the real and mysterious you, has my life acquired an import, a knowledge, an experience that nothing else can give.

Christ calls each of us by name, so that each one of us may feel in his depths the need of satisfaction, of fullness of life.

– Father Julián Carrón

Martha

FOR MANY, the name of Martha is synonymous with anxiety and distraction. When Christ has come as a guest to her home, she begs him to instruct her sister Mary, who sits at his feet, to help her serve the meal. Instead, Christ gently corrects Martha, insisting that Mary has chosen "the better part" (Lk 10:42). But Martha is not a one-sided biblical figure, a mere foil for her contemplative sister. She is a seeker, and, like her sister, desires to respond with her whole self to the call of Christ.

In John's Gospel, it is Martha, the "do-er," who goes out to meet Christ before he even enters the town. There Martha boldly proclaims to Christ her belief that, had he arrived earlier, her brother Lazarus, who has just died, would yet be with them. "Even now," she declares, "I know that whatever you ask of God, God will give you" (Jn 11:22). When Jesus questions her, Martha testifies to her faith in the resurrection of the dead—a pious Jewish belief. But Christ wants to draw her to himself: "I am the resurrection and the life" (Jn 11:25). Martha, undaunted, responds wholeheartedly: "I have come to believe that you are the Messiah, the Son of God, the one who is coming into the world" (Jn 11:27). Despite her anxiety and distraction, something else has been at work in Martha—she has been captured by Christ.

– Lisa Lickona

*The transmission of the Christian faith
consists primarily in proclaiming Jesus Christ in order
to lead others to faith in him.*
(CCC 425)

ALL MISSION BEGINS with the Father sending Jesus to reveal his love. The Father's love is his source of life and joy, and therefore to love us Jesus desires that we know the supreme joy of being loved by the Father. In this way Jesus lives the precept of loving his neighbors as he loves himself. We see this in Saint Andrew who, immediately after encountering Jesus, went and "found his own brother Simon and told him, 'We have found the Messiah'.... Then he brought him to Jesus" (Jn 1:41-42). We see it in the Samaritan woman who declared to her neighbors: "Come see a man who told me everything I have done" (Jn 4:29). We see it in Peter's invitation to the crowds to be baptized on Pentecost. We see it in Saint Paul's mission and in all the missionaries throughout the Church's history.

Saint Augustine writes: "Any good thing that can be shared is not properly possessed unless it is being shared." This applies preeminently to the supreme good of Christian faith. To pass the faith on to others, to evangelize, is to fulfill the commandment to love our neighbors as we love ourselves.

– Douglas Bushman

"*L*OVING CHRIST WITHIN EACH THING,…not stopping at appearances, but passing over to the other shore of each thing, which is him [this is faith],…we may obtain the good things he promised, which exceed every desire" (L. Giussani). Because the desire is for you, Christ, in every thing and within every thing. "Those who love father or mother more than me aren't worthy of me. But those who abandon father, mother, brother, sister for my sake…will have a hundredfold…"–that is, they'll love themselves and their poverty a hundred times more; they'll embrace their misery with mercy a hundred times more; they'll desire, aspire, walk a hundred times more impetuously toward their destiny. To love your woman or man…a hundred times more; to love the things at your hands a hundred times more; to forgive yourself, your neighbor…a hundred times more; to embrace the world a hundred times more.…

If we haven't reached this point, the problem isn't that we're unworthy, but that we haven't done the journey of faith, because without faith, there isn't this satisfaction.… For this reason, even the last remaining discomfort can become the point of departure for making this journey. Who can do it? Only those with an ultimate affection for self. Faith is the ultimate expression of an affection for oneself, a love for oneself.

– Father Julián Carrón

PRAISE AND THANKS TO YOU, O blessed faith! You tell me with certitude that the Blessed Sacrament of the altar, the heavenly Manna, is no longer bread, but my Lord Jesus Christ who is wholly present there for love of me.

One day, O Jesus, full of love and of goodness, you sat beside the well to await the Samaritan woman, that you might convert and save her. Now, you dwell on our altars, hidden in the consecrated Host, where you wait and sweetly invite souls, to win them to your love. From the tabernacle you seem to say to us all: "O men, why do you not come to me, who love you so much? I am not come to judge you! I have hidden myself in this Sacrament of love only to do good and to console all who have recourse to me;" I understand, O Lord; love has made you our prisoner; the passionate love you have for us has so bound you that it does not permit you to leave us.

– Father Gabriel of Saint Mary Magdalen, o.c.d.

Mary of Bethany

IN CONTRAST TO HER SISTER MARTHA, who is "anxious and worried about many things" (Lk 10:41), Mary is the contemplative. Mary sits at the feet of the Lord while Martha serves; she remains grieving at home for her brother, Lazarus, while Martha rushes from the house to meet the Lord. Mary's most celebrated act, however, occurs at the meal in Bethany, where she anoints the feet of Christ with costly perfume and dries them with her hair. In Mary we see the faith that is nurtured in prayer and flowers in flagrant self-gift.

Earlier in John's Gospel, we learn of Christ's great affection for Mary and her siblings, Martha and Lazarus. Meeting Mary as she grieves Lazarus' death, Jesus weeps too, "perturbed and deeply troubled" (Jn 11:33). In Christ, Mary has met the abiding, eternal love of the triune God in a human face. She has never known a love like this. Unlike her sister, Mary does not attempt to put words on this love: she doesn't complain or bargain. She acts. Contemplating his face, meditating upon his words, she can think of naught else but spending herself for Christ. Indeed, she has chosen "the better part" (Lk 10:42).

– Lisa Lickona

"Let us be sober, putting on the breastplate of faith and love and the helmet that is hope for salvation."
(1 Thes 5:8)

THE TONE SET HERE IS SERIOUS and restrained rather than festive. The admonition to sobriety is an admonition to alert awareness of our surroundings. The surrounding land could be dangerous and filled with hidden enemies. We are at war, and so we must be awake.

The war Saint Paul is writing of is spiritual, not physical, and is the more rather than the less dangerous for that. The images of armor and helmet indicate that shrapnel is flying through the air fully able to pierce and slash without warning. By themselves these images could indicate that the appropriate posture of the Christian is defensive and crouching behind protective covering. The world is a dangerous place which we do well to keep at a distance.

Without denying that indiscriminate absorption of our cultural artifacts tends to produce minds closed to the Gospel, the breastplate of faith and hope in God's power and fidelity to his promises and the breastplate of love for God and of the people he died to redeem, gives us warrant to face the world with sobriety, to be sure, but also without crippling fear and also with full confidence in his victory.

– Father John Dominic Corbett, O.P.

*W*HAT FAITH BASICALLY MEANS is just that this shortfall that we all have in our love is made up by the surplus of Jesus Christ's love, acting on our behalf. He simply tells us that God himself has poured out among us a superabundance of his love and has thus made good in advance all our deficiency. Ultimately, faith means nothing other than admitting that we have this kind of shortfall; it means opening our hand and accepting a gift. In its simplest and innermost form, faith is nothing but reaching that point in love at which we recognize that we, too, need to be given something. Faith is thus that stage in love which really distinguishes it as love; it consists in over-coming the complacency and self-satisfaction of the person who says, "I have done everything, I don't need any further help." It is only in "faith" like this that self-ishness, the real opposite of love, comes to an end. To that extent, faith is already present in and with true loving; it simply represents that impulse in love which leads to its finding its true self: the openness of some-one who does not insist on his own capabilities, but is aware of receiving something as a gift and of stand-ing in need of it.

– Pope Benedict XVI

Lazarus

ONE OF THE MOMENTS on the journey of grief is when it becomes hard, maybe impossible, to remember the sound of the deceased's voice. Scripture scholars tell us that aside from the Passion, the story of Lazarus is the longest narrative found in John's Gospel. Yet not once, before he dies or after his return from the dead, do we hear Lazarus speak. It seems odd that after being at the center of one of the most dramatic moments in Jesus' ministry, Lazarus has nothing to tell us. Or does he?

The lack of words does not lessen the power of his story. After all the worry and anger, there is that moment when Jesus stands before the tomb. With tears streaming down his face, Jesus commands, "Lazarus, come out." And he does. The image of Lazarus, soon to be loosed of his burial shroud, offers us the meaning of the story. Jesus calls each of us by name. He desires that we come out of the darkness of anger, despair, and sin. He desires the feelings of shame and fear be torn from us like a burial shroud. Lazarus, whose name means "God is my help," is a symbol of all Jesus wants to do for us today.

– Monsignor Gregory E. S. Malovetz

*T*HE REALIZATION FINALLY DAWNS: **God really ex-ists. Christ really exists. The Church has re-ally been founded by his will, and manifests** his creative activity in history.

The person feels the impulse to belong. His first attempt may be a failure. He drifts away. He is disillusioned by the signs of human weakness he finds there, by the low cultural level, by the narrow spiritual outlook. He is repelled by what is strange or contradictory. But at length conviction matures and he moves towards the reality which is calling him. This is not merely a provisional engagement, one that can be revised in the light of subsequent experiences, but a final irrevocable decision that he makes. He binds his person, by a bond of loyalty, he attaches his inner being to the reality which confronts him. This engagement expresses itself in a profession of faith, and is consummated by the act of baptism, which introduces the new convert to the mystery of an ever creative God, in the "rebirth by water and the Holy Spirit."

Now he bears within him the seed of a new life. He stands upon the threshold of a new existence. A new form of existence presses for recognition, and the life of faith begins with all its manifold duties.

– Monsignor Romano Guardini

Let Freedom Ring!

FREEDOM IS OURS among all created things:
Freedom! It can ring in our hearts,
clear, on the march
or it can clang with the noise that is in us,
around us
distorting our expressions
disordering our air;
we pollute the day with darkness—
our freedom gone awry.
Watch the birds taking flight!
Our humanity they fly!
They do not stray from their goal.
Not so the human heart
gone cold.
But the Christ heart builds the Body
glows
trumpets victory over shining seas
releases those not free
strengthens our vast land
where peoples come with hope
for what's been promised long ago.
What do they find?
Stealth, aggression, over-possession?
Or freedom to look for and breathe
life, liberty, happiness—
all accents, colors, creeds?
Is the promise just our spirit?
Is the Spirit lost in dreams?
Children of the Church, whose victory do we bleed?

– Rita A. Simmonds

Simon of Cyrene

"THEY PRESSED INTO SERVICE A PASSER-BY, Simon, a Cyrenian, who was coming in from the country, the father of Alexander and Rufus, to carry his cross" (Mk 15:21).

Jesus had told his disciples that they must take up their cross, and follow him. He had not told them that one man, this Simon, would quite literally do just that. Scourged within an inch of his life, Jesus fell to the earth while carrying the bitter tree up the path to the Skull Place. Simon then bore the weight upon his own shoulders for awhile, and so an ordinary Jew was granted the high honor of partaking of the sacrifice of his own Savior. It is an honor, then, and a duty, and a joy, granted in turn to every Christian wayfarer.

Simon had come all the way from the coast of North Africa to celebrate the Passover in Jerusalem. He could not have known how profound a role he would play in the ultimate Passover. Saint Mark says that he is the father of Alexander and Rufus, naming them as if they were known friends. If so, then Simon too must have learned to follow Jesus in faith, after he had followed him in suffering.

– Anthony Esolen

What the Catholic faith believes about Mary
is based on what it believes about Christ,
and what it teaches about Mary
illumines in turn its faith in Christ.
(CCC 487)

"BEHOLD, I am the handmaid of the Lord. May it be done to me according to your word" (Lk 1:38). With these words Mary expresses her sense of identity and vocation. By her faith the entire meaning of her life derives from her relation to God and her place in his plan of love that is fulfilled in Jesus Christ. Her whole being is to be the Mother of God and to cooperate in Jesus' mission of redemption. If Mary sees herself as totally involved in the mystery of Christ, how could the Church see her differently? Thus, we can only understand Mary in light of Christ's mission to reveal God's love.

At the same time, Mary's place in this mystery and mission brings home to us God's great regard for human dignity. By contemplating Mary in faith, we discover that God desires our free and active cooperation in the accomplishment of his plan of love. We discover that by the power of his grace we can live up to our vocation. In Mary we discover that by his love for us God desires that we be his friends, his associates, and co-workers in Christ's redeeming love.

– Douglas Bushman

*G*OD CALLS EACH ONE according to his nature and in his own way. In the last resort, becoming a believer always means the same thing: another reality looms before the man who was formerly enclosed in his own being, in his own world; before him, in him, or above him, however we may express it—another reality, belonging to another world, from above, from beyond. This reality, this "beyond," becomes more concrete, grows in strength; its truth, its goodness, its holiness become more definite and demand the allegiance of him who has been called. The decision to entrust one's own existence to the strange reality which surpasses it, the sacrifice of one's own self-sufficiency and of the independence of one's own world, will be difficult. It will mean a rude shock and a gamble. Christ has said: "He who possesses his soul, will lose it; but he who gives his soul, will find it." Hence the soul must first lose itself by recognizing that there is a second goal; and then must recognize that beyond there lies the true goal.

– Monsignor Romano Guardini

The Good Thief

NAMED THE THIEF WHO STOLE HEAVEN, this man nailed to a bar may as well be called the greatest gymnast of all time. For who has made a greater leap of faith than this crucified man casting his eternal lot with a traitor and blasphemer? Or we might call the more accurately named good criminal the greatest wrestler in history, for though pinned to the cross, he escapes its fierce hold and secures victory. Perhaps this convict is convicted by the only words he would ever hear Jesus cry: "Father, forgive them, they know not what they do" (Lk 23:34).

Allowed only a few short verses in Luke, the good criminal will make the most of it by manifesting three outstanding virtues. Despite excruciating pain that dulls the sense, he makes a public confession of his sins that exonerates those who have punished him. He then encloses this grasp of justice within a reverence for God, to whom he recognizes he must ultimately answer. Finally, he places his reverence for God in the heart of Jesus, to whom he turns with a startling act of faith in divine and human mercy. On the most godless stage of human cruelty that warped human justice could erect, the good thief steals our thunder of outburst and complaint, of protest and lament, by believing that even in circumstances from hell he could seize heaven.

– Father Lawrence J. Donohoo

"May you fight a good fight by having faith
and a good conscience. Some, by rejecting conscience,
have made a shipwreck of their faith."
(1 Tm 1:18b-19)

IS IT REALLY POSSIBLE to reject conscience? Yes, of course. The baby is crying. Should I get up to feed him? Yes. Will I get up to feed him? I might not. If not, then I have rejected conscience.

But there is a more radical way of rejecting conscience. It involves not seeing your actions through the lens of right and wrong at all.

Imagine yourself ordering a plate of scrambled eggs for breakfast. Someone asks you if the plate of scrambled eggs is right or wrong. The question makes no sense to you. You think that eggs are tasty or hot or cold, not right or wrong.

There are human beings who evaluate their acts the way you evaluate your eggs. Ask them if they enjoy what they do and they will know what you mean. Ask them if what they do is right or wrong and they won't. Such people are called sociopaths.

Sociopaths are sociopaths because they can't imagine themselves in anyone else's shoes. That's why they can make no sense of the Golden Rule. That's why they can't imagine God putting himself in our shoes. That's why they can't have living faith. May God have mercy on them.

– Father John Dominic Corbett, O.P.

"O LORD, you find your delight in being with us, but do we find ours in being with you? Especially do we, who have the privilege of dwelling so near your altar, perhaps even in your very own house, find our delight in being with you? Oh! how much coldness, indifference, and even insults you have to endure in this Sacrament, while you remain there to help us by your presence!

"O God, present in the Eucharist, O Bread of Angels, O heavenly Food, I love you; but you are not, nor am I, satisfied with my love. I love you, but I love you too little! Banish from my heart, O Jesus, all earthly affections and give place, or better, give the whole place to your divine love. To fill me with yourself, and to unite yourself entirely to me, you come down from heaven upon the altar every day; justly then, should I think of nothing else but of loving, adoring, and pleasing you. I love you with my whole soul, with all my strength. If you want to make a return for my love, increase it and make it always more ardent!" (Saint Alphonsus)

– Father Gabriel of Saint Mary Magdalen, O.C.D.

The Centurion at the Cross

THE DAY STARTED OUT AS USUAL. My squad and I were up early, getting ready for the day's round of executions. One of the criminals had made a real ruckus lately—the whole city seemed to want his head on a platter. So we lit into him pretty good, then led him through the streets, glistening red in the sun. But he kept falling, so we yanked a foreigner out of the crowd to get the beam up the hill. At noon we stuck him to the wood.

That's when the day started getting strange. First he said something to the one on his right: "Today you will be with me in Paradise" (Lk 23:43). It sounded like a door opening. I looked around, but nobody seemed to notice. People were jeering. My men were vying for his clothes. Then I looked over and saw his mother, with a teenager. "Woman, behold, your son" (Jn 19:26). That's what I heard— this kid was now her son. The door inched open some more. What I heard next made me stagger: "Father, forgive them, they know not what they do" (Lk 23:34).

Things were now out of hand. The door was moving, my heart was racing. The teenager looked over—suddenly he felt like my kid brother. That's when it hit me: I wanted to be a son, a child again. I wanted my humanity back. Then he died. Pushing the door wide open, I cried, "This man was innocent beyond doubt. Truly this man was the Son of God!" (Lk 23:47; Mk 15:39).

– Andrew Matt

The Church's faith precedes, engenders,
supports and nourishes our faith.
(CCC 181)

It is not always easy to believe all the time, to practice this virtue of faith. There are many things in our Catholic Faith that may rub us the wrong way on certain occasions. The Church's teachings on contraception, the death penalty, and the indissolubility of marriage, for example, are not the ways of the world. The ways of the world, however, would be much "easier" to accept and embrace. Instead, the theological virtue of faith asks us to submit not to the world but rather to truth himself. Faith requires us to submit our entire intellect and will to the Lord, and not to the latest polls in the *New York Times*.

This might be one reason why the Lord blesses us with his Church, so that we would have a place where we belong, where our life is being lived in union with other people living the same way. The Church strengthens our lives of faith by reminding us of those who have lived this faith before us. The saints, the martyrs, and perhaps even members of our own families have been examples to us for living the faith. The Church brings us all together in that one act of profession of faith.

– Father James M. Sullivan, O.P.

Faith and the Luminous Mysteries of the Rosary

❨ *The Baptism of the Lord* – Baptism is the sacrament of faith. Baptism was instituted to destroy the sin in us so that it could never again give birth to death. May I imitate the gesture of self-emptying Jesus manifests at his baptism. May I constantly turn to the Father in my nothingness and in the confident dependence of faith.

❨ *The Wedding Feast of Cana* – In the miracle of the water made wine at Cana, Jesus revealed his glory, and his disciples began to believe in him. May daily problems and the experience of need move me to place my trust in our Savior's providential care for me. May my struggles deepen my belief in Christ's compassion.

❨ *The Preaching of the Kingdom* – Faith comes through hearing. The preaching of the Church brings me to belief; the Word of God nourishes my faith. May I grow in my conversion and become a credible witness. May God use me to open the hearts and minds of many to the desire for God and for true life.

❨ *The Transfiguration* – The Transfiguration of Jesus aims to strengthen the disciples' faith in anticipation of the Passion. May I believe in the radiant life of holiness Jesus reveals in his Transfiguration. May I grow in my belief that what I behold in the miracle of the Lord's Transfiguration is what he desires me to become.

❨ *The Institution of the Eucharist* – At the Last Supper Jesus blesses us with his supreme gift: the Holy Eucharist, sum and summary of our faith. May my way of thinking become more and more attuned to the Eucharist, and may the Eucharist in turn confirm my way of thinking, filling me with confidence.

– Father Peter John Cameron, O.P.

Mary, the Mother of James and Joses

THIS MARY is the mother of James the younger (traditionally, James, the son of Alphaeus; thus one of the twelve disciples) and of Joses (a "brother," i.e., possibly cousin of Christ). She is a witness to the crucifixion. She is also among the women who follow Christ from Galilee and, at dawn on the first day of the week, go to the tomb with spices in order to anoint the body.

"Who will roll away the stone?" the women ask each other. When they look up, the stone had been rolled away. As they enter the tomb, they see a young man dressed in white who tells them, "Do not be alarmed. He is risen!"

At which point—and who among us would not do the same?—"They went out and fled from the tomb, seized with trembling and bewilderment. They said nothing to anyone, for they were afraid" (Mk 16:8).

Like us, Mary, the mother of one of Christ's disciples, knows that she stands to be scorned and shunned. Like us, she isn't sure what she's seen, nor that she can believe what she's seen. Like us, she is afraid for herself and she also must be terribly afraid for her son.

Think of the courage to go and dress the body of the crucified one. Think of the courage to continue to stand—under the circumstances—with your son, with Christ, with Christ's mother.

– Heather King

The Great Faith of the Saints

FAITH IS A VIRTUE that reveals itself most powerfully when it is put to the test, a lesson we learn from the saints.

It was by faith that Saint Monica, persisting in her prayers and tears, won the conversion of her son Saint Augustine. It was by faith that the priest and religious founder Saint Dominic, fervently offering Mass for a man who had died falling from a horse, obtained the man's restoration to life. It was by faith that the missionary Saint Francis Xavier endured endless months at sea, stifling heat and humidity in Indonesia, and deep snow in Japan to lead souls to God. It was faith that kept the virgin Saint Rose of Lima on her knees before the Blessed Sacrament for over twenty hours from Holy Thursday to Good Friday, knowing that she was in the presence of God. It was by faith that the Vienna archbishop Saint Clement Hofbauer, armed only with his rosary beads, wrought the deathbed conversions of obstinate sinners.

It is faith that has made the saints willing to lose all for the winning of Christ. In March of 1941, the Franciscan priest and martyr Saint Maximilian Kolbe, having been arrested by the Nazis, was in his prison cell when a Gestapo officer became enraged at the sight of his religious habit. The Nazi seized the priest's rosary beads and held up the crucifix before the prisoner's face, shouting, "Imbecile, idiot, filthy priest, tell me if you believe in that." Father Kolbe calmly replied in a strong voice, "Yes, I believe." The Gestapo officer struck the priest across the face twice and asked him again, "Well, do you still believe?" Once more, Father Kolbe answered, "Oh yes, I believe." The Nazi now pummeled the prisoner's face with further blows. Struggling to keep himself erect, Father Kolbe remained face to face with his persecutor. The officer then asked, "And now will you tell me that you still believe?" The priest's answer was the same: "Yes, I do believe." The Nazi thereupon beat and kicked Father Kolbe until he collapsed. After the officer left the cell, the priest told his fellow prisoners, "My friends, you ought to rejoice with me; it is for souls, for the Immaculata!"

Faith gives us certainty about the things that matter most, a certainty that no earthly power can shake.

– James Monti

"Faith, in its deepest essence,
is the openness of the human heart to the gift:
to God's self-communication in the Holy Spirit."
– Blessed John Paul II

Mary, the Wife of Clopas

MARY, wife of Clopas, is mentioned just once in the Gospels. She is a witness of the crucifixion, specifically, to the wrenching moment when, from the cross, Christ turns to his mother and says, "Woman, behold, your son" (Jn 19:26), and then turns to John, "the disciple…whom he loved" (Jn 19:27), and says, "Behold, your mother" (Jn 19:27).

We, too, can stand at the foot of the cross and witness this wrenching intersection of hard news and good news. *I, your beloved son, am dying but I present you with another kind of son. I, your beloved friend, am dying, but here, in Mary, is sister, brother, mother, father, another kind of friend.*

We know something of the Last Supper, but it is interesting to imagine "the Next Supper": the meal on Good Friday night—for even in shock, in trauma, we still hunger. We can picture Mary, Christ's mother, John, Mary of Clopas, and some of the others at table together. Incoherent with grief, barely able to pass the plate and the cup, even so, they must have had the stirrings of the knowledge that Christ is the Way, the Truth, and the Life. Stupefied with sorrow, even then they must have realized that he has given them, in a new way, to each other.

– Heather King

"Deacons must be dignified,…holding fast
to the mystery of faith with a clear conscience."
(1 Tm 3:8-9)

"THE MYSTERY OF FAITH" refers to God's confiding of his loving plan for the saving of the world. The Father confides this plan to his Son who carries it out by his acceptance of a redemptive death on the cross, by his rising from the dead, and by his sending of the Spirit which engrafts all who are willing into his same obedience, death, and rising.

"Holding fast" implies endurance in personally appropriating this mystery. It means holding fast to the Savior's cross as the years lengthen and it becomes ever clearer that God will settle for nothing less than everything.

Having "a clear conscience" is less about minute spiritual bookkeeping and more about access to God. Having a clear conscience is about the ability truly to enter God's presence in worship with nothing in the way. Of course, this is only possible because Jesus our High Priest has already once and for all entered the heavenly sanctuary, come into his Father's presence, and poured out his blood before God on our behalf.

Deacons minister to this mystery. By their words they preach it. By their charitable service they embody it. Their dignity is great.

– Father John Dominic Corbett, O.P.

To proclaim the faith and to plant his reign,
Christ sends his apostles and their successors.
(CCC 935)

FAITH ACCEPTS ALL that God does as unquestionably wise. Throughout salvation history, God works through mediators. He does not need Moses to save Israel from slavery in Egypt, yet he answers the cry of Hebrew slaves by sending Moses to free them. Moses is so closely associated with God that, upon seeing the miracle of their deliverance, the people "believed in him *and in his servant Moses*" (Ex 14:31 emphasis added). This pattern continues throughout the Bible. Because God sends judges and prophets to guide his people, he takes the rejection of his messengers as rejection of himself (Jer 7:21-26).

Jesus stands in continuity with this divine wisdom with respect to the Apostles: "Whoever listens to you listens to me. Whoever rejects you rejects me. And whoever rejects me rejects the one who sent me" (Lk 10:16). Because they are sent by Christ and empowered by the Holy Spirit, faith receives the Apostles' teaching, not as the word of men but as the Word of God (1 Thes 2:13). Our faith is only in God; if it concerns the Apostles, it is because of his wisdom in choosing them, and their successors, to represent him.

– Douglas Bushman

Joseph of Arimathea

AFTER THE SUPREME AGONY of the Passion, in a way recalling the peace of the Christmas beginning, Luke speaks of another man named Joseph, a member of the Sanhedrin, the Jewish supreme court. He starts as a secret disciple of Jesus, but this "virtuous and righteous man" (Lk 23:50), at the hour of trial, courageously stands for acquittal, no longer hiding his faith, as the court condemns Jesus and hands him over to Pilate. And having stood up for Jesus once, his courage waxes on. This Jew dares to approach Pilate to ask for permission to bury Jesus. Finally, in death, Jesus is given over into loving hands. Joseph places him in his own tomb, in the midst of a garden, the Eden that will blossom with resurrected life.

There is a painting by Rogier van der Weyden, *The Descent from the Cross*, which depicts Mary as the New Eve in a posture of swooning which parallels that of the divine corpse: her Son's associate in the depths of his love-suffering. And though Jesus' foster father is dead, there's also a Joseph present at the crucifixion. Van der Weyden shows an older man holding Jesus under the arms, almost certainly Joseph, recalling those paintings that show God the Father upholding the arms of his Son on the cross, in his victorious agony of love. By faith, we too participate in this victory of love.

– J. David Franks

*F*AITH, IN THE CHRISTIAN SENSE, has a unique and exclusive character.... Say to a man, for example, who has given to another not only his respect and his sympathy, but his complete love, involving body and soul and his whole being: "Love is a general feeling which many different kinds of people experience for each other, you, someone else, or anybody at all." He will perhaps look at you skeptically and then turn away. For what kind of an answer can he give to words which wound him so deeply? If he did speak, this is what he would say: "My love is not a mere accident! I do not feel a general love which may be applicable to me or to anybody at all! My love belongs to one person in particular and stands or falls with him. That is its gamble, its pricelessness. That person is my love!" Such a person would immediately understand me should I say that faith cannot be torn from its content.

Faith is its content. It is determined by that which it believes. Belief is the living movement towards him in whom one believes. It is the living answer to the call of him who appears in revelation and draws men to him in grace.

– Monsignor Romano Guardini

Cleopas

ONE OF THE MOST BELOVED PASSAGES in the Easter Gospels recounts the journey of the two disciples on the road to Emmaus—a road that may be understood as the journey of faith. The two disciples, Cleopas and his unnamed companion, are walking to a nearby town on the first Easter evening. A stranger joins them, and they are amazed that he has not heard about all that had happened in Jerusalem in the past several days.

The two disciples know the events but not their significance. The stranger begins to put the events into a new context: that is, he interprets them through passages from the Bible and shows the disciples how these events are part of God's plan for the salvation of the world. The stranger explains the Scriptures, and the disciples' hearts burn within them—a mysterious and beautiful phrase.

But the disciples do not recognize the risen Christ until they encounter him in the breaking of the bread. Thus they move from faith to insight, and so do we. This passage from Saint Luke's Gospel is the oldest account of the structure of the Mass: proclamation of the Scripture, application of it to the people in a homily, and the Eucharistic action. For us, too, our faith is fulfilled when Christ becomes truly present—Body, Blood, soul, and divinity—upon the altar.

– Father Joseph T. Lienhard, s.j.

OH GOD, give me the courage to call you Father. You know that I do not always give you the attention you deserve. You do not forget me, even though I so often live far from the light of your face.

Come close, despite everything, despite my sin however great or small, secret or public, it may be. Give me inner peace, that which only you know how to give. Give me the strength to be true, sincere; tear away from my face the masks that obscure the awareness that I am worthy only because I am your son. Forgive me my faults and grant me the possibility to do good.

Shorten my sleepless nights; grant me the grace of a conversion of heart.

Remember, Father, those who are outside of here and still love me, that thinking of them, I remember that only love gives life, while hate destroys and resentment transforms into hell long and endless days. Remember me, oh God. Amen.

– A prayer by an inmate named Stefan recited during Pope Benedict XVI's visit to the Roman District Prison of Rebibbia, December 18, 2011

*F*AITH MAY ALSO BE RE-WON in the most varied ways. If it is achieved through a proper deepening of the personality, once one arrives at a certain maturity reality is accepted for what it is, without capitulating before it, strong in one's faith. Such faith makes sure of its independence with regard to the world. It becomes more deeply rooted in its own ground and may oppose to existence an attitude which does not expect agreement, but extricates itself from all opposition or disappointment deriving from reality, and emphasizes itself, as against such reality, by an "And nevertheless!" Such a person may even find a deep, grim satisfaction in acknowledging that the world does not agree with him, that struggle is everywhere inevitable, and that the life of faith is itself a combat.

We may express this again in the following way: faith grows in character. To have character means that conviction maintains itself in the face of reality. Trust, discipline, perseverance all enter into faith; a tenacious struggle with reality, the maintenance of a position even when a successful outcome can hardly be predicted in the near or distant future.

Such is the faith of one who has matured, of the man or woman who lives by steadfastness without any illusions.

– Monsignor Romano Guardini

Mark the Evangelist

THE ROMAN NAME MARCUS is added to his own Jewish name John. His mother Mary makes her home a refuge for Peter upon his release from prison. So she sets a model of faith for her son. Mark's cousin, the Apostle Barnabas, takes him with Paul to Antioch. Not an Apostle himself, Mark is a sort of sidekick, all the while observing events with a keen eye. Paul seems to have been irritated when Mark returns to Jerusalem, and does not take him on his second apostolic trip. "One Lord, one faith, one baptism" (Eph 4:5) does not require one and the same personality. Faith unites the faithful without homogenizing them. Paul will write of Mark who finds the courage to go to Rome, though he must have dreaded it. Mark may also have gone to Asia Minor, for Paul asks Timothy to bring Mark back to Rome "for he is helpful to me in the ministry" (2 Tm 4:11).

Mark may witness the execution of Paul. He is also like a "son" to Peter who is about to be crucified (1 Pt 5:13). He writes the Gospel account of what the Apostles have told him, and some of which he may have seen himself. Faith enables him to help very different characters who might have found each other hard to live with, had they not shared "the peace of God that surpasses all understanding" (Phil 4:7).

– Father George William Rutler

"The love of money is the root of all evils,
and some people in their desire for it have strayed
from the faith and have pierced themselves
with many pains."

(1 Tm 6:10)

LOVE FOR MONEY is as much a symptom as a root of evil. Love of money can come from many places in our soul. It can come from chronic insecurity. It can come from desire for status and fuel desire for status. It can come from desire for power and can inflame that desire. It can come from love of luxury and leisure and plunge one further into the addictions that they bring.

There are three common reasons that people devoured by love of money stray from the faith. First of all they stray from the faithful. People tend to find time to spend with people who share their priorities. Someone in love with money has little in common with someone in love with God. Secondly, they stray from the commandments. Appetite clouds and sharpens perception, and someone alert to profit might be less alert to the demands of justice.

Finally, the love of money is never satisfied. That is why once it worms its way into the heart it is for ever pierced with dissatisfaction and can never find rest and contentment in the particular providences in which God directs our lives or say, "The LORD is my shepherd; I shall not want" (Ps 23:1).

– Father John Dominic Corbett, O.P.

*T*O BELIEVE MEANS to be aware of the living reality of God; but since God is love, the believer necessarily begins to seek love. The commandment to love God and to love neighbor as oneself leads us to become aware of and to live by the most profound force which springs from our relationship with God: namely charity. Saint Paul is always speaking about it: in his First Epistle to the Corinthians (1 Cor 13:2), he says: "If I should have all faith, so that I could remove mountains, and have not charity, I am nothing." Saint John sums up everything in charity, so that the pressing invitation to love becomes the primary law of Christian life. And Saint James does not hesitate to say that the faith which does not manifest itself in good works remains "dead." There is indeed a kind of faith without charity; but what the Apostle says of this shows what a frightful condition it is: You believe that there is one God. You do well. The devils also believe, and tremble. Faith without charity is a faith mixed with terror. Hence charity is the purest effect of faith; it emerges from it like the flower from the stock and roots....

At the beginning of faith love must be present. The faith of which Scripture speaks must have its roots in love.

– Monsignor Romano Guardini

*The Apostle's Creed associates faith in the forgiveness
of sins not only with faith in the Holy Spirit,
but also with faith in the Church and
in the communion of saints.*
(CCC 976)

To BELIEVE IN CHRIST is to believe in God's mercy and the forgiveness of sins. Christ reveals the Father's mercy (Parable of the Prodigal Son), forgives sins (the paralytic, the penitent woman, the woman caught in adultery, the repentant thief, Saints Peter and Paul), and offers himself in sacrifice. Faith in God's mercy and forgiveness is inseparable from faith in the Holy Spirit, the Church, and the communion of saints because these are the fruit of Christ's sacrifice for sins. He sends the Holy Spirit so that sins may be forgiven (Jn 20:22-23). He institutes the sacraments and sends the Apostles to continue his "ministry of reconciliation" (2 Cor 5:18), empowering them by the Holy Spirit. Christ's forgiveness of sins thus continues through the action of the Holy Spirit, working through the Church's hierarchy and sacraments, and through the intercessions and merits of all who are united in the communion of saints. The saints pray for what Christ prays and dies for, namely, the forgiveness of sins. The apostolic Church, then, is the place where we encounter God's merciful love and our sins are forgiven.

– Douglas Bushman

Mary, the Mother of Mark

P ETER HAS JUST ESCAPED FROM PRISON. The angel has come in the night, loosened his chains, helped him pass the first and second guard, and let him through the iron gate leading into the city of Jerusalem.

Immediately, he goes to the house of Mary, "the mother of John who is called Mark, [i.e., Mark the Evangelist], where there were many people gathered in prayer" (Acts 12:12).

A maid goes to the gate and reports back, astonished, that it is Peter. The consensus inside the house is: "You are mad." Nonetheless, floored with joy, they admit him. He tells them of the angel, asks them to report back to James and to the brethren, and departs.

That is all one kind of miracle, but maybe another kind is that during this time of persecution, "many people gathered in prayer" together—presumably all through the night. Peter knows just where to go. He knows where the people of faith would be gathered, and he knows that they would be praying. Perhaps Mark himself is there that night, at the house of his mother. Perhaps he is thinking of the time Peter knocked at the gate when later he will write: "Watch, therefore; you do not know when the lord of the house is coming" (Mk 13:35).

– Heather King

*T*O BELIEVE IN GOD means to have a certain "vision" of him; to experience to a certain extent that he is there, that the world exists and is centered on him, as Saint Paul says in his Epistle to the Romans: "From the creation of the world, his invisible attributes are seen by his works, his eternal power also and his divinity" (cf. Rm. 1:20). God emerges from all that is around me, from what I am, and from what constitutes the framework of my existence. But how ambiguous all these terms are! Obviously nature does not reveal God to us the way the needle of a barometer indicates the air pressure. It rather suggests him both as an explanation and as a mystery. The world speaks of God, but in an ambiguous way, because it speaks through the confusion and chaos of sin. By listening to its words, one man will hear the echo of divine wisdom; another will only perceive cold indifference, or even ill will and betrayal. For the world reveals God, but hides him at the same time: God is indeed its creator and its model image, but he is also the Other One, the Unknown, hidden by evil. Moreover, when the "works" in question are men, the world of men, or the history of men; when it is myself who is involved— what appears to or happens in me—how dubiously all this speaks of God!

– Monsignor Romano Guardini

Rhoda

Poor Rhoda! She must have been teased for years. As the servant of Mary, the mother of John Mark, she answers the knock at the gateway door. "She was so overjoyed when she recognized Peter's voice that, instead of opening the gate, she ran in and announced that Peter was standing at the gate" (Acts 12:14). Peter is supposed to be in jail, not standing outside her door. Luke, the author of Acts, relishes the comic picture of the first pope, just miraculously released by an angel from chains, two guards, and an iron city gate, only to be left stranded outside the Christian safe-house by the maid.

Despite her forgetfulness, Rhoda is truly a model of faith. Unlike Thomas the Apostle, she doesn't have to see in order to believe: she only hears Peter's voice, and she grasps that God has worked a wonder. And, like the women who first saw Jesus, her "story seemed" to the listeners "like nonsense" (Lk 24:11). They insist, "You are out of your mind," but she holds her ground. They relent: "It is his angel" (Acts 12:15). They resolve the argument by opening the door and beholding Peter, who explains everything and departs. Rhoda knows in her bones that nothing is impossible for God, so she is quick to believe when others doubt. And she is a great patron saint for those of us who tend to absent-mindedness.

– Angela Franks

*T*o LOVE, from the human point of view, is first of all to admit the existence of a being greater than myself, who demands a sacrifice on my part. To love means to be prepared to meet the Most High, not to shun this encounter, but to seek it in order to realize that it is only in the gift that this encounter will involve that I can truly find myself. This attitude awakens in me all that speaks of God, and enables me to see him.

But, God has revealed himself in a special and precise way in Jesus Christ; so that "he who sees me, sees the Father." In Christ "came a light into the world," this world namely created by the "Word" who is the same as Christ.... For God has spoken; his messengers have brought his Word to us to instruct our minds, to direct and fortify our hearts....

With regard to the Son it is said: "no one can come to him unless the Father who sent me draw him."... Of Christ we know that men have not received him, they have hardened their hearts against him. Finally, it is said that the Word of God cannot be understood unless the heart is touched and the mind opened, yet the devil can certainly tear him from the heart in spite of the most sustained effort. In order to be perceived by man, the revelation of God in Christ, the Word of God, demands a lively readiness, grace, and love.

– Monsignor Romano Guardini

"I am already being poured out like a libation,
and the time of my departure is at hand.
I have competed well; I have finished the race;
I have kept the faith."

(2 Tm 4:6-7)

HERE IS JOY. Here is confidence. Here is someone who knows salvation is very near. He is filled with confidence, not ignorance or arrogance or presumption. How can he be so sure?

He is confident because he knows his God. He knows that the fidelity and mercy of him who has called him to preach the Gospel will sustain him in the grace that has already saved so many.

He is confident because, as he feels the time of his natural life drawing to a close, he can also feel his spirit being lifted up by the will of God who is pouring it out in love and in sacrifice and in adoration.

He is confident because he knows so much of his life has already been disposed of by God. Yet if it is true that, as the philosophers say, we do not possess our life in any single instant but only successively in each moment, then it follows that we can only give it away in each moment and can only give it completely over in love as it ends. Paul feels this moment approach, and he cannot contain his joy.

May we so live that we may so die. Amen.

– Father John Dominic Corbett, O.P.

OW DOES THE MOTHER love her child? How does this love come about? He who does not yet exist but will someday be formed in her blood is first of all loved by the mother through her disposition to conceive him. Then she feels in herself something alive, and her love grows in proportion as this body develops distinct from her own. Through this love she becomes aware of it, and believes in the purpose and realization of the existence of this child. And when she has brought him forth into the world and looks at him in her arms, her eyes are then capable of the most profound kind of knowledge, for her heart has now passed through the hard school of patience and love.… God is independent and free, he is essentially "himself," but he assumes shape and appearance with regard to me; he presents himself to me according as I am; he demands to be received into my thought and into my life, to become "my God." To believe fully, does this not mean that God has become my God? That he "is born in me," as the masters of the spiritual life say? But this mystery only takes place in love—and the first act of love consists in giving oneself to God in the light of this mystery.

– Monsignor Romano Guardini

Luke the Evangelist

LUKE'S IS THE FIRST non-Jewish voice to record its impressions of the new fact of Christ in the world. The only Gentile author in Holy Scripture, Luke is a Greek. And like any outsider, there are many things that strike him differently than the way they strike others. For example, only in his Gospel do we hear the parable of the Prodigal Son and the Good Samaritan (Lk 10:30-37). And only Luke tells us of the sinful woman in the house of Simon the Pharisee (Lk 7:36–50), and the raising from the dead the son of the widow of Nain (Lk 7:11-17). And where would we be without his telling of the Christmas story and of the first years of the Church (Acts)? Thus, with a desire for accuracy (Lk 1:3; 3:1-2) that befits his profession as a doctor (Col 4:14) and detailed observer of humanity, he chronicles the life of Christ and the Church.

He discovers in Christ that the work of God aims first of all not at the powerful (Lk 16:19-31), or even the righteous or the good (Lk 15:11-32), but at the forgotten (Lk 16:19-31), the ostracized, and the repentant. He carries us along with him in his sense of amazement at what God is doing, leaving us amazed too.

– Father Vincent Nagle, F.S.C.B.

WE CAN DO NOTHING BETTER to promote the growth of our faith than to open our heart to love. To be generous enough to desire the existence of a Being who surpasses us, to wish to encounter the Most High in order to give ourselves to him. To adopt the bold, joyous attitude of one who does not fear for himself, for he knows that the gift of oneself is stronger and more creative than self-containment can be.

But all this remains still very much an earthly matter. We must open our heart to the mystery of love which comes from God, which is given by him in whom this love is a "theological virtue," is divine energy by which and in which God reveals himself to himself: the Father to the Son, the Son to the Father, and both in the Holy Spirit. It is this mystery in which grace allows us to share. God is "given" to us in grace and in love. It is by this mystery that faith lives. We must cling to this mystery if we wish to learn to know a living faith.

We may escape from the risk of indefiniteness and indifference if we adopt a serious attitude towards love there where it is felt most concretely: namely with regard to our neighbor.

– Monsignor Romano Guardini

When the Church celebrates the sacraments,
she confesses the faith received from the apostles....
The law of prayer is the law of faith:
the Church believes as she prays.
(CCC 1124)

THE SACRAMENTS are actions of God's love by which he imparts saving grace to us. He desires our free cooperation, and this requires that we understand the nature of his love. This is why revelation is always an invitation, and this invitation is repeated in every sacrament. God respects our free will, and says, in effect: Now that you know what it means for me to love you, will you consent actually to be loved? Will you allow me to love you?

We see this in Mary's faith at the Annunciation. Through Gabriel, God reveals his desire to make the supreme gift of his Son to Mary, and he awaits her consent. She does not conceive until the moment of her "Yes" in faith. In response, Mary is overshadowed by the Holy Spirit. She is loved in a new way by God, and by this love she is transformed to be the Mother of God.

Similarly, in the sacraments, God comes to love us, and faith, fully informed about what this means, freely consents to being loved by him.

– Douglas Bushman

Transfigured

WE JOURNEYED
with Jesus
on foot
up a high mountain.

At its peak
we closed our eyes.

Then there was light,
so much light
we could no longer sleep.
Another world
had broken in.

Where is my Lord?
What have you done to him?

The Master is not gone;
He is fully arrived—

God the Son
descends with us
cloaked in humankind.

– Rita A. Simmonds

Matthias

WHAT IF YOU FLIPPED A COIN in deciding if you should marry? Would you consider rolling dice in determining which job you should take? One might think that a risky way of making a choice. It was a part of the process by which Matthias is chosen as the one to replace Judas Iscariot among the Twelve. There are criteria: the one chosen has to have been an eyewitness to the ministry of Jesus and has to have experienced the risen Jesus. And they pray that the Holy Spirit will guide them. Matthias is chosen in the casting of lots. After that moment he is never mentioned again in the Scripture. All other information about him is legendary, vague, or contradictory.

Yet Matthias stands as a powerful witness to Christians who will come after him. Matthias could have said, "No, thank you," and walked away. Instead, he says, "Yes"—with no thought that anyone centuries later will remember anything he does. He understands that discipleship is revealing Jesus to others in the present moment, with no real concern about what will happen next week. To be guided by the Spirit means taking the risk in the present to live as an eyewitness of Gospel love.

– Monsignor Gregory E. S. Malovetz

*W*HEN AT THE END OF EACH DAY we look back on what we have done we are always conscious of our deficiencies; yet, in spite of this, we remain confident, for a time at least. We say to ourselves: The next time things will go better. Then gradually we become skeptical and ask ourselves where the redemption is of which faith speaks. Am I not a Christian? It is said that grace is in me and that a new man is to be born: what happens to him?... Life passes, its opportunities vanish and do not return; habit, resignation, and routine set in, and we ask ourselves anxiously, if not with despair: Where is the renewal of which faith spoke? This is the time really to grasp what hope which is against all hope means. This amounts to saying that the heavenly life is in us, even though we do not feel it; it grows in us despite all our efforts, thanks to God; our task is to remain calm, be patient, and always begin again. Instances of discouragement, hardening, and frustration are not mere simple appearances but the bitter truth: the blind resistance of worldly reality to redemption. And yet this inner life develops apace, for, coming from heaven, it triumphs over the world.

– Monsignor Romano Guardini

O GOD, all-powerful and all-knowing, without beginning and without end, you who are the source, the sustainer, and the rewarder of all virtues, grant that I may abide on the firm ground of faith, be sheltered by an impregnable shield of hope, and be adorned in the bridal garment of charity. Grant that I may through justice be subject to you, through prudence avoid the beguilements of the devil, through temperance exercise restraint, and through fortitude endure adversity with patience. Grant that whatever good things I have, I may share generously with those who have not and that whatever good things I do not have, I may request humbly from those who do. Grant that I may judge rightly the evil of the wrongs I have done and bear calmly the punishments I have brought upon myself, and that I may never envy my neighbor's possessions and ever give thanks for your good things.

– Saint Thomas Aquinas

Joseph, Candidate for Apostle

FOLLOWING THE TREACHERY OF JUDAS—who, having betrayed the Master, promptly goes off and hangs himself—it fell to the Apostles to find a fitting candidate to take his place. Two names are put forward, that of Joseph and Matthias, the latter of whom being chosen, poor Joseph is left to languish in second place. What becomes of this shadowy figure who misses the opportunity to be numbered among the Apostles by what appears to be a mere luck of the draw (Acts 1:26)?

The Scriptures of course are wholly silent on the matter. But surely the obvious inference is that while God may have chosen not to include him among the Apostles, he certainly wished him to remain a disciple. To what end? I think to remind the rest of us that the Son of Man has came to call everyone, including even those who finish second, because sanctity is not a self-help enterprise but a work of grace, dispensed by One the outcome of whose own life, seen in secular terms, was anything but a photo finish. A Crucified God is not a witness to worldly success. But, then, success, unlike faithfulness, was never a biblical category. So do not think poorly of this saintly man, who, as runner-up, failed to make first place. When we gain heaven we win the whole blooming sweepstakes.

– Regis Martin

Baptism is the sacrament of faith (Cf. Mk 16:16)....
It is only within the faith of the Church that each
of the faithful can believe.
(CCC 1253)

"FAITH COMES FROM WHAT IS HEARD, and what is heard comes through the word of Christ" (Rom 10:17). Faith is our response to Christ's witness to the Father and his love, and to the witness of the Holy Spirit and the Apostles to Christ. This witness is pure gift of love, and faith receives it as a gift. Faith itself is a gift, coming from God himself, through the community of believers, the Church. Though coming to faith and living in faith require an effort of co-operation on our part, no one achieves, earns, or gives himself faith, just as no one achieves, earns, or gives himself baptism.

By baptism the Church gives spiritual birth to her sons and daughters. They become members of God's family. Just as children are their parents' heirs, so baptism makes us God's children who inherit the Church's faith. The Church labors on behalf of her children, by evangelizing and pro-claiming this faith through the example and words of her members. Then at baptism parents and godparents are entrusted to catechize; representing the Church, they are the first apostles whom Jesus sends to witness to and to teach the Church's faith to their children.

– Douglas Bushman

*I*T IS NECESSARY FOR US to pay our due to reality, to recognize the real seriousness of evil and corruption. Man must also make his way, plunged in darkness which seems to make the path of the redeemed as impossible as the work of the Redeemer. Here too we must believe. The victory will not be vouchsafed to us in this world; redemption cannot be seen from here in all its fulfillment. Fulfillment will come only beyond the grave. But there is an assurance which enables us to bear up until we get there, namely hope.

In the last few sentences we have used the words faith and hope interchangeably, and with reason. Faith and hope are not identical, but they reveal, in different ways, one and the same life. This is the life we call faith, in order to designate the consciousness we have of the reality of God in Christ and our faithfulness towards him. But it is also an awareness of victory and achievement, in spite of an apparently preponderant opposition; it is the certainty of salvation, in spite of the objection of the world which deems the thing impossible. From this point of view, we call it hope.

– Monsignor Romano Guardini

Stephen

IT IS A WONDER what drug store reading glasses can do. Words and letters that are blurry before you purchase the glasses become clear as you drive away. Stephen is chosen as one of several to serve as deacons so that the Apostles can do the work of teaching and preaching. We are told that he has the face of an angel, and through signs and wonders leads others to know Jesus. Stephen encounters religious leaders whose vision is not only blurry. They are blinded by ego and complacency. Stephen is led before them, and in a beautiful speech (Acts 7:2-53) explains how the current leaders are as blind and misguided as their ancestors. The rage of the leaders becomes murderous, and they order Stephen to be stoned. Before he dies, he looks up into the heavens and sees Jesus.

In our lives, we may clearly see Jesus in times of joy and in moments of service. But our vision may become blurry when there are disagreements or we face someone's anger. It is Stephen who encourages us not to look down in despair. He challenges us to look up and realize that not even the tensions and tragedies of life can cloud the presence of Jesus.

– Monsignor Gregory E. S. Malovetz

*"We are not among those who draw back and perish,
but among those who have faith and will possess life."*
(Heb 10:39)

Aunt Bertha was a pleasantly aging "matriarch" of her family. No one would ever suspect she was full of anxiety over many things, especially her *pleasantly aging* and losing touch with the younger generation. And so she drank. It helped to take the edge off her anxiety. She drank more and more as the years rolled by, and every night would cross an invisible line into alcoholic oblivion. She drew back from everyone who noticed that Aunt Bertha had a drinking problem. She was filled with denial, fear, and isolation. And when she woke up one morning in a holding cell of the local jail, having driven her car onto the sidewalk and into a storefront, she had no faith that things would ever be better.

Any addiction robs us of our physical, mental, and spiritual life. It robs us of the daily rhythm of our family's dance; we escape; we draw back; we perish.

Faith assures us that God wants us to be. Whatever anxiety we find ourselves in, we know that God will not abandon us. We do not have to perish well before we die, but accept life on life's terms, and trust that God brings about the good, even in our most desperate circumstances. And we not only hear the music; we get up and dance.

– Father Jacob Restrick, O.P.

*M*ANY THINGS SEEM POSSIBLE FOR...faith which others would deem difficult or impossible. When apparently insoluble problems like the following arise: How can eternal God have created time and the finite? How could he have loved this perishable human creature planted on this atom of dust which is the earth? How could he have developed on the latter a Sacred History? How is it possible for God to have become man? How can he remain for all eternity and yet sacrifice himself for man? Then such faith has a ready answer full of sanctity: "Love does such things." This is, for such a type of faith, the ultimate answer....

In the last resort, the criteria of this form of faith are: that is possible which can be achieved by love; that is true which is believable on the part of love; that is good which enables love to exist and grow. These criteria assume particular significance from the fact that the one who loves is God and that love possesses his holy magnanimity and his infinite power. In this way a perspective opens up, a transmutation takes place of all our value judgments concerning the world which are essential to the Christian life.

– Monsignor Romano Guardini

Philip

PHILIP is one of the first seven deacons or servers ordained in Jerusalem (Acts 6:5). Later in the Book of Acts, Paul and Luke meet Philip in the seacoast town of Caesarea. There he is identified as "the evangelist"; and further, we read that he has four unmarried daughters with the gift of prophecy (Acts 21:8-9).

Acts 8 narrates several events in Philip's life. After the martyrdom of Stephen a persecution breaks out in Jerusalem, and the Christians there are dispersed. Philip goes north to Samaria and preaches with great success. He even converts and baptizes Simon the Magician there.

Then an angel sends Philip south to Gaza, where he meets the Ethiopian eunuch, who is riding in his carriage reading the prophet Isaiah. Philip is running next to the carriage. The Ethiopian invites him into the carriage and asks about the meaning of a passage in Isaiah. Philip explains how it refers to Christ; the eunuch comes to faith and asks for baptism. Philip deserves the title "the evangelist," the one who proclaims the saving Gospel of Jesus Christ. He can also be a patron for the Year of Faith, interceding for all who read the Scriptures and inquire about the Christian faith. Like Philip, we might run alongside them and encourage them in their journey to faith.

– Father Joseph T. Lienhard, S.J.

What faith confesses, the sacraments communicate.
(CCC 1692)

GIFT AND LOVE GO TOGETHER. Love's proper act is to bestow gifts. So, to confess the greatness of God's gifts is to make an act of faith in his love. "We have come to know and to believe in the love God has for us" (1 Jn 4:16). Love begins with a desire, an intention of something good for those we love. Yet, we often confront the limitations of our own love, finding ourselves unable to confer the intended gift. It is not so with God. God's love is effective, and believing this is the foundation for faith in the sacraments as signs that cause the grace they signify. Grace cannot be verified in any way. We can only know it has been imparted by faith in Christ's promise. In baptism, water is seen and words heard, and we believe that grace is given and sins are forgiven. In the Eucharist, we believe that bread and wine become the Body and Blood of Christ, making love itself present to us. Like the centurion who believed in the power of Christ's word (Lk 7:6-9), we believe that the Word of love Christ speaks in the sacraments enriches us with grace.

– Douglas Bushman

*T*HE MIND SEEKS TRUTH because it can only live by truth. The existence of things which cannot be explained depresses him. The obscurity of causes and effects bothers him and disturbs him. It is only after having grasped the central significance of being, and the finality of the movement of existence, that such a person can really live. The "truth" which he seeks is not merely the exactness of a general law which can always be attained, but the substantial fulfillment which corresponds to his search, the ultimate explanation, the finality of order. And once he perceives that this sublime light, this ultimate achievement, this peace in which the mind finally rests content, cannot be attained in the world itself, he perceives also that it must have its source in Revelation. That is so, not because the truth of the world is too limited, but because the heart demands another kind of truth, the holy truth of the living God. But this cannot arise from any world… To know that and to accept it, is faith. For a person like this to believe means to have penetrated into the realm of ultimate truth which, through the intermediary of Christ, comes from God; it means to have made contact with that supreme truth in its holy essence, its causes and its effects, to be aware that God is the Light.

– Monsignor Romano Guardini

The Ethiopian Eunuch

ONE OF THE HEROES of our faith is an Ethiopian eunuch, among the first baptized Gentiles. His story is brief, but blazes across the pages of Scripture like a comet. Who is this obscure yet resplendent figure? He's the queen of Ethiopia's money manager, "in charge of her entire treasury" (Acts 8:27). When we meet him, however, he's doing something strange: returning from a pilgrimage to Jerusalem and reading about the Suffering Servant (Is 53:7-8). Here is a prestigious pagan who has it all, but he's looking for something more.

What happens next, as if in answer to the eunuch's longing, is that God reveals his love for him in a stunning ecclesial encounter. Inspired by the Holy Spirit, Philip the deacon chases down the Ethiopian's chariot and asks, "Do you understand what you are reading?" (Acts 8:30). The eunuch replies like a beggar, "How can I, unless someone instructs me?" (Acts 8:31). Akin to Jesus on the road to Emmaus, Philip then unveils the mystery of Christ's Passion hidden within Isaiah's prophecy. Heart aflame, the eunuch exclaims, "Look, there is water. What is to prevent my being baptized?" (Acts 8:36). Philip baptizes him on the spot. Nourished by Word and sacrament, the Ethiopian "continued on his way rejoicing" (Acts 8:39). Though a eunuch, he will now be like Philip: a father of the faith.

– Andrew Matt

WE ENCOUNTER STILL another type of faith…. What we call reality does not seem to be truly real to them; they consider it rather as a shadow. Whence comes this feeling? Does it come from a slackening will to live…from a tiredness of the heart, or from some other cause? In any case, they recognize what readily escapes men gifted with much greater powers of vitality—namely the contingency and unreal character of life. Such persons long for what can give them a full experience of life, something which is no longer precarious, dull, half-defined, but massive and capable of satisfying their thirst. They wish to attain a reality which has nothing to do with a mere appearance, in order thus to feel truly real themselves. Their road is often a long one. First they may perhaps think that they have found what they are seeking in the passions, in the drunkenness of enjoyment, in the desire to work, in the will to fight—until the day when they discover that all this merely hides the emptiness. This emptiness is found everywhere and cannot be filled by any earthly thing. They then become aware that God alone can heal this wound…. He can bring it about that a finite creature, which is only half alive, can become aware of true life.

– Monsignor Romano Guardini

Tabitha

WOULD IT BE EASY to return to this world after experiencing death? I have a friend who was medically dead for several minutes while doctors frantically worked to restart his heart. He says that he did not want to come back, since the presence of Jesus was so real that he wanted nothing other than to stay with our Lord for ever. And yet God sent him back: his work was not yet done.

So too with Tabitha: she has died, and Peter is sent for. He puts all the mourners outside, kneels, and prays. "Then he turned to her body and said, 'Tabitha, rise up.' She opened her eyes, saw Peter, and sat up" (Acts 9:40). Her work is not yet done; she must return to the Church.

So too Jesus' work after his Resurrection is not yet done, even though he has returned to his Father. He continues his work on earth through new means, through the Church—through Peter and the other Apostles and their successors, and through the sacraments they give. This is perhaps why Peter imitates Jesus so precisely: Jesus too raised someone, after putting out the mourners, taking her hand, and saying, "'*Talitha koum*,' which means 'Little girl, I say to you, arise!'" (Mk 5:41).

Do I think that Jesus is dead and gone, or do I have faith that he continues to work his miracles in the Church?

– Angela Franks

HE EYE OF FAITH opens to the light of grace and grasps all the more clearly this reality of God which is revealed. Such a knowledge is nothing but the growth of faith. But this knowledge takes place in "experience," that is, in the concrete approaching, probing, getting the feel and the taste of something. It is only in this way that the content of faith flowers, like a bud, full of truth and value; it presents itself clearly to the mind and penetrates to the very heart....

Fundamentally faith is the obedience of man to God...the attentive submission of finite humanity to the reality of its Creator and Lord who, in revealing himself, has disclosed man's sinful state and nothingness. There is a gulf of dissimilarity here which nothing can fill; faith always remains the obedient acceptance of the incomprehensible reality of God towards which humanity is directed.... The only knowledge possible is founded on obedience: it comes from...acceptance... which abandons the glorification of self. It is achieved in the constant abandonment of self to the judgment of holy God. Knowledge in faith, according to the nature and object of faith, is extinguished as soon as faith is...a genuine knowledge, a living "knowledge," in the sense of an inner presence, a penetration.

– Monsignor Romano Guardini

*"Faith is the realization of what is hoped for
and evidence of things not seen."*
(Heb 11:1)

MY MOTHER LOVED SOAP OPERAS and knew the characters on her "soaps" like they were her friends and relatives. One day I was home sick and joined her in the middle of *Search for Tomorrow.* She tried to explain the circumstances but soon realized I would never understand it because every character was interwoven in years of complex situations.

How much of life is like that. We only see our tiny, limited, corner of the world—our personal soap operas. But we have within us a longing to know everything; it never ends. We have a longing to experience new things; we know that when we love someone there is so much more to discover about that person. We only see a little part of God's love and presence in the world, but we know that there is so much more—that God's love is unlimited and his presence all around us, which ordinary eyes do not see, but the eyes of faith do! Faith is a knowledge beyond the visible, beyond what the five senses experience. Faith reveals a whole world that is more real than the complexities of our daily soap operas… and that gives us real hope in our "search for tomorrow."

– Father Jacob Restrick, O.P.

*Faith is the theological virtue by which
we believe in God and believe all that he has said
and revealed to us.*
(CCC 1814)

MADE IN GOD'S IMAGE, we are made for the truth. Instinctively we know that truth is discovered, not manufactured, and that it is objective, not alterable. Both of these characteristics of truth are perfectly realized in God. He is creator, before all else that is. Unmade, God is the measure of all things that are made. And God is unchanging, not like an inert substance, but like the most faithful and constant of friends. We believe in him, then, because God is truth itself. This is why the ultimate explanation for all that God does is that he is faithful to himself.

Faith allows us to participate in this fidelity of God to himself. God and his Church's teachings become the measure of all we do, think, and say. Because God and the Church's teachings are constant, so is our faith, and so are the friendships we make based on faith. To be made for the truth is to be made for the constancy that only faith can give. When we are not constant and manipulate the truth to suit our whims, faith—that is God and his truth—calls us to conversion in order to conform ourselves to the truth.

– Douglas Bushman

Paul

Paul's conversion to faith begins at his extraordinary meeting with the risen Lord, who challenges him: "Why are you persecuting me?" (Acts 9:4; cf. 22:7; 26:14) This question opens his eyes to recognize in faith Christ relating all to the Father. From a zealous oppressor of others he becomes an ardent Apostle of the Church. He urges us, as temples of the Holy Spirit, to "offer your bodies as a living sacrifice…your spiritual worship" (Rom 12:1). He teaches that by worthily participating in the Eucharist we are transformed into one body, Christ's, and so share his risen life of glory.

Paul's faith is not based on an abstract theory or the Law, but on Christ. In his cross Paul sees God's power and wisdom surpassing human reason (1 Cor 1:18ff.) and recapitulating all things (Eph 1:10). His conviction that Christ "lives in me" (Gal 2:20) impels him to witness faith working in love. To know the heart of Paul, as a Father of the Church puts it, is to know the heart of Christ. It is through his encounter with Paul that Saint Augustine, in his restless quest for happiness, learns to believe and live the truth of the Gospel.

May Paul's letters inspire us to perceive the revitalizing qualitative difference made by faith in the grace coming from Christ.

– Father Michael L. Gaudoin-Parker

Faith and the Sorrowful Mysteries of the Rosary

◀ *The Agony in the Garden* – In his agony, Jesus begs that the Father's will be done. His prayer reveals that Jesus loves the Father's will more than his own life. May I live such trusting abandonment, completely given over to the will of God. May the suffering I encounter in my daily life make me strong and steadfast in faith.

◀ *The Scourging* – That someone could look at Jesus and not love him is the most fearsome thing in life. A life lived in defiance of Jesus Christ results in such anger, hatred, and hostility. May I be saved from whatever would tempt me to resist Jesus Christ, to reject him, or to revile him. By Christ's wounds we are healed.

◀ *The Crowning with Thorns* – Even in the soldiers' mockery and derision, the truth is revealed: Jesus Christ is King, and to be human is to confess him as such. Even in my betrayals, even when I am lost in sin, may I know my need for Jesus, and may the mercy of Christ the King draw me out of the darkness.

◀ *Jesus Takes up His Cross* – To be one with Jesus in taking up the cross is to embrace the Father's will and the love that pours forth from that sacrifice. Faith gives the promise of an indestructible love. And faith increases as we witness Jesus' body being destroyed in the brutality of the Passion. For this is not the end.

◀ *The Crucifixion* – We have gained access by faith to the grace in which we stand, and we even boast of our afflictions. For faith means choosing to stand with the Lord so as to live with him. God proves his love for us by dying for us sinners. We place all our faith in that love. We believe, hoping against hope.

– Father Peter John Cameron, O.P.

Faith and Public Life

CHRISTIAN FAITH demands much of us. In fact, it demands everything of us: "If any man would come after me, let him deny himself and take up his cross and follow me" (Mt 16:24 RSV). Faith in Christ is always faith in him who died for our sins; it is born of an encounter with Christ who, while risen, still bears the marks of crucifixion.

By worldly standards, the cost of discipleship is high, but faith assures us that the Lord's invitation to go with him to Calvary is also an invitation to share in the unceasing joy of the Resurrection. When put in those terms, the cost of discipleship is counted as nothing and we begin to see just how gratuitous a gift faith is.

As Saint Paul writes: "I have been crucified with Christ; it is no longer I who live, but Christ who lives in me; and the life I now live in the flesh I live by faith in the Son of God" (Gal 2:20 RSV). Faith, because it transforms us, always has public consequences; not only because the precepts of faith guide the decisions we make as citizens, but because if Christ truly lives in us, then our very lives—including our public lives—are not ours, but his, and must bear witness accordingly.

Faith, like love, is never a solitary affair; it is always personal, but never truly private. Since it is no longer we who live, but Christ who lives in us, no part of our life can ever be partitioned off from the faith or withheld from the demands of discipleship. A branch cut from the vine bears no fruit but withers and dies (Jn 15:4-7). Christ is not *part* of our life, he is *the* Life. He is integral to our very being.

We see this integrity manifest in the great saints who proclaim Christ by their lives. What heart would not be stoked to love by a sister like Saint Thérèse of Lisieux or a brother like Saint Ignatius? Who would not grow more self-less with Saint Francis as a neighbor or Joseph of Nazareth as a co-worker?

If living in the company of saints would be a blessing, would not our own holiness be likewise for everyone we encounter? This is the vocation we all receive in baptism. No one could give a greater gift to his family and friends, co-workers and neighbors—or indeed, to his nation—than to live a life worthy of the Sonship he shares with Christ through baptism. Nothing has more radical public consequence than holiness.

By living faithful lives of radical conversion we give public testimony to the Truth who is Christ, who alone reveals man to himself. As such, there can be no greater citizen than one who is, as Saint Thomas More put it, "the king's good servant, and God's first." There can be no greater citizen than a saint.

– **Stephen P. White**

Ananias

WHILE HIS APPEARANCE is brief and easily overshadowed by the far weightier presence of another, the part played by Ananias in the conversion of Saul seems a perfect example of both the importance of faith and the mediating power of signs in doing God's will. For no sooner has lightning blinded the fire-breathing Saul, who in his fury against the Way is bound for Damascus in search of fresh blood, than the voice of God is addressing Ananias in a dream, instructing him to go "lay [his] hands on him, that he may regain his sight" (Acts 9:12).

And, yes, for an instant Ananias does waver in his resolution to carry out the command, reminding God of Saul's reputation, of the evils he has inflicted upon "your holy ones in Jerusalem" (Acts 9:13). But God is not intimidated and urges him to get on with it, "for this man is a chosen instrument of mine to carry my name before the Gentiles, kings, and Israelites" (Acts 9:15). Which Ananias at once sets out to do, stirred by the grace of faith to go and lay hands on Saul, thus mediating a miracle whose ultimate outcome will be Christ's conquest of the world.

– Regis Martin

GRANT THAT I MAY always observe modesty in the way I dress, the way I walk, and the gestures I use, restrain my tongue from frivolous talk, prevent my feet from leading me astray, keep my eyes from wandering glances, shelter my ears from rumors, lower my gaze in humility, lift my mind to thoughts of heaven, contemn all that will pass away, and love you only. Grant that I may subdue my flesh and cleanse my conscience, honor the saints and praise you worthily, advance in goodness, and end a life of good works with a holy death. Plant deep in me, Lord, all the virtues, that I might be devout in divine matters, discerning in human affairs, and burdensome to no one in fulfilling my own bodily needs. Grant to me, Lord, fervent contrition, pure confession, and complete reparation. Order me inwardly through a good life, that I might do what is right and what will be meritorious for me and a good example for others. Grant that I may never crave to do things impulsively, nor disdain to do what is burdensome, lest I begin things before I should or abandon them before finishing. Amen.

– Saint Thomas Aquinas

*"By faith we understand that the universe was ordered
by the word of God, so that what is visible came
into being through the invisible."*
(Heb 11:3)

UNCLE HARRY was my favorite uncle because he was
an amateur magician, and my sister and I were his best
audience. He would pull real quarters out of my ears and
make them disappear in an instant. I still love to watch
magicians do the most incredible things right before our
eyes. Even if our grownup sophisticated minds know it's
all tricks and sleight of hand, smoke and mirrors, there's
something in us that loves to see the invisible appear, like
the bunny out of the hat!

Our faith is not magic; it's not a trick of the mind or
sleight of hand. God, we know, is not a magician, but created our universe with incredible order and beauty. We
can look up at night and marvel at the cosmic display of
stars and planets and look through a microscope at the
tiniest universe within a living cell. Faith understands that
God does not create by sleight of hand or trickery, but by
his Word. He has "it" in his mind, and he "speaks" it, and
it comes to be.

Faith knows this because it's reflected in our own experience. We think of a word before we speak, and "create" whole sentences and paragraphs and the "book" of
our life. It's not magic—it's real!

– Father Jacob Restrick, O.P.

*I*N ORDER TO RECOGNIZE the content of faith we must first experience it. "If you abide in my word...you shall know the truth." If for example I am told that everything which happens is owing to Providence, that over the whole life of man and over each detail of this life there is the hand of God, this assertion will remain a dead letter as long as I have not experienced it. Only when I decide to consider everything which happens to me, both the good and the bad, as coming ultimately from God, do I understand what that means. This is easy to say but difficult to do: infinitely difficult for the human will in despair about its own powerlessness and yet obstinately at grips with it, so lazy and lax, yet so rebellious and proud. But it is only when I act thus, and to the extent that I really do so, that this belief in Providence is revealed to be true. It is only when I am quite convinced that I have received a special mission from God, that every event offers me the opportunity of fulfilling it. It is only when I persevere in this consciousness, through joy and sorrow, through success and failure, that I become aware of the existence of a force which directs and sustains me—and this is precisely the "truth" of faith which we mean here.

– Monsignor Romano Guardini

Cornelius

CORNELIUS, the first Gentile baptized by the Apostle Peter, has received the grace of faith before ever meeting Peter. He is described in Acts as a "God-fearing" Gentile, i.e., one who believes and prays to the God of the Jewish people. In fact, the vision of God instructing him to send men to summon Peter occurs during his daily prayers.

His faith is manifested by his immediate obedience to the vision; and we see his exceptional certainty when he invites his relatives and friends to await Peter's arrival. Cornelius has complete confidence that anyone sent by God is worth waiting for, and this confidence (*con-fide* = "with faith") turns him into a fearless missionary.

When Peter arrives, Cornelius proclaims that he and his friends are "in the presence of God" (Acts 10:33) and ready to listen. As Peter speaks, the Holy Spirit is poured out, and Cornelius' faith is fulfilled when he is finally baptized by Peter.

Cornelius is an example of the openness of heart that faith in God brings us. Before encountering Peter, Cornelius' acknowledgment of the God of Israel, and his desire to be in relationship with him in prayer, predisposes him to welcome the encounter with Christ when Christ arrives in his life in the person of Peter.

– Father Richard Veras

*T*HE PRINCIPAL LABOR of the Christian is to believe that divine love is the breadth and length and height and depth, and that there is simply nothing above, below, or beyond it. It is our home; it enfolds us and is our utmost security both in this life and in death and beyond. We are speaking of faith, not of feelings or intellectual grasp. For faith means a blind trust in and surrender to the God of love, and this love is too great for our human heart and mind. We are to live life no longer as our own, relying on our own pathetic vision of reality and of how God is to us, but clinging, mind and heart, to the Son of God who "loved me and sacrificed himself for me" (Gal 2:20). We must train ourselves to renounce our natural mode of seeing and evaluating. This must be at the service of faith, yet must not be taken for faith. Without realizing it, we can call "faith" that assent we give to our own manageable ideas of God. True faith takes us into the unknown. It calls for blind trust; it calls for profound humility and surrender. This is real asceticism, the self-denial that Jesus tells us is essential if we are to be his disciples.

– Sister Ruth Burrows, O.C.D.

Barnabas

A REBIRTH OF APOSTOLIC ZEAL could break out in your parish. You could be a new Barnabas! Ablaze with evangelical fire, Barnabas was crucial for the missionary expansion of Christianity. If we ask his intercession, that same fire will fall upon us as we pursue the New Evangelization, to bring about a rebirth of faith in the modern world, filling our churches again.

Barnabas was sent by the Church in Jerusalem to investigate a new thing, occurring in Antioch: Gentiles, not just Jews, were being preached to. And they were coming in! Would this surprising movement of the Spirit be ratified by the Church's Jewish core? If God does something unexpected, will we be happy or aggrieved? Luke describes Barnabas as "a good man, full of Holy Spirit and of faith" (Acts 11:24 RSV). What praise! A man of faith is open to God's surprising initiatives: "When he arrived and saw the grace of God, he rejoiced and encouraged them all to remain faithful to the Lord in firmness of heart" (Acts 11:23).

The Letter to the Hebrews has been attributed to Barnabas. Here is a Levite convinced that the faith of Israel finds its fulfillment in the faithfulness of Christ, the eternal Priest of the universal sacrifice of the cross. This "son of encouragement" (Acts 4:36) always teaches that faith is the very substance of things hoped for.

– J. David Franks

When it is deprived of hope and love,
faith does not fully unite the believer to Christ and
does not make him a living member of his Body.
(CCC 1815)

BY ITS NATURE, faith is meant to produce a life that is
ordered according to God's truth and plan of love for us.
The actions by which we take our place in this plan of love
are the "works" that are so many fruits of faith when it is
united with hope and love. Sadly, it happens that some who
are baptized end up living as if God did not exist. They do
not renounce their faith in an act of heresy or apostasy,
yet they sin against love of God and love of neighbor, or
against hope, at least by acts of omission (such as failing
to attend Sunday Mass; not confessing grave sins; not witnessing to their faith). To underscore the seriousness of
this state, Blessed John Paul II called it a silent apostasy.
In this state a person is like a tree that does not yield fruit.
It is still alive; God does not give up on it. He provides it
with water and nutrients (Church teaching and the sacraments) in the hope that it will produce fruit. But, if in the
end it does not, it will be cut down and burned (Lk 13:6-9).

– Douglas Bushman

*F*aith must grow from experience to knowledge. We have to do with the inner history of faith, which is unfolded when the believer lives with the object of his faith. In his daily life he encounters the contents of his faith; sometimes one aspect or another is revealed to him more clearly; the deeper levels begin to appear more distinctly; the object of faith is seen both as a suggestion and demand: he becomes aware of what it requires of him. He directs his life according to his faith, he molds his life according to it, he makes it the standard of his existence. Thus he comes to know what the powers contained in his faith are, how it assures him stability, support and security. What he received first as teaching, story, message, changes in consistency, density, and weight; it is found to be reality. All these things are in keeping with human experience: action, life, challenge, and bold decisions; but in all this it is God who is acting, for faith is grace. The light of God develops the content of belief in knowledge. Under the guidance of God the obedience of faith finally arrives at joyful possession. God himself, the All-Holy, is revealed as a living reality in that which obedience has enabled us to retain and to think.

– Monsignor Romano Guardini

James "the Brother of the Lord"

THE IDENTITY OF JAMES has long been a focus of curiosity and inquiry, because he is called "the brother of the Lord" (Mt 13:55; Mk 6:3; Gal 1:19). Since the *Da Vinci Code* a spate of books has bizarrely seen this in a literal sense. Jerome explains that this expression means "cousin," as in oriental usage. Understood this way, the traditional faith is preserved about Mary's virginity and, moreover, about Jesus' uniqueness as Son of God.

James is one of those to whom the risen Lord appears (1 Cor 15:7). Like all the disciples, he witnesses to God's desire revealed by Jesus to relate all people as his children. This is fulfilled not by blood ties nor by desire nor human will. Thus, when told that his relatives are looking for him, Jesus indicates that deeper than family relationship is the truth about being bonded to him in faith (Mk 3:31ff.).

James teaches that faith is the key and real code for interpreting everything regarding Christ. Leader of the Jerusalem community, he is present at the first Church Council where he voices the decision of crucial significance about welcoming non-Jewish converts. He is later martyred for this. In his important epistle, he insists that faith in Christ is not alive unless it is expressed through deeds of practical caring service.

– Father Michael L. Gaudoin-Parker

*S*OME HAVE PORTRAYED the mystical experience as something of dubious value, dangerous for the purity and integrity of the Christian faith.... Others have seen in it something interesting from the psychological point of view, or as an object of literature or amusement.... All such attitudes leave out of account the Christian evidence which is based on Scripture, the lives of the saints, the conscience of a believing people: namely, that God is the living God, and in Christ God is near at hand. That it is in him that "we have movement, life, and being." That he is love and liberty and grace—and that no power of this world, no scientific theory, no theological syllogism can prevent him from touching the soul when it pleases him. A faith which has been assumed humbly and seriously; a faith which receives from God the longing for the immediacy of love and which has not let this longing die, but which has unceasingly prayed for the fulfillment of this desire, however long the waiting period may be: a faith which is not content with temporary satisfactions, but with the confidence of the child of God remains anchored in the essential; such a faith doubtless always ultimately arrives, more or less, at that which we mean by the "mystical," unless we prefer to speak simply of the fullness of faith.

– Monsignor Romano Guardini

*"Since we are surrounded by so great a cloud of witnesses,
let us…persevere in running the race
that lies before us while keeping our eyes fixed on Jesus,
the leader and perfecter of faith."*
(Heb 12:1-2)

I KNOW A YOUNG WOMAN who just entered the convent. After the ceremony each sister gave her the "kiss of peace" and a personal word of welcome. It's amazing to witness such a moment. It takes faith to give oneself so unreservedly to Christ and to the service of the poor. I spoke later with one of the novices who had been through the reception ceremony three years ago, and I asked her what her "word of wisdom" was to the new sister. And she said without hesitation: "Keep your eyes fixed on Jesus."

One could certainly say that to any bride and groom today too. They are surrounded by a cloud of witnesses on their wedding day, and it takes great faith to give oneself, each to the other, "until death do us part." Even for a single person or a widowed man or woman, it takes great faith to persevere in living the Christian life today. And the same grace and word of wisdom can be given to each one: *keep your eyes fixed on Jesus*. The way before us is always uncertain and will call forth patience, forgiveness, prayer, and above all love. Jesus is the Way that is "perfect" because he is the Truth and the Life.

– Father Jacob Restrick, O.P.

There are three theological virtues:
faith, hope, and charity.
They inform all the moral virtues and give life to them.
(CCC 1841)

FAITH, HOPE, AND CHARITY are called theological virtues because they are God-centered in every way. First, they are gifts that only God can bestow. We must cooperate, since God will never override our free will, but they remain gifts of grace. Second, we can only know about them by way of divine revelation. God has made known to us that these virtues are necessary for salvation. To have faith, hope, and charity is to be blessed by God. Most importantly, they make us sharers in God's own life. By faith, hope, and charity we are in communion with God, knowing what he knows and loving what he loves.

God does not want to be alone in his knowing and loving. If a Frenchman deeply desired to speak with a person who did not speak French, he might wish he could infuse knowledge of French into that person's mind. It is like that with God. In order to communicate to us his life of truth and love, he makes us able to understand him and to receive his life, and he does this by infusing faith, hope, and charity into the souls of those who open themselves to his love.

– Douglas Bushman

Silas (Silvanus)

SILAS MUST HAVE WORN OUT plenty of sandals in his travels to preach the Word. He was sent by the Apostles in Jerusalem to deliver their decision to the Gentile believers, that they were not bound by the law of circumcision. He sojourned with Saint Paul across the plateau of Asia Minor, setting sail then for Greece. He was with Paul in Corinth and Athens and Thessalonica. If he's the same man we know as Silvanus, we find him years later with Saint Peter in Rome, working as his secretary.

But his hearty faith is best shown in Philippi, where he and Paul are stripped, beaten, and thrown into prison. What did Paul and Silas do then? They "were praying and singing hymns to God as the prisoners listened" (Acts 16:25). Paul had chosen Silas deliberately; the two must have been close friends. They were certainly of one mind and heart here, preaching by their joy! When an earthquake shatters their chains, they do not run off, as their jailer fears. They call out to the man, who falls at their feet. "Sirs, what must I do to be saved?" he asks (Acts 16:30). The answer to him and to us is as straight as can be: "Believe in the Lord Jesus" (Acts 16:31).

– Anthony Esolen

*O*UR PERSONAL FAITH draws its life from the totality of faith around us, which goes back from the present into the past; but that means the Church.

"The Church" means the "us" in faith; it is the sum total, the whole community of believers; it is the believing collectivity. It is not merely Christian prayer which ought to say "us," but also faith. The latter is equally rooted in "us," understood as a whole. The true "us" is more than a mere sum of individuals. It is a movement proceeding from them all. A true collectivity or totality is something more than a simple grouping of a few individuals; it is a vast living structure of which each individual is a member. A hundred men who stand before God as an *ekklesia* represent something more than the mere addition of a hundred individuals; they constitute a living and believing community—we do not mean merely a simple "community" in the purely subjective sense of the term, a convenient designation for a feeling arising from the communal needs of the individual. No, the origin of the community we are referring to here, its consistency and its value, are drawn from something outside the communal needs of the individual; they come from elsewhere, they derive consistency and value from elsewhere: I refer to the "Church."

– Monsignor Romano Guardini

M_Y G_{OD},

I bless thee that thou hast given me the eye
    of faith,/ to see thee as Father,
    to know thee as a covenant God,
    to experience thy love planted in me;
For faith is the grace of union
    by which I spell out my entitlement to thee:
Faith casts my anchor upwards
    where I trust in thee
    and engage thee to be my Lord.
Be pleased to live and move within me,
    breathing in my prayers,/ inhabiting my praises,
    speaking in my words,/ moving in my actions,
    living in my life, /causing me to grow in grace.
Thy bounteous goodness has helped me believe,
    but my faith is weak and wavering,
        its light dim,/ its steps tottering,
        its increase slow,/ its backslidings frequent;
It should scale the heavens, but lies groveling
        in the dust.
Lord, fan this divine spark into glowing flame.
When faith sleeps, my heart becomes
    an unclean thing,
    the fount of every loathsome desire,
    the cage of unclean lusts
    all fluttering to escape,
        the noxious tree of deadly fruit,
        the open wayside of earthly tares.
Lord, awake faith to put forth its strength
    until all heaven fills my soul
    and all impurity is cast out.

– A Puritan Prayer

Apollos

GIFTED ORATOR and revered theologian, Apollos is a Jewish convert from Alexandria. With "ardent spirit" (Acts 18:25) he boldly proclaims the Gospel with great zeal and accuracy. But Priscilla and Aquila see troubling lacunae in his teaching, and noting both his predicament and promise, they undertake his instruction. Endowed with a deeper grasp of the faith, Apollos sets out anew with the brothers' support to proclaim the Gospel, and engages in vigorous apologetics. Saint Paul's high praise contrasts his own planting with Apollos' watering, and he ranks him alongside Saint Peter and himself (1 Cor 3:6, 22). This suggests that this teacher and preacher becomes a missionary of the first order.

Apollos is likely one of the first to emphasize precision and nuance in communicating the truths of the faith. If the Gospel reveals the most important truths about God, Christ, ourselves, salvation, and destiny, it is important to get these right and to recognize that God is in the details. Combining accuracy with vigorous zeal, Apollos understands that Scriptural faith, which reaches to God himself, is a response to grace. Appealing to head and heart, faith is no less complex than we are. Yet Apollos' success in the end arises because he bends down and submits humbly to the corrections of his betters.

– Father Lawrence J. Donohoo

The Wood of the Cross

"By his wounds, you have been healed."
(1 Pt 2:24)

Wood of the Cross:
Walking Stick
Heavy Door
Treasure Chest
Splintered Floor

Tree of Loss and Gain,
Sentence and Release,
Bloodied Roots
Solid Beams
carried
dropped
lifted
propped
abhorred, ignored, adored—
All for One
Body
ravaged
restored.

– Rita A. Simmonds

*H*OWEVER FINE a thing spontaneity of life may be—the time will necessarily come when we must stand firm, choose, take sides. Faith also involves maturity, character, and coming of age. Properly understood and lived, dogma really means character in faith. Upon encountering dogma, a spontaneous and living faith may also become involved in a crisis: we must resign ourselves to this as something inevitable. But if faith always emerges victorious, if it assimilates dogma, it then acquires a spirit of decision and an awareness of responsibility and of destiny which are simply irreplaceable. It need not lose its vibrant energy. It has only to gain by the seriousness and pain of discussion.

This is the way faith broadens and matures, until finally dogma gradually penetrates the life and attitude of the believer. It penetrates to the extent that—except at certain moments of warning and demand—it influences the life of the believer, no longer mainly as a conscious directive force or rule, but more as a guide on the road towards a higher liberty.

– Monsignor Romano Guardini

> *"Remember your leaders who spoke the word of God*
> *to you…and imitate their faith."*
> *(Heb 13:7)*

BEFORE CHRISTMAS LAST YEAR, Pope Benedict XVI met with all the cardinals and bishops who head the various offices which make up the Roman Curia. It's like the chief shepherd gathering all the other shepherds before going to the manger in Bethlehem. He wanted to thank them for their service to the Church and to highlight his own special moments of grace in the past year. One of the most moving experiences for the Holy Father was World Youth Day in Madrid. His own faith was enlivened by the joy, enthusiasm, and prayerfulness of the millions of young people who cheered him, listened intently to him, and devoutly prayed with him.

The young people, on the other hand, have their own youthful faith enlivened and made joyous and prayerful by the words of the Holy Father, and by his loving them and wanting to be with them. More than words it is his faith that enthralls them. They live in a neo-pagan world which promotes self-centeredness to the max, and they experience the banality of it all. They want a spiritual depth and substance to their lives, and they see and hear this in Pope Benedict and in their own bishops and priests and faithful laity who listen to God's Word and let it direct their lives. That's something to imitate!

– Father Jacob Restrick, O.P.

Timothy

TIMOTHY IS ONE of Paul's most trusted collaborators, having sent a number of letters in conjunction with Paul, and receiving two letters from him in which the Apostle calls Timothy his "child" in the faith.

Paul is filled with joy at Timothy's "sincere faith" (2 Tm 1:5). Indeed, it is Timothy's faith that has propelled him, at a young age, to be entrusted with pastoral responsibility in Ephesus (1 Tm 1:3).

When Paul first meets Timothy in Lystra, the young man has already gained the respect of the Christians in that community, and Paul's invitation to Timothy to accompany him is both a reward for Timothy's faith as well a graced opportunity to deepen that faith.

Paul admits all of his previous sinfulness to Timothy (1 Tm 1:12-16), and Timothy recognizes in Paul the very presence of Christ. Timothy would have been well-educated by Paul's teaching that the Church is the Mystical Body of Christ and would not have been scandalized that Christ would be present in the frail, earthen vessel of Paul. This, in turn, is what likely gives Timothy the courage and grace to become a pastor himself at such a young age. For it is not in his abilities that he trusts, but rather in his faith in Jesus, who forms Timothy through the tender and firm fatherhood of Paul.

– Father Richard Veras

*B*ELIEVING IS NOT MERELY ACTION, thought, willing, behavior; it involves the essence of being. More precisely, belief means that the created being is on the road towards God. It is this process which, coming from God, takes hold of the being of man, namely the new birth, the invasion of divine love or of divine life from which a new existence comes to be by the grace of God—and the new-born man then makes this process personally his own in the tension of faith. Faith is a movement which is continually being born in the mystery of that transubstantiation which takes place in the sacrament.

But in this mystery it is not a question of individual existence. God takes hold of humanity and the individual in it. He grasps the individual, but only in the whole. He grasps the whole, that is the Church, in order to get at the individual through it; or again, the individual in order that the Church may be.

God visits man redeemed by Christ and brings him back to himself. It is he himself, we are even tempted to say, who believes in place of man. In the process of regeneration he gives man his own life that it may become man's life; in faith, the one who has become a Christian returns to God, but it is the life of God which draws him.

– Monsignor Romano Guardini

Faith and the Glorious Mysteries of the Rosary

◀ *The Resurrection* – Faith is already the beginning of eternal life. It is a foretaste of the knowledge that will make us blessed in the life to come. May faith in the risen Lord move me to turn to God alone as my ultimate goal. May I never prefer anything to him or substitute anything for him. Jesus Christ is my life.

◀ *The Ascension* – Faith involves a shift from dependence on the visible and practicable to trust in the invisible. As the Lord ascends into heaven, and we see his physical body no more, we are drawn to exercise a deeper faith. And we are drawn into deeper communion with those who follow Jesus in faith.

◀ *The Descent of the Holy Spirit* – With the gift of the Spirit at Pentecost, the disciples understand more perfectly the man Jesus they have faithfully followed. May the Spirit of Truth give us insight to live by faith in every circumstance. May he strengthen our witness of faith, making us fervent, active, and courageous.

◀ *The Assumption* – I cannot believe without being carried by the faith of others. As the Blessed Virgin Mary is carried up to heaven, she continues to mediate her faith that unites me with her Son. May the knowledge of our Lady's intercession from heaven increase my faith and deepen my trust in God.

◀ *The Coronation of the Blessed Virgin Mary* – As Mary is crowned Queen of heaven and earth, the world is blessed with a Mother who cares for us more than we can care for ourselves. Mary's Queenship extends to our every need, our every weakness, our every failing. May our Lady show her power and reign in our life.

– Father Peter John Cameron, O.P.

> *By faith, we believe…all…that Holy Church*
> *proposes for our belief.*
> *(CCC 1842)*

FAITH HAS AN ALL-OR-NOTHING QUALITY. Saint James expressed it: "For whoever keeps the whole law, but falls short in one particular, has become guilty in respect to all of it. For he who said, 'You shall not commit adultery,' also said, 'You shall not kill.' Even if you do not commit adultery but kill, you have become a transgressor of the law" (Jas 2:10-11). Notice the emphasis on God, who spoke each commandment. His love and truthfulness stand behind everything he has revealed and that the Church teaches authoritatively. Consequently, to disregard any one thing revealed and taught is to reject God's personal authority.

To pick and choose what to believe is to stand in judgment of the Church, or even of God. Then one is trusting more in oneself than in God's authority, and faith's foundation is eroded. In such a case, the motive for assent is no longer God's truthfulness or his promise to guide the Church. Rather, it is the person's own judgment. The attitude this displays is: I will decide what is reasonable and true. Yet, this is precisely what divine revelation and the Church's teaching save us from. Faith saves us from self-deception and error.

– Douglas Bushman

Eunice and Lois

Timothy is a beloved confidant and fellow traveler of Paul. "I recall your sincere faith," Paul writes, a faith "that first lived in your grandmother Lois and in your mother Eunice and that I am confident lives also in you" (2 Tm 1:5).

In the 1648 Rembrandt painting, *Timothy and His Grandmother*, Timothy is a child, lingering at Lois' ample knee as she sternly but lovingly points out a line of Scripture. She is dressed humbly, in a black head covering, a black shawl, and a long wine-colored skirt, evocative, among other things, of the rich bloodline through which Timothy receives his instruction.

At the time Paul writes his Second Letter to Timothy, he is in prison awaiting execution. Timothy, too, as bishop of Ephesus, will be martyred in his old age, dragged through the streets and stoned to death for censuring a pagan festival.

Legend has it that as he breathes his last, Timothy sees the heavens open and Christ come down with a double crown, saying, "Thou shalt receive this of my hand."

He receives it first at the hand of those two great women who teach him the power and treasure of Scripture: Eunice and Lois.

– Heather King

*I*N BELIEVING, we entrust ourselves to the knowledge acquired by other people. This suggests an important tension. On the one hand, the knowledge acquired through belief can seem an imperfect form of knowledge, to be perfected gradually through personal accumulation of evidence; on the other hand, belief is often humanly richer than mere evidence, because it involves an interpersonal relationship and brings into play not only a person's capacity to know but also the deeper capacity to entrust oneself to others, to enter into a relationship with them which is intimate and enduring.

It should be stressed that the truths sought in this interpersonal relationship are not primarily empirical or philosophical. Rather, what is sought is the truth of the person—what the person is and what the person reveals from deep within. Human perfection, then, consists not simply in acquiring an abstract knowledge of the truth, but in a dynamic relationship of faithful self-giving with others. It is in this faithful self-giving that a person finds a fullness of certainty and security. At the same time, however, knowledge through belief, grounded as it is on trust between persons, is linked to truth: in the act of believing, men and women entrust themselves to the truth which the other declares to them.

– Blessed Pope John Paul II

"Consider it all joy, my brothers,
when you encounter various trials,
for you know that the testing of your faith
produces perseverance."
(Jas 1:2-3)

I COULD LOOK into the laboratory windows of Memorial Sloan-Kettering Hospital in New York from my bedroom window across the street. I called the corner of East 68th Street and York Avenue the corner where God pulls the rug out from under us. The rug, of course, is a diagnosis: *you've got cancer…*

There are many "rugs" in our lives: the loss of a loved one; the hardship of unemployment; the heartbreak of separation; the acceptance of illness or failure; the ravages of addictions and terrible mistakes.

Trials put our faith in God on trial. In the bearing of trials, we either strengthen our faith or lose our faith. If our faith has sustained us throughout the little ups and downs of life, when a tragedy or trial comes our way, we draw on our faith, and it gives us strength. Faith is a knowledge, and such faith knows that God loves us and permits everything in our lives. Even in the worst times, he will bring something good out of it all.

This is experienced as a deep and quiet joy. Not raucous or artificial hilarity, it may even be accompanied with copious tears and mourning. But deep down is the knowledge of God's love and presence, for he is the Weaver of the rug.

– Father Jacob Restrick, O.P.

once a week and invited our family and friends to join us. Whether someone joined us or not, what matters is that we desired to pass it on.

This is the Year of Faith. This is your time to make a deeper commitment. It is not about results; it is about your choice to do your very best. The greatest gift is when we take our gift of faith and give it away.

We have an important call as witnesses for Christ, but if our youth do not see our witness of an abundant life, then it is all in vain. Many years ago, I used to go to 6:30 AM Mass with my friend T. J. When I encouraged him to start going on his own, my words fell on deaf ears. Although he stopped going to Mass, we remained close friends. Then just last month T. J. told me he had made a commitment to go to daily Mass for the rest of his life, and his dad is going with him and seeking help at Alcoholics Anonymous. My witness and encouragement paid off. It taught me that one of the greatest gifts is sharing the source and summit of our Catholic Faith—the Holy Sacrifice of the Mass.

– Justin Fatica

" ORD, IF IT IS YOU, bid me come to you upon the water." When the Lord said "Come" Peter climbed out of the boat and began to walk on the water. This is what he could do through the power of the Lord; what by himself? Realizing how violently the wind was blowing, he lost his nerve, and as he began to sink he called out, "Lord, I am drowning, save me!" When he counted on the Lord's help it enabled him to walk on the water; when human frailty made him falter he turned once more to the Lord, who immediately stretched out his hand to help him, raised him up as he was sinking, and rebuked him for his lack of faith.

Think, then, of this world as a sea, whipped up to tempestuous heights by violent winds. A person's own private tempest will be his or her unruly desires. If you love God you will have power to walk upon the waters, and all the world's swell and turmoil will remain beneath your feet. But if you love the world it will surely engulf you, for it always devours its lovers, never sustains them. If you feel your foot slipping beneath you, if you become a prey to doubt or realize that you are losing control, if, in a word, you begin to sink, say, "Lord, I am drowning, save me!" Only he who for your sake died in your fallen nature can save you from the death inherent in that fallen nature.

– Saint Augustine

O LORD MY GOD, you are all my good. And who am I that I should dare to speak to you? I am your poorest and meanest servant, a vile worm, much more poor and contemptible than I know or dare to say. Yet remember me, Lord, because I am nothing, I have nothing, and I can do nothing. You alone are good, just, and holy. You can do all things, you give all things, you fill all things: only the sinner do you leave empty-handed. Remember your tender mercies and fill my heart with your grace, you who will not allow your works to be in vain. How can I bear this life of misery unless you comfort me with your mercy and grace? Do not turn your face from me. Do not delay your visitation. Do not withdraw your consolation, lest in your sight my soul become as desert land. Teach me, Lord, to do your will. Teach me to live worthily and humbly in your sight, for you are my wisdom who knew me truly, and who knew me even before the world was made and before I was born into it.

– Venerable Thomas à Kempis

Damaris

DAMARIS IS A WOMAN OF ATHENS, one of the few of either gender converted by Paul's preaching in the Areopagus; her name appears nowhere else in Greek literature.

Paul is preaching the resurrection of the dead, a scandal in any era, and it is humbling to consider the unlikeliness that anyone is ever converted at all. It is humbling to remember that we go back in an unbroken line to these first few converts who were willing to believe what we want to believe but can hardly bring ourselves to believe: that death is not the end; that a lowly carpenter from the backwater of Nazareth entered human space, time, and history, and vanquished death.

I once attended a prison orientation in order to be able to share the story of my alcoholism with the inmates. For three hours the trusty went on about the hardened criminals, the crafty criminals, the criminals who would come for the coffee but not for the message. But to have broken through the prison walls yourself is to know that someone else can, too. At the end, I raised my hand. "A hundred won't hear, but one will," I said. "That is why we come."

That is how our faith is spread, then, as now.

Paul preaches. Damaris hears.

– Heather King

Our moral life has its source in faith in God who reveals his love to us. Saint Paul speaks of the "obedience of faith" (Rom 1:5; 16:26.) as our first obligation.
(CCC 2087)

Obeying God's commandments is a function of believing that love is his motive in giving them. Love desires what is best for the one who is loved. God desires our fullest happiness, and his commandments specify what we must do and avoid doing in order to live that fullest happiness. The conviction of faith that God loves us overturns the great lie of the serpent, who led Adam and Eve to doubt God's love. As long as they believed that love was his motive for giving the commandment not to eat the forbidden fruit, they obeyed the commandment, thinking that indeed it was best for them. As soon as they doubted his love, they disobeyed.

Thus, we see that the obedience of faith is our first obligation and that it encompasses all obligations. Because God is love, we can entrust ourselves, our very happiness and fulfillment, to him. Mary is the perfect model of this obedience of faith. She received God's revelation about her place in his plan of love, and she faithfully fulfilled everything that was hers in that plan. A deep conviction of faith that God loves us is the truth that sets us free to obey his commandments.

– Douglas Bushman

*"Did not God choose those who are poor in the world
to be rich in faith and heirs of the kingdom
that he promised to those who love him?"*
(Jas 2:5)

"TOOTHLESS TESSIE, that's me name," she said beaming a toothless smile. I was a tourist looking out for movie stars on the corner of Hollywood and Vine, when Toothless Tessie came up to me and asked for a cigarette. I didn't have a cigarette, but I smiled back and asked her what her name was. We chatted like old friends meeting by chance in Hollywood. Tessie wanted to be an actress fifty years ago "before I lost me teeth!" she exclaimed with a toothless laugh.

I gave Tessie ten dollars toward a pack of cigarettes which she graciously accepted, blessed me for it, and promised to pray for me. "I'm in the middle of a novena to Saint Theresa, me patron saint," she informed me with nonchalant certitude. "What are you praying for?" I asked. "To quit smoking; it's too darn expensive."

I laughed at the incongruity of it all, and Tessie laughed with me. I learned in that brief encounter that Tessie was a daily communicant and made a holy hour of Eucharistic adoration every afternoon. She also had a chronic cough and an itchy scalp, but she was getting by. She lived in a cardboard box. I watched her two-step down the street and waved goodbye. I smiled and went home; I had met a star.

– Father Jacob Restrick, O.P.

*T*HE BELIEVER IS ALWAYS threatened with an uncertainty that in moments of temptation can suddenly and unexpectedly cast a piercing light on the fragility of the whole that usually seems so self-evident to him…. That lovable Saint Thérèse of Lisieux, who looks so naïve and unproblematical, grew up in an atmosphere of complete religious security; her whole existence from beginning to end, and down to the smallest detail, was so completely molded by the faith of the Church that the invisible world became, not just a part of her everyday life, but that life itself. It seemed to be an almost tangible reality that could not be removed by any amount of thinking. To her, "religion" really was a self-evident presupposition of her daily existence; she dealt with it as we deal with the concrete details of our lives. Yet this very saint, a person apparently cocooned in complete security, left behind her, from the last weeks of her passion, shattering admissions that her horrified sisters toned down in her literary remains and that have only now come to light in the new verbatim editions. She says, for example, "I am assailed by the worst temptations of atheism." Her mind is beset by every possible argument against the faith; the sense of believing seems to have vanished; she feels that she is now "in sinners' shoes."

– Pope Benedict XVI

My Angel

THE GLORY WE SHARE
is the Face you clearly see.
You fight my invisible foe,
the anger that flares
from who knows where?
You counter the dagger glare—
Oh the crossfire in my soul!
There you go—
Giver of good thoughts,
catalyst and companion
constant in kind deeds,
Guardian Angel,
free and faithful
deputy.

– Rita A. Simmonds

*T*HEN PETER…with his usual impulsiveness, says, "Master, we don't understand what you say either, but if we go away from you, where will we go? You alone have the words that explain life. It's impossible to find anyone like you. If I don't believe in you, I can't believe my own eyes, I can't believe in anything any more." It's the great, true, real alternative: either the nothingness in which everything culminates—the nothingness of what you love, of what you esteem, the nothingness of yourself and your friends, the nothingness of sky and earth, the nothingness, everything is nothing because everything will end up in ashes—either this or that man there is right; he is who he says he is. So Peter says to him, "Only you, only you explain everything," which means you set everything right again, and you make us see the connection between everything; and you make life great, intense, useful, and you give us a glimpse of its eternity.

– Monsignor Luigi Giussani

*Faith in God's love encompasses the call
and the obligation to respond with sincere love
to divine charity.*
(CCC 2093)

OUR LOVE FOR GOD is a response to his love for us: "We love because he first loved us" (1 Jn 4:19). Faith in God's love cannot remain mere data to be acknowledged because love desires to make a gift of itself. God reveals his love so that we might receive it. He wants us to know that he loves us because he wants us to desire to be loved. At that moment, we desire what he desires; God's will is done on earth as it is in heaven.

God's love is transformative, making us participate in his own love. This in turn orders all of our loves. Because he is infinite in perfection and goodness, we love God without measure, with *all* our heart, soul, mind, and strength (Mk 12:30). Our love for others, including ourselves, is rightly ordered when we love them as God loves them, desiring their happiness, which comes by fulfilling his plan for their lives, that is, their vocation. We love others for God and because of God by supporting them—by prayer, example, teaching, encouragement—to respond to God's love by embracing their vocation in order to live fully his plan of love.

– Douglas Bushman

*T*HE ONLY RATIONAL THING is the "yes." Why? Because the reality that is proposed corresponds to the nature of our heart more than any of our images. It corresponds to our thirst for happiness, which constitutes the reason for living, the nature of our I, the need for truth and happiness. Indeed, Christ corresponds to this more than does any image we can construct. Think what you want: just show me someone who's better than this man as he's described in the New Testament! Tell me, if you can think of one! You can't; he corresponds to your heart more than anything we can possibly imagine....

The obstacle on the road to the truth is a form of falsehood. It's called preconception. One has already formed, already fabricated, his opinion of him. Christ is to the opposite of what I would like: the political I, I in love, I who thirst for money, I who desire a career, I who want a healthy life. He's the opposite from whatever I place my hope in. And I do so in vain; because nothing hoped for ever comes about. The "no" is born solely of preconception.

– Monsignor Luigi Giussani

Lydia

Having arrived with Timothy and Luke in Philippi—
after he has been invited in a "vision" (Acts 16:10)—Paul
encounters Lydia at the riverbank outside the city. Lydia
is a working woman—a cloth merchant—a Gentile "wor-
shiper of God." She is converted at once. And right away
she extends an invitation to Paul and his companions: "If
you consider me a believer in the Lord, come and stay at
my home" (Acts 16:15). They *are* convinced, but on the way
there Paul angers the local authorities when he delivers a
clairvoyant girl of an evil spirit. He and his companions
are thrown into jail. A miraculous jailbreak follows. But
despite all the excitement, Lydia is still on their minds, and
they make their way at last to her house.

Paul's stay in Philippi, incredibly brief, but action-
packed, is bookmarked by the encounter with Lydia. And
Lydia is, no doubt, on Paul's mind when he writes his letter to the Philippians, so full of affection and encouragement. As if by a miracle (like the miracle of the loaves and
the fish), the Church in Philippi grows in grace and truth
from its humble beginnings in the home of Lydia.

– Lisa Lickona

*T*HE LITTLE WORD *CREDO* contains a basic option vis-à-vis reality as such; it signifies…a fundamental mode of behavior toward being, toward existence, toward one's own sector of reality, and toward reality as a whole. It signifies the deliberate view that what cannot be seen, what can in no wise move into the field of vision, is not unreal; that, on the contrary, what cannot be seen in fact represents true reality, the element that supports and makes possible all the rest of reality. And it signifies the view that this element that makes reality as a whole possible is also what grants man a truly human existence, what makes him possible as a human being existing in a human way. In other words, belief signifies the decision that at the very core of human existence there is a point that cannot be nourished and supported on the visible and tangible, that encounters and comes into contact with what cannot be seen and finds that it is a necessity for its own existence.…

Belief has always had something of a…leap about it, because in every age it represents the risky enterprise of accepting what plainly cannot be seen as the truly real and fundamental. Belief…has always been a decision calling on the depths of existence, a decision that in every age demanded a turnabout by man that can only be achieved by an effort of will.

– Pope Benedict XVI

*F*AITH IS THE FINDING of a "you" that upholds me and amid all the unfulfilled—and in the last resort unfulfillable—hope of human encounters gives me the promise of an indestructible love that not only longs for eternity but also guarantees it. Christian faith lives on the discovery that not only is there such a thing as objective meaning but that this meaning knows me and loves me, that I can entrust myself to it like the child who knows that everything he may be wondering about is safe in the "you" of his mother. Thus in the last analysis believing, trusting, and loving are one, and all the theses around which belief revolves are only concrete expressions of the all-embracing about-turn, of the assertion "I believe in you."...

The believer will repeatedly experience the darkness in which the contradiction of unbelief surrounds him like a gloomy prison from which there is no escape, and the indifference of the world, which goes its way unchanged as if nothing had happened, seems only to mock his hope. We have to pose the question, "Are you really he?" not only out of intellectual honesty and because of reason's responsibility, but also in accordance with the interior law of love, which wants to know more and more him to whom it has given its yes, so as to be able to love him more.

– Pope Benedict XVI

> *"What good is it, my brothers,*
> *if someone says he has faith but does not have works?*
> *Can that faith save him?"*
> (Jas 2:14)

BLESSED TERESA OF CALCUTTA did not win the Nobel Prize for Peace because of her faith. There is no Nobel Prize for heroic faith in God, for belief in divine revelation given to the world by Christ, for never missing Mass on Sunday or holy days. Mother Teresa was honored because of her "works." She certainly deserved such a distinction. And the whole world admires her for what she and her sisters did... and continue to do, namely, to care for the poorest of the poor.

The world doesn't really reflect on the deeper reality, that Mother Teresa and a whole litany of saints do what they do for love of Christ. She took the Lord at his word: Whatever you do to one of these least ones, you do unto me.

We know that faith is an "action-noun." Love is an "action-noun" and an "action-verb." And when we live by faith in God, when we "practice" the faith, we love one another. We also don't have to do heroic, Nobel-prize-winning works to love. Another Thérèse never left the confines of a Carmelite monastery and discovered her vocation was to be love at the heart of her Mother, the Church. Every little gesture can be an act of love when done for the Lord. And charity begins at home.

– Father Jacob Restrick, O.P.

*S*OMETHING ABSOLUTELY CENTRAL becomes visible here, namely, that faith has to do, and must have to do, with forgiving; that it aims at leading man to recognize that he is a being that can only find himself in the reception and transmission of forgiveness, a being that needs forgiveness even in his best and purest moments....

This means that faith is located in the act of conversion, in the turn of one's being from worship of the visible and practicable to trust in the invisible. The phrase "I believe" could here be literally translated by "I hand myself over to," "I assent to." In the sense of the Creed, and by origin, faith is not a recitation of doctrines, an acceptance of theories about things of which in themselves one knows nothing and therefore asserts something all the louder; it signifies an all-encompassing movement of human existence; to use Heidegger's language, one could say that it signifies an "about-turn" by the whole person that from then on constantly structures one's existence.

– Pope Benedict XVI

Paul's Jailer

HE IS A REALIST, this jailer. He feels secure being of use to the ruling power by guarding the prison that holds those seen as enemies of that power. When they "instructed the jailer to guard [Paul and Silas] securely" (Acts 16:23) he knows his life depends on it. Awoken by the earthquake, he sees the open doors and empty chains and knows it is all over. Not waiting for his life to be taken, he decides to take it himself. Then there they are, those two prisoners begging him not to do it. His eyes open. The real power is not with those who built this prison. It is with the God of these two men. He "fell down before Paul and Silas" (Acts 16:29) asking, "what must I do to be saved?" (Acts 16:30). As a realist, he knows that you have to serve somebody, and here is the power of someone who cares. He brings them home, "bathed their wounds; then he and all his family were baptized at once" (Acts 16:33). The jailer had served the power of violence, but was lost. The exceptional presence of these two men leads him to do the only realistic thing and beg for salvation, for himself and those whom he loves, from the God who loves him.

– Father Vincent Nagle, F.S.C.B.

*T*HE DRAMATIC STRUGGLE over the question, "Who is, who was Christ?"…shook the Church in the fourth and fifth centuries. This striving was not concerned with metaphysical speculations; such things could not have shaken those two centuries down to their very foundations and down to the simplest people living in them. On the contrary, the question at issue was this: What happens when I myself become a Christian, when I enroll myself under the banner of this Christ and thereby accept him as the authoritative man, as the measure of humanity? What kind of shift in being do I thus accomplish; what attitude to the business of being a man do I adopt? How deep does this process go? What estimate of reality as a whole does it involve?…

It is characteristic of faith that it comes from hearing, that it is the reception of something that I have not thought out, so that in the last analysis thinking in the context of faith is always a thinking over of something previously heard and received.

In other words, in faith the word takes precedence over the thought, a precedence that differentiates it structurally from the architecture of philosophy.

– Pope Benedict XVI

GRANT ME YOUR GRACE, O most merciful Jesus, that it may be with me, and work with me, and remain with me to the very end. Grant that I may always desire and will that which is most acceptable and pleasing to you. Let your will be mine. Let my will always follow yours and agree perfectly with it. Let my will be one with yours in willing and in not willing, and let me be unable to will or not will anything but what you will or do not will. Grant that I may die to all things in this world, and for your sake love to be despised and unknown in this life. Give me above all desires the desire to rest in you, and in you let my heart have peace. You are true peace of heart. You alone are its rest. Without you all things are difficult and troubled. In this peace, the selfsame that is in you, the Most High, the everlasting Good, I will sleep and take my rest. Amen.

– Venerable Thomas à Kempis

*F*AITH IS NOT SOMETHING thought up by me but something that comes to me from outside, its word cannot be treated and exchanged as I please; it is always foreordained, always ahead of my thinking....

The primary factor for belief is, as we have seen, the proclaimed word. While a thought is interior, purely intellectual, the word represents the element that unites us with others. It is the way in which intellectual communication takes place, the form in which the mind is, as it were, human, that is, corporeal and social. This primacy of the word means that faith is focused on community of mind in a quite different way from philosophical thinking. In philosophy, what comes first is the private search for truth, which then, secondarily, seeks and finds traveling companions. Faith, on the other hand, is first of all a call to community, to unity of mind through the unity of the word. Indeed, its significance is, a priori, an essentially social one: it aims at establishing unity of mind through the unity of the word. Only secondarily will it then open the way for each individual's private venture in search of truth.

– Pope Benedict XVI

Phoebe

PHOEBE IS A CLOSE FRIEND OF PAUL'S, and she is probably entrusted with the delivery of his letter to the Romans. Hence his reference to her: "I commend to you Phoebe our sister, who is [also] a minister of the church at Cenchrae, that you may receive her in the Lord in a manner worthy of the holy ones...for she has been a benefactor to many and to me as well" (Rom 16:1-2). The word "minister" here (sometimes translated "deaconess") can be distracting. The word literally means "servant," and, as Pope Benedict XVI says, "Although at that time the title had not yet acquired a specific ministerial value of a hierarchical kind, it expresses a true and proper exercise of responsibility on the part of this woman for this Christian community." Indeed, Paul could not have managed without Phoebe and her peers, who were "helpers of many."

Paul here expresses concretely what he develops elsewhere concerning the Church as the Body of Christ: "As a body is one though it has many parts, and all the parts of the body, though many, are one body, so also Christ... Now you are Christ's body, and individually parts of it." (1 Cor 12:12, 27). You, whether Jew or Greek, priest or lay, man or woman, have a mission in the Church and the world that only you can complete. You can have faith that the Father has equipped you to do it.

– Angela Franks

*H*E WHO TRIES TO BE a mere observer experiences nothing…. The reality "God" can only impinge on the vision of him who enters into…the experiment that we call faith…. The verbal strife with the unbelieving interlocutor has finally reached the point at which the latter admits that he must make a choice about God. But he would like to avoid the leap, to possess a mathematical certainty: "Is there no way of illuminating the darkness and of seeing the face of the cards?" "Yes, Scripture and all the other testimony of religion." "Yes, but my hands are tied and my lips are closed…. I am so made that I cannot believe. What am I to do?" "So you admit that your inability to believe does not come from reason; on the contrary, reason leads you to belief; the reason for your refusal lies elsewhere. There is therefore no point in trying to convince you any further by piling up the proofs of the existence of God; you must above all fight against your passions. You would like to reach faith, but you do not know the way? You want to cure yourself of unbelief, and you ask for a remedy? Take a lesson from those who were earlier racked by doubts like yourself…. Follow the way by which they began; by acting as if they believed, by taking holy water, by having Masses said, and so on. This will bring you quite naturally to believe and will stupefy you."

– Pope Benedict XVI

"Faith of itself, if it does not have works, is dead."
(Jas 2:17)

Bᴵᴸᴸ Wᴵᴸꜱᴏɴ ᴡᴀꜱ ᴀ ᴅʀᴜɴᴋ. He had made many promises to his wife, Lois, that he would stop drinking. He told God he wouldn't drink again. But he did. When he was on a business trip, very close to breaking all his promises again, he didn't have faith anymore that he could really stay sober. But he made a phone call before going into the hotel bar, and that led him to meeting a Dr. Bob Smith, who was also trying to stay sober. And they met and talked to each other for hours. They didn't drink. They sought out others who didn't have faith in sobriety or that God would free them from their addiction. And all they did was talk.

This was the beginning of Alcoholics Anonymous in 1935. Today there are groups of men and women talking to each other all over the world. Bill W. eventually wrote down twelve steps to describe this program of recovery. And the Twelfth Step states that "having had a spiritual awakening as a result of these steps, we tried to carry this message to alcoholics, and to practice these principles in all our affairs."

For such men and women, faith is not dead, but is increased by "giving it away" to others.

– Father Jacob Restrick, ᴏ.ᴘ.

*T*HE PERSON OF JESUS *IS* HIS TEACHING, and his teaching is he himself. Christian faith, that is, faith in Jesus as the Christ, is therefore truly "personal faith." What this means can really be understood only from this standpoint. Such faith is not the acceptance of a system but the acceptance of this person who is his word....

Jesus did not call himself unequivocally the Messiah (Christ); the man who gave him this name was Pilate, who for his part associated himself with the accusation of the Jews by giving in to this accusation and proclaiming Jesus on the cross, in an execution notice drawn up in all the international languages of the day, as the executed king (= Messiah, *Christus*) of the Jews. This execution notice, the death sentence of history, became with paradoxical unity the "profession of faith," the real starting point and taproot of the Christian faith, which holds Jesus to be the Christ: as the crucified criminal, this Jesus is the Christ, the King.... His existence is thus his word. He *is* word because he is love. From the cross faith understands in increasing measure that this Jesus did not just do and say *something*; that in him message and person are identical, that he is all along what he says.

– Pope Benedict XVI

A Gospel Litany of Faith

Lord Jesus,

◖ Once the shepherds saw you in the manger, they left proclaiming the Good News to the world.
– *May your presence move me to live by faith.*

◖ On the storm-tossed sea, you called Peter to come to you, walking across the water.
– *Rid me of fear—save my faith from faltering.*

◖ When blind Bartimaeus begged you for sight, you declared, "Your faith has healed you."
– *Give me the vision and the insight of true faith.*

◖ When the woman with a hemorrhage touched your hem you said, "Your faith has cured you."
– *Make my faith stronger than any dread or worry.*

◖ Jairus knelt before you in belief, begging you to come and raise his daughter from her deathbed.
– *Let me live this truth: what is needed is trust.*

◖ To the lame man by the Sheep Pool you asked, "Do you want to be healed?"
– *Help me to believe in your desire to heal me.*

◖ You marveled at the widow's mite because she gave more than all who donated great sums.
– *Make my life one of a total gift of self in faith.*

◖ Struck with wonder at his healing, the leper returned to you; his faith was his salvation.
– *Let my faith be marked by humility and thanks.*

◖ When the centurion saw your suffering, he confessed, "This man was the Son of God."
– *May my suffering lead to deeper faith.*

◖ When you saw the faith of the men carrying the stretcher of the paralytic, you healed him.
– *May my faith bear fruit for the world.*

– Father Peter John Cameron, O.P.

Faith, Witness, and Mission

IN THE YEARS when I was coming to believe, a phrase that Jesus pronounces many times bothered me a bit: "Your faith has saved you," he says (cf. Mk 5:34; Mk 10:52; Lk 7:50, etc.). I thought that there was something not quite right about that. After all, right before Jesus speaks these words in the fifth chapter of Mark, the Evangelist explains that Jesus perceived "at once that power had gone out from him" (Mk 5:30). Evidently, it was Jesus who was saving these people, not them saving themselves through their "faith." So, what role does faith play?

A great teacher of faith answered this one day when he offered to me this definition: "Faith is the recognition of the presence of Jesus here and now." I was stunned. This understanding of faith was completely revolutionary for me. I realized at once that this definition made clear what Jesus means by "Your faith has saved you." Jesus was referring to the people's ability to recognize in him the presence of the one who saves. Their faith made them come near to him and beg of him their salvation. His presence provoked this response in them, this faith. In turn, he healed them.

The question of faith came alive for me. Up to that moment, I had lived the mission of faith by holding and defending certain fundamental propositions or notions, such as, "Jesus is the Son of God." Now I saw that propositions such as these were the necessary *fruit* of faith. Faith itself is that thing that happens which allows a person to point and say, "It is the Lord!" (Jn 21:7). "Faith," says Pope Benedict XVI, "is an encounter with the man Jesus."

The mission of faith, then, is not primarily arguing about certain ideas. Rather, it is the wide-open availability to people so that they might be invited to meet Christ in the Church, among the faces that make up the Body of Christ. Witnessing to the faith is a matter of embracing people exactly where they are and as they are. Thus, in allowing people to share my life, they can, with grace, make the very same discovery of that presence, the presence that lets them say with Saint Peter and me, "You are the Messiah, the Son of the living God" (Mt 16:16).

– Father Vincent Nagle, F.S.C.B.

The acts of faith, hope, and charity enjoined by the first commandment are accomplished in prayer.
(CCC 2098)

IT IS DIFFICULT to converse with a stranger. Who is this? What shall I say? What if this person is not interested in what I say? For people of faith, God is no stranger. All of Jesus' prayers—the Our Father, his prayer before raising Lazarus, his prayer in the Garden of Gethsemane, his priestly prayer, his prayer at the Last Supper—are addressed to the Father. They concern the Father's plan of love and Jesus' place in it. Faith enables us to pray like Jesus because by faith we receive what he has revealed about the Father and his plan of love. Even more, faith makes it possible for us to pray through, with, and in him; Jesus prays in us, and we pray in him. In him, prayer is communion with God, in thought and in action. This faith-inspired prayer fulfills the first commandment because we turn to the one, true God, the Father revealed by Jesus, and we embrace his plan of love by fulfilling the vocation that he gives us, ordering our lives to the hallowing of his name, the coming of his kingdom, and his will being done on earth as it is in heaven.

– Douglas Bushman

*C*HRISTIAN FAITH IS...above all things a looking forward, a reaching-out of hope....

Christian faith is not based on the atomized individual but comes from the knowledge that there is no such thing as the mere individual, that, on the contrary, man is himself only when he is fitted into the whole: into mankind, into history, into the cosmos, as is right and proper for a being who is "spirit in body."...

Being a Christian means essentially changing over from being for oneself to being for one another....

Of course, the principle of love, if it is to be genuine, includes faith. Only thus does it remain what it is. For without faith, which we have come to understand as a term expressing man's ultimate need to receive and the inadequacy of all personal achievement, love becomes an arbitrary deed. It cancels itself out and becomes self-righteousness: faith and love condition and demand each other reciprocally. Similarly, in the principle of love there is also present the principle of hope, which looks beyond the moment and its isolation and seeks the whole. Thus our reflections finally lead of their own accord to the words in which Paul named the main supporting pillars of Christianity: "so faith, hope, love abide, these three; but the greatest of these is love" (1 Cor 13:13).

– Pope Benedict XVI

Priscilla

With her husband Aquila, Priscilla (also known as Prisca) actively worked with Paul in the establishment of Christianity in Corinth and Ephesus. After Phoebe, they head up the long list of people whom Paul thanks in Romans 16: "Greet Prisca and Aquila, my co-workers in Christ Jesus, who risked their necks for my life, to whom not only I am grateful but also all the churches of the Gentiles" (Rom 16:3). Paul, who has ordained many through the laying on of hands, here singles out first, not another cleric, but a lay couple as exemplary "co-workers in Christ Jesus." They remind us that the Church is more than the priesthood, as essential as it is: priests are to bring the sacraments to the laity, who must be receptive soil for the seed of the Word if Christianity is to take root and flower.

Priscilla and Aquila were tent-makers (Acts 18:3); they brought the saving truth of Jesus to the everyday world of commerce. They also had a house-church, a safe place where Christians gathered for the Eucharist: "Aquila and Prisca, together with the church at their house send you hearty greetings in the Lord" (1 Cor 16:19 rsv). Thus they allowed the Gospel to penetrate into two essential fields: work and family. Pope Benedict XVI summarizes their example: "Every house can be transformed into a small church."

– Angela Franks

"Indeed, someone may say, 'You have faith and I have works.' Demonstrate your faith to me without works, and I will demonstrate my faith to you from my works."

(Jas 2:18)

"A" FOR ADULTERY! I was in high school when I first read Nathaniel Hawthorne's *The Scarlet Letter*. I couldn't imagine the "Puritan" practice he wrote about, not to mention the hidden surprise in the plot.

More noted than any of Nathaniel Hawthorne's great books was a daughter named Rose who married and had a child, who died in childhood. The first remarkable thing about Rose is that she became a Catholic. More remarkable, after her marriage ended, her heart (now formed by faith) turned with compassion toward people with terminal cancer who had no one to take care of them. She brought them into her home and dressed their wounds. Another woman joined her in this corporal "work" of mercy. Together they became Dominican Third Order religious, and a new congregation of sisters was born. Over a hundred years later, "Hawthorne Dominican Sisters" are still carrying on the "work" of their foundress, Mother Alphonsa Hawthorne. The difference between them and dedicated agnostic caregivers is huge. It's the life of faith which blossoms into loving service. We don't wear a sign for all to see, except the "sign" of the cross. Faith spilling over into works.

– Father Jacob Restrick, O.P.

*D*IVINE WISDOM gently coaxes us to submit to being purified of self, to being comforted in our helplessness and poverty; it persuades us to surrender control, and to abandon ourselves blindly to love. Without such a period of prayer it is hardly possible for our faith in the sacraments to have the depth that will enable us to receive them fruitfully. Nor is it likely that we shall recognize and respond to God's self-gift in the humdrum of our daily life.

Our senses do not necessarily support our life of faith; on the contrary they can shout denial. God longs for us to live by the faith of Jesus. We are blind; such is the fallen human condition. We do not "see" God, but Jesus does. God has made *him* our wisdom. We choose to live by *his* "knowing" the Father, his faith—a faith that was expressed in total abandonment to his Father and a trust in him throughout all life's vicissitudes, and supremely in his acceptance of death by crucifixion. The "immeasurable greatness of his power" by which God the Father accomplished the exaltation of Jesus is now at work in us who believe (Eph 1:17-23). We are enabled to live our lives in this certitude all the time, not just sometimes—and not just in some matters, but in all.

– Sister Ruth Burrows, O.C.D.

Education in the faith *by the parents should begin
in the child's earliest years....*
*Family catechesis precedes, accompanies, and enriches
other forms of instruction in the faith.*
(CCC 2226)

GOD SENDS PARENTS to their children as the first missionaries to proclaim his love through their actions and words. Everyone, Blessed John Paul II taught, is by nature a philosopher. He meant that life is a classroom, and the mandatory curriculum for all people is the meaning of life. Because of our free will, life is a great test of choosing for Christ or against Christ, who came that we might attain a blessed life: "I came so that they might have life and have it more abundantly" (Jn 10:10). Faith says "Yes" to the abundant life of Christ. This is why the best way to learn the meaning of life is by seeing it in those who, by faith, have discovered it and live it in Christ: the saints of God's family. Living with meaning in Christ brings joy in knowing that as images of God we are made for love, that in Christ we possess that love, and that nothing can separate us from it (Rom 8:37-39). The power of evangelization is the joy of living faith.

– Douglas Bushman

*T*RUST CAN BE AN EXPECTATION based on probabilistic calculations or on ordinary experience: to trust means to anticipate that an object or a person will be as reliable as it or he used to be (to trust one's car, to trust a debtor or a physician). In personal contacts another sense of "trusting" emerges; a non-calculated confidence, an acceptance of another person in advance, no matter whether we have ever had the opportunity to verify her or his reliability and even if we have reason to doubt it. This comes closer to what a believer feels in his attitude to God. God is not reliable and cannot be trusted on the basis of a historical record showing that whenever his children asked for his help, it was invariably given according to their wishes; they cannot escape the conclusion that fortune and misery are distributed at random and not in agreement with the rules of justice as they normally understand it. They accept God's will as it is manifested in the chaotic mass of incomprehensible accidents, of blindly operating laws of nature, of patent injustice in human affairs. They trust God before his wisdom and goodness are experimentally tested and irrespective of the results of possible tests. Such results indeed are never conclusive: occasionally they seem to be positive, more often they defeat expectations; yet trust is not shaken precisely because it is not based on empirical evidence but given *a priori*. Once it is given, but not before, believers can perceive God's hand at work in events and they frequently have the feeling of a world being wisely governed in spite of all the horrors that seem to defy such an assessment.

– Leszek Kolakowski

ENLIGHTEN ME, good Jesus, with the brightness of internal light, and take away all darkness from the habitation of my heart. Restrain my wandering thoughts and suppress the temptations which attack me so violently. Fight strongly for me, and vanquish these evil beasts—the alluring desires of the flesh—so that peace may come through your power and the fullness of your praise resound in the holy courts, which is a pure conscience. Command the winds and the tempests; say to the sea: "Be still," and to the north wind, "Do not blow," and there will be a great calm. Send forth your light and your truth to shine on the earth, for I am as earth, empty and formless until you illumine me. Pour out your grace from above. Shower my heart with heavenly dew. Open the springs of devotion to water the earth, that it may produce the best of good fruits. Lift up my heart pressed down by the weight of sins, and direct all my desires to heavenly things, that having tasted the sweetness of supernal happiness, I may find no pleasure in thinking of earthly things.

Snatch me up and deliver me from all the passing comfort of creatures, for no created thing can fully quiet and satisfy my desires. Join me to yourself in an inseparable bond of love; because you alone can satisfy him who loves you, and without you all things are worthless.

– Venerable Thomas à Kempis

Titus

TITUS IS A GREEK, not a Jew, and a trusted companion of Saint Paul (Gal 2:1, 3; Paul also mentions Titus often in 2 Cor). At the time when Paul is at odds with the Christian community in Corinth, Titus is Paul's companion and a mediator in the dispute. Titus also completes the collection that Paul is making to help the poor Christians in Jerusalem.

Later, Paul addresses a letter to Titus, after Paul had left him behind in Crete to organize the Church there. In the letter, Paul instructs Titus to set up stable Christian communities in Crete and to appoint presbyters or bishops in each town.

Throughout the letter, Paul emphasizes true faith and sound doctrine. The true faith, our Christian faith, is not a vague affirmation of optimism, but the firm confession of who God is and what he has done for us in Jesus the Christ, as we say each Sunday: "I believe in one God, the Father almighty…I believe in one Lord Jesus Christ…I believe in the Holy Spirit." When he writes of sound doctrine, Paul refers to it as the authentic message (Ti 1:9). He had already encountered irresponsible teachers, who had swerved from the truth and were upsetting whole families (Ti 1:11, 14). The Church has preserved the authentic message and handed it on to us—Thanks be to God!

– Father Joseph T. Lienhard, S.J.

*O*NE MAY RETORT that if God indeed wants to convey to us meaningful signs of his rule, his actions appear counter-productive since we are not capable of comprehending them. What is the purpose of speaking to people in a language they do not know and can never properly learn? But this is to beg the question. Whoever believes in God's presence in the world, has to admit that empirically his presence is ambiguous. Clearly, there would be no need of faith if the course of world affairs followed directly and unmistakably the norms of justice; this would mean that we live in Paradise. Adam and Eve did not believe in God's existence in the sense that their descendants were to (exception being made for Abraham, Moses and a few mystics); they lived in a real theocracy, under God's direct and visible government. Life in exile is bound to be ambiguous, God's signs are never clear, trusting him is inevitably to defy the limits of natural knowledge.

– Leszek Kolakowski

*"See how a person is justified by works
and not by faith alone."*
(Jas 2:24)

My MOTHER COLLECTED bisque figurines. Her favorite was a seated little girl holding a pear. The figurines were on display in our living room, and instilled since toddler-ville was the admonition: *"No, no. Don't touch!"* My fat little teenage hands, however, were allowed to touch, and even to dust. And that's when the little girl holding a pear slipped out of my hands and smashed to smithereens!

I wanted to die on the spot! I had faith in God's mercy and forgiveness, although I wasn't so sure of my mother's. I was spared martyrdom, and came to believe in my mother's mercy, love, and forgiveness because I experienced it firsthand. My mother knew I was truly contrite. She had faith in me, even when I made mistakes.

I also wanted to "make up" for my clumsiness—it's in our human makeup to be "justified," to make up for our sins. Only after I worked and saved money, bought another figurine, and then saw my mother's joy, did I feel justified.

We are justified before God because we belong to Christ—he is our justification. And because he lives in us, we strive to love one another. *See the Christians, how they love one another.*

– Father Jacob Restrick, O.P.

*I*F WE ARE AT TIMES CONSCIOUS of our weakness, faith reminds us that, since God is himself our strength and our support, we have nothing to fear, even when the world and the devil join forces against us....

This is most evident in the wondrous change wrought by the Holy Spirit in the Apostles. Armed at his coming with the power of God, they, who up to this time had been timid and slothful, go courageously to meet all kinds of trials—scourgings, imprisonment, and death itself—glad to undergo suffering in the name of Jesus....

Faith is likewise a *source of comfort*, not only in the midst of tribulations and of humiliations, but also when we have the misfortune of losing our dear ones. We are not among those who sorrow without hope....

Our chief consolation is the doctrine of the *Communion of Saints*. While awaiting the day when we shall be reunited to those that have departed this life, we are even now bound to them by the most intimate ties in Christ Jesus. We pray that their time of trial be shortened and their entrance into heaven hastened; they in their turn, now assured of their salvation, ardently pray that we may one day join them.

– Father Adolphe Tanquerey, s.s.

All Souls

EACH DROP OF RAIN
makes its own circular splash;
so fast
the puddle grows,
and how many souls
have come and gone
to be somewhere else
carried on?

A mother always knows
a soul she has enclosed;
in a moment long
she knows
what's come and gone.

The puddle grows
and who's to blame?
All
fall
silent.
We watch
and cannot stop
the rain.

– Rita A. Simmonds

"In this you rejoice…that the genuineness of your faith, more precious than gold that is perishable even though tested by fire, may prove to be for praise, glory, and honor at the revelation of Jesus Christ."
(1 Pt 1:6a-7)

W E LIKE THINGS THAT ARE GENUINE. Think of a handbag or a wallet that is stamped: "Genuine Leather" and one that only looks like leather. I've had both genuine leather shoes and artificial leather shoes, and over time, the artificial leather shoes crack and wear away, while the genuine leather become softer and pliable. I still have them, while the fake leather shoes I tossed years ago.

Saint Peter's faith was sorely tried, and for all his bravado, he denied that he even knew the Lord. But his failure turned out for strengthening his in a more genuine way. He was the first Apostle to see the Lord risen from the dead, and that was what he proclaimed for the rest of his life, which was full of trials and ended in crucifixion. Genuine faith is tested and purified like gold, which is considered the most precious of metals.

Our faith is our most precious gift which sustains us through every kind of hardship and trial and suffering. It endures, and in the end will soften our hearts and make them pliable. Then the Holy Spirit can form us into vessels of praise and others will see that our faith is for real.

– Father Jacob Restrick, O.P.

*E*VERY PERSON has a basic religious attitude, because man is made to yearn for an all-embracing meaning of life. We cannot carry out a single action without implying—perhaps unawares, against our own theoretical convictions—the ultimate meaning of things. This affirming, perhaps unconsciously, of the ultimate meaning of life is called the *religious sense*, since it is born of the most elementary and impressive evidence that we can ever have: the evidence that the ultimate meaning is "more" than we, and that we depend on it totally. The religious sense of its very nature is the soul of all other interests, particularly because all our interests move us towards our happiness, our destiny; in other words, our ultimate meaning.

I am not the measure of all things: an Other is. So life consists in living for an Other, in affirming an Other. The Greeks used to speak of Fate; the Stoics of necessity; Christians speak of Providence. But over and above the differences, everyone has a clear awareness of this supremely evident reality: the fact that we depend.

– Monsignor Luigi Giussani

Philemon

IF WE ACCIDENTALLY CAME UPON someone's email or personal letter, our first reaction might be, "I shouldn't be looking at this." One could think the same thing in looking at the letter Philemon received from Paul. The shortest of all Paul's letters, it is a private one, yet it delivers one of Paul's most challenging messages.

Philemon is a Christian leader in Colossae. It is believed he was a wealthy man and that the local church met in his home. One of Philemon's slaves runs away, eventually meets Paul, and becomes a Christian. Paul advises the slave to return to Philemon. Of course the slave is fearful of punishment, so Paul writes a letter appealing to Philemon's faith in Christ. Paul encourages Philemon to receive his slave back into his home with forgiveness and mercy. Philemon is challenged to remember that no matter what the status each has in the world, both he and his slave are now brothers in Christ (Phlm 16). This is a radical and challenging direction, given that slavery is an accepted part of the culture. Paul confidently tells Philemon that he will be given the grace to do what seems hard. Philemon's problem poses a challenge for us: what does it mean to forgive?

– Monsignor Gregory E. S. Malovetz

*C*HRISTIANITY IS AN EVENT. There is no other word to indicate its nature, neither the word *law*, nor the words *ideology, concept,* or *plan.* Christianity is not a religious doctrine, a series of moral laws, or a collection of rites. Christianity is a fact, an event. All the rest is a consequence. The word "event" is therefore crucial. It indicates the method chosen and used by God to save man: God became man in the womb of a fifteen-to-seventeen-year-old girl named Mary, in "the womb…where our desire did dwell," as Dante says. The manner in which God entered into relationship with us to save us is an event, not a thought or a religious sentiment. It is a fact that took place in history, a fact that reveals who God is and points out what God wants from man, what man must do in his relationship with God. As a way of communicating himself to man, God could have chosen direct enlightenment, so that each individual would have to follow what God suggested to him in his thoughts and in his heart. This would have been by no means an easier or safer road, since it would be constantly exposed to the fluctuation of feelings and thoughts. But the way God chose to save us is an event, not our thoughts!

– Monsignor Luigi Giussani

*"Be sober and vigilant. Your opponent the devil
is prowling around like a roaring lion looking for
[someone] to devour. Resist him, steadfast in faith,
knowing that your fellow believers throughout the world
undergo the same sufferings."*

(1 Pt 5:8-9)

SISTER MARY BARUCH lived in a cloistered monastery all her life. On her Fiftieth Jubilee she was asked what sustained her faith all these years. She said: "Realizing that my life was not about me. We don't engage in any active works, but we realize that we belong to the Mystical Body of Christ. We have temptations, discouragement, trials of faith. I've stood in the cloister hearing the devil whisper in my ear: 'What if it's not all true!' I've wrestled with resentment and envy over what other sisters have. I had to learn to keep my poor mind from entertaining impure thoughts and desires. I have to keep watch over food and drink and over-work. It's like the devil takes a quiet stroll around the cloister waiting to attack us in moments of weakness. I know I'm just like others who must endure greater temptations and suffering than I. But I also know I'm not alone. We're all making the journey to God, alone, together."

Sister Mary Baruch told me she copied out these words of Saint Peter and taped it by her bed. "It reminded me to put the 'Big Cat' out every night."

– Father Jacob Restrick, O.P.

*F*OR REASON, owing to its own very original dynamic, cannot fulfill itself unless it recognizes that reality is rooted in Mystery. Human reason reaches its apex, and so is truly reason, when it recognizes things for what they are, and things as they are proceed from an Other. What intensity of life is promised to those who grasp, instant by instant, the relationship of everything with the origin! Each instant enjoys a definitive relationship with the Mystery, and so nothing is lost: this is what we exist for, and this is our happiness.

Yet there is a wound in man's heart that distorts something inside him and he cannot, by his own strength, remain in truth. He fixes his attention and his desire on particular and limited things. The original plan, that for which man is created, was altered by the arbitrary use of freedom. Thus men tend towards a particular, which, when detached from the whole, is identified as life's aim. The experience we live every day is that men tend to identify the totality of life with something partial and limited. Escaping this partiality is not in our hands. None of us can, alone, recover a true way of looking at reality.

– Monsignor Luigi Giussani

Contemplation is a gaze of faith, fixed on Jesus.
(CCC 2715)

FAITH MAKES JESUS the focus of life and prayer. He reveals everything: the truth about God, about man, and about God's plan of love for man. Jesus is the pearl of great price, the treasure hidden in a field. We would sell everything to possess him (Mt 13:44-46). When faith contemplates him, we are aware of being in possession of our entire meaning, purpose, and happiness. At this point, prayer becomes a simple gaze of faith, fired by love. All that we have learned about our faith, celebrated in the sacraments, lived and prayed as his disciples—all of this is present in him. By faith we are conscious of being in the presence of the pure and Holy One. By faith we know that his nature is love, and that therefore he is making a gift of himself to us, right here, right now. By faith we can consent to being loved, because by faith we know what his love means. In his loving look upon us and our loving look upon him, everything that faith can say is said. The gaze of faith is an exchange of love, our participation in the "eternal exchange of love" (CCC 221).

– Douglas Bushman

*T*HE DYNAMIC OF FAITH, as it emerges within Christian revelation, is quite different. Here it is no longer our reason that explains, but our reason that opens up—thus perceiving the fulfillment of its dynamic—to God's self-revelation. In this way the divine Mystery communicates its nature, its "thoughts" and "ways," manifesting itself in time and space. While religious experience springs from the need for meaning that is awakened by the impact with the real, faith is the recognition of an exceptional Presence that corresponds totally to our destiny, and the adherence to this Presence. Faith means to recognize that what a historical Presence says of itself is true.

Christian faith is the memory of a historical fact: a Man said something about himself that others accepted as true, and that I, too, accept because of the exceptional way in which that fact still reaches me. Jesus is a man who said, "I am the way, the truth and the life."… Paying attention to what that Man did and said to the point of saying, "I believe in this Man," adhering to his Presence, and affirming what he said as the truth: this is faith. Faith is an act of reason moved by the exceptional nature of a Presence that brings man to say, "This man who is speaking is truthful. He is not lying, I accept what he says."

– Monsignor Luigi Giussani

Onesimus

THE EXPRESSION "you can't go home again" is a reminder that we cannot live in the past. When Onesimus receives the direction to go home from Paul, he may have been shocked. He is definitely afraid. Onesimus is a slave who ran away from his master, Philemon, a Colossian church leader. After meeting Paul, Onesimus is converted to Christianity. Ready to begin a whole new life, he may have expected Paul to send him into the world to preach. Instead, Paul tells him to return to his master and seek reconciliation. In a world in which slavery is commonly accepted, Onesimus knows this is not a good idea. Paul sends a letter to the master, appealing to his Christian faith on behalf of "my child Onesimus…my own heart" (Phlm 10, 12).

This Letter to Philemon, the shortest of all Paul's letters, is a challenge for Christians. Are we willing to live what we say we believe, or do I put limits on how I live my faith? For Onesimus, it means trusting in the power of the Holy Spirit not only to return and make amends. It means a willingness to live with the consequence of his actions. Onesimus does return and some believe he later becomes a bishop, but that is disputed. What we do know is he shows us what it means to trust God's grace and live reconciliation.

– Monsignor Gregory E. S. Malovetz

*T*HE ENCOUNTER WE HAVE HAD…in time becomes…the true form by which I look at… myself, at others, and at things. When an encounter is all-embracing, it becomes the shape…of relationships. It…is the form by which they are conceived of and lived out.

The attitude of one who is struck by the Christian event, who recognizes it and adheres to it, is called "faith."

Our position regarding the event of Christ is the same as that of Zacchaeus before that Man who stopped under the tree that he had climbed, and told him, "Come down, quickly, I am coming to your place." It is the same position as that of the widow whose only son had died, and who heard Jesus saying, in a way that appears so irrational to us, "Woman, do not weep!" It is absurd to say such a thing to a mother whose only son has died. For them, as for us, it was the experience of the presence of something radically different from what we imagine, and at the same time something that totally and originally corresponds to the profound expectations of our person…. Since our heart is made for this correspondence, it should be something normal in life, but, on the contrary, it never happens. When it does happen, it is an exceptional experience. Faith is having the sincerity to recognize, the simplicity to accept, and the affection to cling to such a Presence.

– Monsignor Luigi Giussani

"The victory that conquers the world is our faith."
(1 Jn 5:4)

A NUMBER OF YEARS AGO there was a British comedy called *Bless me, Father*. The principal characters were an old pastor and his young curate. The young priest was devoted to serving the poor of the parish and was involved in many programs to that effect, while the old pastor visited the well-to-do parishioners and took care of them. The young priest became exasperated at the old priest's "ministry" and verbally objected to it: "Why do you spend all your time catering to the rich; it's the poor who need us!" The old priest (and I'm paraphrasing) smiled and said: "Yes, but when the chips are down, the rich know that money can't save them."

We all live in our own worlds, as it were. And when that world strikes us with hardship, be it chronic illness, addiction, tragic losses, or sadness, we also know that money, power, fame, influence, experience, and education do not "save us." Knowing (and faith is a knowledge) that God is present; God is for real; God loves us; God's grace will get us through, is the victory that conquers our world. When our world has its rug pulled out from under us, and we are losing our balance, our faith bids us to "offer it up" for our good and the good of all his holy Church.

– Father Jacob Restrick, O.P.

*E*SSENTIALLY, faith is recognizing a Presence that is different…. What is exceptional does not normally happen, and when it happens one says, "This is something quite different. There is a superhuman power here!"…

Just as Christ gives himself to me in a present event, he brings to life within me the capacity for grasping it and recognizing it in its exceptionality. Thus my freedom accepts that event, and acknowledges it. So in us, faith is both the recognition of the exceptional that is present and the simple and sincere adherence that says "Yes" and does not object. Recognition and adherence are part of the moment in which the Lord reveals himself to us through the power of his Spirit. They are part of the moment when the event of Christ enters our life. To recognize him in life is a gift of the Spirit, which always implies a simplicity of heart…. For God creates us with our eyes and heart wide open to reality, positively reaching out to it, so that when we meet something we can say, "This is it." God creates man with this positive outlook and this affection for reality.

Recognizing Christ is a grace, and it is a gift of ourselves to him in original simplicity. The event of Christ is God's love for man recognized by man's love for God.

– Monsignor Luigi Giussani

*"Beloved…I now feel a need to write
to encourage you to contend for the faith that was once
for all handed down to the holy ones."*

(Jude 3)

Humpty Dumpty once sat on the Wall of Faith. He could see things from a higher perspective. The Church and the faith handed on to him from his youth was a strong wall which was a rampart keeping out the attack of an atheistic secular world. Humpty Dumpty sat on the Wall of Faith and knew a communion with God and with his holy ones, the saints in heaven, and those on earth who knew they were sinners striving to be saints.

Humpty Dumpty sat on the wall; Humpty Dumpty had a great fall. He lost his faith in God and in his Church; he lost his communion with God's people, and became "scrambled egg" on the floor. All the king's horses and all the king's men couldn't put Humpty Dumpty together again.

Sometimes the Lord allows us to fall off the wall. Sometimes the Lord allows us to lose our faith, so we may regain it again in a way we never knew before. We're all Mr. or Ms. Dumpty whenever we fall into sin. All the king's horses (money, celebrity, medicine) can't "put us together again." But Christ, our King, can and did! In him we are made his "Beloved" by his grace. And so we may sit on the Wall of Faith again and again, and gaze upon the gate into Eternal Life.

– Father Jacob Restrick, o.p.

*F*AITH IS THE "ACKNOWLEDGMENT" that God has become a factor of present experience. As acknowledgment, it is an act of reason, a judgment, rather than a feeling or a state of mind. Faith is the fulfillment of human reason. It is the intelligence of reality in its ultimate horizon, the recognition of that in which everything consists. Natural intelligence cannot reach this ultimate horizon. It is only through something that has happened, through the event of God-made-man, through his gift, that our renewed intelligence can recognize and touch him. Thus faith reaches an apex beyond reason: without faith, reason is not complete, whereas, in faith, reason becomes the ladder of hope.… For man, adhering with his freedom means unhesitatingly recognizing with simplicity what his reason perceives as exceptional.…

This exceptionality "captures" man's heart (think of the Samaritan woman) so that we can recognize it and adhere to it in virtue of a correspondence we have perceived. This perception leads us to welcome it without delay and to adhere to it wholeheartedly; the entire self, intelligence and affection, is moved in this acknowledgment laden with love. Thus man can say, "All that you have done, all that you have said corresponds so deeply to me that I cannot help recognizing present in you that which you are."

– Monsignor Luigi Giussani

Jude

LITTLE IS KNOWN OF HIS LIFE, save that he was the brother of James, author of the Letter of James, and that he himself wrote a letter, tantalizingly short, found near the end of the New Testament, the single chapter of which covers two pages and twenty-five verses. But brief being best, the message it imparts is fraught with an urgency that transcends the time of its composition.

And what a testimony it provides, too, concerning the sheer passion of the man who wrote it! Seething with a divine impatience to protect the Good News, to ensure that others may be moved to fall in love with Christ, the Epistle becomes a rallying cry for churchmen to defend "our common salvation…that was once for all handed down to the holy ones" (Jude 3). The sacred deposit having come under attack by those who would subvert the bedrock of belief, which is nothing less than God's enfleshment in the world, men of faith are obliged to resist. To deflect the Gnostic assault, and thus to remain God's beloved, you must, says Jude, "build yourselves up in your most holy faith" (Jude 20), awaiting in hope the promised deliverance in Christ Jesus. To whom—here he ends on a sublime doxological note—"be glory, majesty, power, and authority, from ages past, now, and for ages to come. Amen" (Jude 25).

– Regis Martin

*O*FFERING IS THE ULTIMATE consequence of faith. It is just saying, "O Lord, you know I love you." Offering does not require a tremendous effort, but only "I recognize who you are."…

The encounter that happens today is a source of memory because it means coming across a presence that begins in the past. Polycarp, bishop of Smyrna, was deeply moved whenever he told of his teacher John (who was already old when they first met), and of how he would talk of that afternoon when, with Andrew, he had set eyes on Jesus for the first time. (Polycarp would later give up his life for Christ, burned at the stake.) He had his encounter with Christ through John. For him, the encounter with Christ had the face, the characteristics, the form of John, the Christians of Smyrna and the leader of that community. Yet that encounter that gave rise to Polycarp's faith drew all its value, its content, its consistency from Jesus of Nazareth, born of Mary: the Man who, that afternoon, after receiving baptism from John the Baptist, had gone home followed by those two who did not dare speak to him. This is why an encounter is the source of memory. What struck Polycarp in that moment was a fact in the present: "Jesus is the same yesterday, today and forever!" but it was a fact that had begun years before.

– Monsignor Luigi Giussani

*The most common yet most hidden temptation
is our lack of faith. It expresses itself less by declared
incredulity than by our actual preferences.*
(CCC 2732)

PETER BELIEVED that Jesus was the Messiah, but he resisted the revelation that Jesus would be killed. He had to learn that Jesus was a suffering Messiah. His faith had to be purified. As with Peter, in prayer there are confrontations between deeply imbedded desires (our preferences) and God's will. Always at stake in a faith-based dialogue with God (that is, prayer) is our operating vision of what it means to be fully human, fully alive, and happy. We must be prepared, like Peter, to amend what is false in our vision. Desires rooted in the American dream, or a superficial understanding of the role of suffering in God's plan, must die so that desires based on the Good News revealed by Jesus Christ can mature. God loves us too much to allow us to cling to false expectations regarding his love, and we cooperate with him by praying: "I do believe; help my unbelief" (Mk 9:24). We should prefer what God has revealed about a fully human life in his Son, Jesus Christ, the perfect model of what it means to be fully human, and in the many models of this fullness of life, the saints, above all, Mary.

– Douglas Bushman

*I*T WAS MRS. BARRETT who gave me the first impulse toward Catholicism. It was around ten o'clock in the morning that I went up to Kathryn's to call for her to come and play. There was no one on the porch or in the kitchen. The breakfast dishes had all been washed. They were long railroad apartments, those flats, and thinking the children must be in the front room, I burst in and ran through the bedrooms.

In the front bedroom Mrs. Barrett was on her knees, saying her prayers. She turned to tell me that Kathryn and the children had all gone to the store and went on with her praying. And I felt a warm burst of love toward Mrs. Barrett that I have never forgotten, a feeling of gratitude and happiness that still warms my heart when I remember her. She had God, and there was beauty in her life.

All through my life what she was doing remained with me. And though I became oppressed with the problem of poverty and injustice, though I groaned at the hideous sordidness of man's lot, though there were years when I clung to the philosophy of economic determinism as an explanation of man's fate, still there were moments when… life was shot through with glory. Mrs. Barrett in her sordid little tenement flat finished her breakfast dishes at ten o'clock in the morning and got down on her knees and prayed to God.

– Dorothy Day

*G*RACE GIVES US the thirst for God, for God's bliss, and no other kind. That alone can satisfy our craving, even though we may not know it. We may stay a long while without realizing, may carry this germ about inside us for a long while without anything very much showing. At most, an obscure uneasiness may warn us that, despite a happy or thrilling life as commonly regarded, we are not satisfied; and then we find ourselves dreaming from time to time of something new, unexpected, extraordinary which never actually comes. Then, one day, the uneasiness becomes a call, an invitation to set out; we realize that down there and far away there is something waiting for us, and that this something is someone, and that this someone is God, God's bliss, a mystery which the eyes of man have not seen nor the ears of man heard, something unheard of and unfathomable. Then we set out in Christ's footsteps, like sheep following their shepherd, not in fact knowing where he is leading, since we know nothing whatever about this mysterious bliss in store for us. We only know that it is happiness, true happiness, our happiness, the happiness for which we were created, and that is all we want to know.

– Father Bernard Bro, O.P.

"Build yourselves up in your most holy faith;
pray in the holy Spirit."
(Jude 20)

"BLESS ME, Father, for I have sinned. I am a scoffer."
I wasn't sure I heard correctly. "You're a what?" "A scoffer."
(I thought he had said he was a "golfer.") He was my first,
and so far only, "scoffer," at least a self-identified one. The
author of the Letter of Jude speaks about scoffers, right
before the above verse. A scoffer is one who lives by one's
own godless desires and ridicules those who strive to live
the spiritual life. The scoffer causes divisions within families, within the Church, within the parish.

My penitent scoffer helped me to reflect on my own
tendencies to be a scoffer. It comes out when I'm upset and
my ego has been wounded. I can feel it bubbling up when
I'm grumbling over things; or when gossip becomes the
prelude to denigrating someone's reputation or judging a
person's actions in an uncharitable, negative way.

The contrary of a scoffer is one who builds up others;
who wants to mend divisions and heal wounds, in other
words, one who allows the Holy Spirit to bring about unity
and peace. Our "most holy faith" unites us to God and to
one another. The sacrament of reconciliation heals us and
changes us. "Go in peace, and scoff no more!"

– Father Jacob Restrick, O.P.

*J*T IS PART OF THE MYSTERY OF GOD that he acts so gently, that he only gradually builds up *his* history within the great history of mankind; that he becomes man and so can be overlooked by his contemporaries and by the decisive forces within history; that he suffers and dies and that, having risen again, he chooses to come to mankind only through the faith of the disciples to whom he reveals himself; that he continues to knock gently at the doors of our hearts and slowly opens our eyes if we open our doors to him.

And yet—is not this the truly divine way? Not to overwhelm with external power, but to give freedom, to offer and elicit love. And if we really think about it, is it not what seems so small that is truly great? Does not a ray of light issue from Jesus, growing brighter across the centuries, that could not come from any mere man and through which the light of God truly shines into the world? Could the apostolic preaching have found faith and built up a worldwide community unless the power of truth had been at work within it?

– Pope Benedict XVI

A Closing Prayer
for the Year of Faith

Based on Porta Fidei *by Pope Benedict XVI*

LOVING FATHER,

We thank you for the blessing of this Year of Faith. It has been a time to rediscover the journey of faith and to experience with renewed vigor the joy and enthusiasm of the encounter with Christ. May I constantly live out this Year's summons to an authentic and renewed conversion to the Lord. May I always remember that faith means choosing to stand with the Lord so as to live with him. Through the grace of faith, our thoughts and affections, our mentality and conduct are slowly purified and transformed. Faith working through love becomes a new criterion of understanding and action that changes the whole of our life. Faith expands our hearts in hope and enables us to bear life-giving witness. Faith commits every one of us to become a living sign of the presence of the risen Lord in the world. May I continuously profess the faith in fullness and with fervent conviction, certainty, and hope. Make me capable of opening the hearts and minds of many to the desire for God and for true life without end. May I ever remain united in faith with the Mother of God who was proclaimed blessed because she believed. I ask this with great confidence and with a heart filled with gratitude united with Jesus Christ the King of the universe and our Lord, now and for ever. Amen.

– Father Peter John Cameron, O.P.

BRIEF BIOGRAPHIES OF CONTRIBUTORS

Monsignor Lorenzo Albacete is a theologian and former scientist, responsible for the Fraternity of Communion and Liberation in the USA, based in New York. He is author of *God at the Ritz* (Crossroad Publishing).

Douglas Bushman is director of the Institute for Pastoral Theology at Ave Maria University. He received his S.T.L. degree from the University of Fribourg, Switzerland.

Father Peter John Cameron, O.P., is editor-in-chief of MAGNIFICAT and author of *Blessing Prayers: Devotions for Growing in Faith* (MAGNIFICAT).

Father Romanus Cessario, O.P., serves as senior editor for MAGNIFICAT and teaches theology at Saint John's Seminary in Boston, MA.

Father John Dominic Corbett, O.P., teaches fundamental moral theology at the Dominican House of Studies in Washington, DC. He also preaches retreats and gives spiritual direction.

Father Lawrence Donohoo is associate professor of systematic theology at Mount Saint Mary's Seminary in Emmitsburg, MD, and assigned priest for Saint Anthony Shrine/Our Lady of Mount Carmel Parishes.

Anthony Esolen is professor of English at Providence College, a senior editor of *Touchstone Magazine*, and a regular contributor to MAGNIFICAT. He is the translator and editor of Dante's *Divine Comedy* (Random House) and author of *The Beauty of the Word: A Running Commentary on the Roman Missal* (MAGNIFICAT).

Justin Fatica is co-founder of Hard as Nails Ministries, a non-profit Catholic/Christian organization that has impacted over one million young people in the last decade.

Angela Franks is director of Theology Programs for the Theological Institute for the New Evangelization (TINE) at Saint John's Seminary in Boston, MA. She and her husband David homeschool their five children.

J. David Franks teaches systematic and moral theology at Saint John's Seminary, Boston, MA, and serves as the vice president for mission of the Seminary's Theological Institute for the New Evangelization (TINE). He is currently chairman of the board for Massachusetts Citizens for Life.

Father Michael Gaudoin-Parker, a British priest, has been living near Assisi, Italy, for over twenty years. He is the author of *Hearts Aflame with Hope* (Alba House, 2012), a four-volume series on persons inspired by the Eucharist.

Father J. Anthony Giambrone, O.P., is a Dominican priest of the Province of Saint Joseph and a doctoral student in Sacred Scripture at the University of Notre Dame.

John Janaro is a professor emeritus of theology and the author of *Never Give Up: My Life and God's Mercy* (Servant Books).

Father William M. Joensen, a priest of the Archdiocese of Dubuque, IA, is dean of Campus Spiritual Life at Loras College, where he also teaches philosophy and is spiritual director for seminarians.

Heather King is a contemplative laywoman and convert who lives in Los Angeles, CA. She is the author of three memoirs and blogs at shirtofflame.blogspot.com.

Lisa Lickona is a wife and mother to nine children whom she schools on a farm in upstate New York.

Father Joseph T. Lienhard, S.J., teaches patristics in the Department of Theology at Fordham University. He is currently translating Saint Augustine's commentaries on the Old Testament.

Monsignor Gregory E. S. Malovetz is a priest of the Diocese of Metuchen, NJ, and serves as pastor of Saint Charles Borromeo Church in Montgomery Township, NJ.

Father Guy Mansini, O.S.B., is pastor of Saint Isidore the Farmer and Holy Cross parishes in southern Indiana and teaches theology at Saint Meinrad Seminary.

Regis Martin is professor of theology at Franciscan University in Steubenville, OH, and the author of half a dozen books, including most recently *Still Point: Loss, Longing, and the Desire for God* (Ave Maria Press).

Andrew Matt is a member of the MAGNIFICAT editorial team and holds a doctorate in comparative literature. He lives with his wife and two sons in Chester, CT.

James Monti is the author of the forthcoming book, *A Sense of the Sacred: Roman Catholic Worship in the Middles Ages* (Ignatius Press, 2012), as well as *The Week of Salvation: History and Traditions of Holy Week* (Our Sunday Visitor).

Father Vincent Nagle, F.S.C.B., is a member of the Missionaries of Saint Charles Borromeo and currently serves in Immaculate Conception Parish in Bir Zeit, Palestinian Authority.

Father Jacob Restrick, O.P., is a Dominican priest of the Province of Saint Joseph. He is presently chaplain to the Hawthorne Dominican Sisters at Rosary Hill in Hawthorne, NY.

Father George William Rutler is pastor of the Church of Our Saviour in New York City. His latest book is *Cloud of Witnesses* (Scepter Publishers).

Rita A. Simmonds is an award-winning poet. She lives in Brooklyn, NY, with her husband and two children.

Father J. M. Sullivan, O.P., serves as novice master for the Dominican Province of Saint Joseph at Saint Gertrude Priory in Cincinnati, OH.

Monsignor James Turro, professor emeritus of New Testament Studies, Seton Hall University, Orange, NJ, is currently professor of New Testament Studies at Holy Apostles Seminary in Cromwell, CT.

Father Richard Veras is pastor of the Church of Saint Rita in Staten Island, NY, and a regular contributor to MAGNIFICAT. He is author of *Jesus of Israel: Finding Christ in the Old Testament* (Servant Books) and *Wisdom for Everyday Life from the Book of Revelation* (Servant Books).

Paul C. Vitz, a professor at the Institute for the Psychological Sciences and professor emeritus at New York University, writes on integrating psychology and the faith.

Stephen P. White is a fellow in the Catholic Studies Program at the Ethics and Public Policy Center in Washington, DC.

MEDITATION & PRAYER BIOGRAPHIES

Saint Anselm († 1109) was an abbot, bishop, philosopher, and theologian.

Saint Augustine († 430) is called the Doctor of Grace.

Father Jordan Aumann († 2007) was an American Dominican priest, founder of the Institute of Spiritual Theology, and founding editor of the Cross and Crown Series in Spirituality.

Father Benedict M. Ashley is an American Dominican priest, a prominent theologian, and the author of several books.

Father Hans Urs von Balthasar († 1988) was an eminent Swiss Catholic theologian who wrote prodigiously.

His Holiness Benedict XVI was elected to the See of Saint Peter in 2005.

Saint Bonaventure († 1274) was a Minister General of the Franciscans. He is a Doctor of the Church.

Father M. Eugene Boylan († 1964) was a monk of the Cistercian Abbey of Mount Saint Joseph, Roscrea, Ireland.

Father Bernard Bro is a French Dominican priest, a distinguished theologian, and the author of many books.

Sister Ruth Burrows is a Carmelite nun at Quidenham in Norfolk, England. She is the author of a number of best-selling books.

Father Julián Carrón is a Spanish priest and professor of theology at the University of Milan.

Father Jean-Pierre de Caussade († 1751) was a French Jesuit priest, a writer, and a revered spiritual director.

Pope Clement XI († 1721) reigned as pope from 1700 until 1721.

Father Francis L. B. Cunningham († 1963) was a Dominican priest of Saint Rose Priory, Dubuque, Iowa. He was the author of *The Christian Life* and *The Indwelling of the Trinity*.

Blessed Charles de Foucauld († 1916), contemplative and mystic, lived among the Tuareg people of Algeria.

Servant of God Dorothy Day († 1980) co-founded the Catholic Worker movement with Peter Maurin.

Servant of God Catherine de Hueck Doherty († 1985) was born in Russia and founded Madonna House in Combermere, Canada.

Saint Francis Xavier († 1552) was a great Spanish Jesuit missionary to Asia.

Monsignor Luigi Giussani († 2005) was a priest from Milan, Italy, who was the founder of the ecclesial movement Communion and Liberation.

Saint Gregory of Narek († 1003) was an Armenian monk, poet, mystical philosopher, and theologian.

Monsignor Romano Guardini († 1968) was born in Italy and became a renowned professor of philosophy and theology in Germany.

Blessed Guerric of Igny († 1157) was an abbot and a close friend of Saint Bernard of Clairvaux.

Father Walter Hilton († 1396) was a canon of the Augustinian Priory of Thurgarton, England.

Saint Ignatius of Loyola († 1556) was the founder of the Society of Jesus.

Father Bede Jarrett († 1934) was a Dominican priest from England widely esteemed for his preaching, his lectures, and his many books on theology and spirituality.

John the Solitary (early fifth century) was a major writer of the early Syriac Church.

Blessed John Paul II († 2005) reigned as pope from 1978 until 2005.

Venerable Thomas à Kempis († 1471) was a German priest and monk who wrote many spiritual works.

Monsignor Ronald A. Knox († 1957) was a British Catholic apologist and translator of the Bible.

Leszek Kolakowski († 2009) was an acclaimed philosopher from Poland, best known for his trenchant critique of Marxist thought.

Father Henri-Dominique Lacordaire († 1861) was a great Dominican preacher who re-founded the Order of Preachers in France after the French Revolution.

Servant of God Elisabeth Leseur († 1914) was a French married laywoman.

Father André Louf († 2010) served for thirty-five years as abbot of the Cistercian monastery of Mont-des-Cats, France, and was an esteemed spiritual guide and author.

Saint Louis de Montfort († 1716) was a great French missionary preacher especially renowned for fostering devotion to the Blessed Virgin Mary.

Venerable Louis of Granada († 1588) was a Spanish Dominican priest who preached and wrote spiritual works primarily for the laity. His life and writings were lauded by Saint Teresa of Ávila and Saint Charles Borromeo.

Little Sister Magdeleine of Jesus († 1989) was born in Paris, France, and was inspired by the life and writing of Charles de Foucauld. She founded the Little Sisters of Jesus in the Algerian Sahara.

Father Thomas Merton († 1968) was a Trappist monk at the Abbey of Gethsemani, Kentucky, and a prolific author.

Josef Pieper († 1997) was an eminent Catholic philosopher from Germany who authored many books on philosophy, theology, and spirituality.

Father Servais Pinckaers († 2008) was a Belgian Dominican priest and professor of moral theology at the University of Fribourg, Switzerland.

Father Antonio Royo († 2005) was a Spanish Dominican priest who taught ascetical and mystical theology at Saint Stephen's in Salamanca, Spain.

Father Gabriel of Saint Mary Magdalen († 1952) was a Belgian Carmelite priest, teacher, and spiritual director.

Monsignor Robert Sokolowski is professor of philosophy at the Catholic University of America and the author of many books.

Father Adolphe Tanquerey († 1932) was a French Sulpician priest and theologian. His work *The Spiritual Life: A*

Treatise on Ascetic and Mystical Theology is considered a classic.

Saint Teresa Benedicta of the Cross (Edith Stein; † 1942) was a German philosopher and a convert from Judaism who became a Carmelite nun. She was put to death at Auschwitz.

Blessed Teresa of Calcutta († 1997) founded the Missionaries of Charity and was awarded the Nobel Peace Prize.

Saint Thomas Aquinas († 1274) was a Dominican priest from Italy. He remains one of the Church's premier doctors.

Father Simon Tugwell is a Dominican priest, the author of several books on theology and spirituality, and a member of the Dominican Historical Institute.

Father Gerald Vann († 1963) was an English Dominican priest and a popular preacher, lecturer, and author.

Charles Wesley († 1788), an English clergyman, is considered one of the greatest hymn writers of all time.

Lieutenant André Zirnheld († 1942) was a French professor of philosophy who served in the British S.A.S. during World War II. The prayer printed in this booklet was found on his body when he was killed in action in Libya.

Index of Meditations

Index of Meditations

Bibliography for Prayers

Act of Faith, cited in *Manual of Prayers*.	198
Anselm of Canterbury (Saint), cited in *Manual of Prayers*.	213
Bonaventure: The Soul's Journey Into God, The Tree of Life, The Life of St. Francis, Ewart Cousins, Tr. © 1978, Paulist Press, Inc., Mahwah, NJ. www.paulistpress.com. Used with permission.	82
Charles de Foucauld (Blessed), *Prayer of Abandonment*. www.liturgy.co.nz. All rights reserved.	27
Clement XI (Pope), *The Universal Prayer*. www.catholic.org/prayers/prayer.	134, 150
Doherty, Catherine de Hueck (Servant of God), *Fragments of My Life*. © 1979, Ave Maria Press, Inc., PO Box 428, Notre Dame, Indiana 46556, www.avemariapress.com.	99
Francis Xavier (Saint), a *Prayer*, Gerard Manley Hopkins, s.j.,Tr. www.feastofsaints.com/stfxavier.htm. All rights reserved.	166
Gabriel of Saint Mary Magdalen (Father), *Divine Intimacy: Meditations on the Interior Life for Every Day of the Liturgical Year*, Discalced Carmelite Nuns of Boston, Trs. © 2008, Baronius Press. www.baroniuspress.com. Used with permission.	279, 291
Gregory of Narek (Saint), cited in *The Rediscovery of Prayer* by Father Bernard Bro, o.p., John Morriss, Tr. © 1966, The Society of St. Paul, St. Pauls / Alba House, Staten Island, NY. www.albahouse.org. Used with permission.	64
Ignatius of Loyola (Saint), *The Spiritual Exercises*, paraphrased by David L. Fleming, s.j. © 2007, Saint Ignatius, Chestnut Hill, MA. All rights reserved.	42
John Paul II (Blessed), *Ecclesia in America*, January 22, 1999. Used with permission of the Libreria Editrice Vaticana. www.vatican.va.	116
Kempis, Thomas á (Venerable), *The Imitation of Christ*, Aloysius Croft and Harold Bolton, Trs. © 2003, Dover Publications, Inc., Mineola, NY.	373, 389, 405
Manual of Prayers: Pontifical North American College, Rome, Revised by Rev. James D. Watkins. © 1996, The American College of the Roman Catholic Church in the United States. Reprinted by permission of Midwest Theological Forum, Publisher.	255
Puritan Prayer, *The Valley of Vision: A Collection of Puritan Prayers & Devotions*, Arthur Bennett, Ed. © 1975, Arthur Bennett, The Banner of Truth Trust, Carlisle, PA. All rights reserved.	357
Stefan (inmate's prayer), December 18, 2011. Used with permission of the Libreria Editrice Vaticana. www.vatican.va.	304
Thomas Aquinas (Saint), cited in *Manual of Prayers*.	230, 246
Thomas Aquinas (Saint), *The Aquinas Prayer Book: The Prayers and Hymns of St. Thomas Aquinas*, Robert Anderson, Ed., Tr., Johann Moser, Ed., Tr. © 2000, Sophia Institute Press, Manchester, NH. www.sophiainstitute.com. Used with permission.	322, 343
Wesley, Charles. Public domain.	180
Zirnheld, André. *An S.A.S. Soldier's Prayer*, Public domain.	12

ACKNOWLEDGMENTS

Most Scripture selections are taken from the *New American Bible with Revised New Testament and Psalms.* Copyright © 1991, 1986, Confraternity of Christian Doctrine, Inc., Washington, DC. Used with permission. All rights reserved. No portion of the *New American Bible* may be reprinted without written permission from the copyright holder.

The formatting of some texts may be altered in keeping with guidelines required by the USCCB.

Some Scripture selections are taken from *The Holy Bible: Revised Standard Version, Catholic Edition,* copyright 1946 (New Testament), copyright 1965 (The Catholic Edition of the New Testament) by Division of Christian Education of the National Council of Churches of Christ in the United States of America.

No part of this book may be used or reproduced in any manner whatsoever without written permission, except in the case of brief quotations embodied in critical articles or reviews. For information, address MAGNIFICAT, PO Box 834, Yonkers, NY 10702. www.magnificat.com

The trademark MAGNIFICAT depicted in this publication is used under license from and is the exclusive property of Magnificat Central Service Team, Inc., A Ministry to Catholic Women, and may not be used without its written consent.

Published with the approval of the Committee on Divine Worship, United States Conference of Catholic Bishops.

© MAGNIFICAT Inc., New York, 2012.

Printed in Germany by CPI-CLAUSEN & BOSSE.

Cover: *Christ Walks on the Water and Saves Peter,* mosaic (12th century), Cathedral of Monreale, Palermo, Sicily, Italy. © Enzo Lo Verso.

The Magnificat®
Year of Faith Companion

Publisher: **Pierre-Marie Dumont**
Editor-in-Chief: **Father Peter John Cameron, o.p.**
Senior Editor: **Father Romanus Cessario, o.p.**
Managing Editor: **Catherine Kolpak**
Editorial Assistant and Proofreader: **Andrew Matt**
Administrative Assistant: **Nora Macagnone**
Senior Managing Editor: **Frédérique Chatain**
Permissions: **Diaga Seck-Rauch**
Cover and Inset: **Solange Bosdevesy**
Iconography: **Isabelle Mascaras**
Translator: **Janet Chevrier**

Contributors:
  Monsignor Lorenzo Albacete
  Douglas Bushman
  Father John Dominic Corbett, o.p.
  Father Lawrence Donohoo
  Anthony Esolen
  Justin Fatica
  Angela Franks
  J. David Franks
  Father Michael Gaudoin-Parker
  Father J. Anthony Giambrone, o.p.
  John Janaro
  Father William M. Joensen
  Heather King
  Lisa Lickona
  Father Joseph T. Lienhard, s.j.
  Monsignor Gregory E. S. Malovetz
  Father Guy Mansini, o.s.b.
  Regis Martin
  James Monti
  Father Vincent Nagle, f.s.c.b.
  Father Jacob Restrick, o.p.
  Father George William Rutler
  Rita A. Simmonds
  Father James M. Sullivan, o.p.
  Monsignor James Turro
  Father Richard Veras
  Paul C. Vitz
  Stephen P. White

YEAR OF FAITH COMPANION

ORDER EXTRA COPIES
—as low as $1.95 per copy!

ONLY AVAILABLE IN THE UNITED STATES AND CANADA	
QUANTITY	PRICE PER COPY
1-4	US $6.95
5-9	US $4.95
10-49	US $3.95
50-99	US $2.95
100-499	US $2.45
500+	US $1.95

SHIPPING AND HANDLING		
Per order	USA	Canada
Up to US $7.99	US $1	US $2
US $8 to US $15.99	US $2	US $4
US $16 to US $49.99	US $5	US $10
US $50 to US $99.99	US $8	US $16
US $100 to US $299.99	US $16	US $32
US $300 and above	6% of the order	9% of the order

	Quantity	Price per copy	Total
YEAR OF FAITH COMPANION		x US	=
If you live in Colorado, please include CO sales tax (3%)	Shipping & Handling (see chart above)		+
		TOTAL	=

MY INFORMATION

Title/First Name

Last Name

Institution/Parish

Address

City   State

Zip   Country

Phone

Email

METHOD OF PAYMENT

❏ **Check enclosed** *payable to* MAGNIFICAT-BCR *(US $ only).*

❏ **Visa**   ❏ **MasterCard**   ❏ **Discover**

Card No: ⌶⌶⌶⌶ ⌶⌶⌶⌶ ⌶⌶⌶⌶ ⌶⌶⌶

Exp. date: ⌶⌶⌶ ⌶⌶⌶   Security Code: ⌶⌶⌶

Signature:

Please mail this completed order form with payment to:

MAGNIFICAT-BCR
1331 Red Cedar Circle - Fort Collins, CO 80524

or call: 1-970-416-6670 to order by phone
or fax: 1-970-224-1824
or email: specialissue@magnificat.com
or visit: www.magnificat.com

If you liked the MAGNIFICAT YEAR OF FAITH COMPANION you will love MAGNIFICAT

If you would like to receive regularly each month a resource that would help you to develop your prayer life…

MAGNIFICAT *is the answer.*

If you would like to have a companion to accompany you each day in the growth of your spiritual life…

MAGNIFICAT *is the answer.*

If you would like to benefit from a worship aid that helps you participate in the Holy Mass with greater fervor…

MAGNIFICAT *is the answer.*

If you desire to find a way to a more profound love for Our Blessed Savior…

We invite you to become part of the growing worldwide MAGNIFICAT family.

$\mathscr{A}$N ANNUAL SUBSCRIPTION TO MAGNIFICAT

promises thirteen issues—one per month with a special issue for Holy Week—filled with spiritual insight, exquisite art, and invaluable inspiration. You will discover the most beautiful prayers, readings, and hymns of the Church in this lavishly printed, easy-to-read, pocket-sized worship aid. MAGNIFICAT provides a fitting way to enter fully into the Church's liturgical rhythms and spiritual legacy.